Lecture Notes in Computer Science   10300

Commenced Publication in 1973
Founding and Former Series Editors:
Gerhard Goos, Juris Hartmanis, and Jan van Leeuwen

More information about this series at http://www.springer.com/series/7408

Johann Blieberger · Markus Bader (Eds.)

Reliable Software Technologies – Ada-Europe 2017

22nd Ada-Europe International Conference
on Reliable Software Technologies
Vienna, Austria, June 12–16, 2017
Proceedings

 Springer

Editors
Johann Blieberger
Institute of Computer Aided Automation
Vienna University of Technology
Vienna
Austria

Markus Bader
Institute of Computer Aided Institute
Vienna University of Technology
Vienna
Austria

ISSN 0302-9743   ISSN 1611-3349   (electronic)
Lecture Notes in Computer Science
ISBN 978-3-319-60587-6   ISBN 978-3-319-60588-3   (eBook)
DOI 10.1007/978-3-319-60588-3

Library of Congress Control Number: 2017943008

LNCS Sublibrary: SL2 – Programming and Software Engineering

Printed on acid-free paper

This Springer imprint is published by Springer Nature
The registered company is Springer International Publishing AG
The registered company address is: Gewerbestrasse 11, 6330 Cham, Switzerland

Preface

The 22nd edition of the International Conference on Reliable Software Technologies (Ada-Europe 2017) took place in Vienna, returning to Austria 15 years after 2002. The previous editions of the conference were held in Spain (Santander, 1999, Palma de Mallorca, 2004, Valencia, 2010, Madrid, 2015), France (Toulouse, 2003, Brest, 2009, Paris, 2014), the UK (London, 1997, York, 2005, Edinburgh, 2011), Switzerland (Montreux, 1996, Geneva, 2007), Sweden (Uppsala, 1998, Stockholm, 2012), Germany (Potsdam, 2000, Berlin, 2013), Italy (Venice, 2008, Pisa, 2016), Belgium (Leuven, 2001), and Portugal (Porto, 2006).

TU Wien was the lead organizer for this edition, with aid from an international core team that included members of Ada-Europe, the organization that oversees and sponsors the conference series.

The conference took place in the week of June 12–16, 2017, with a rich program for both technical content and social opportunities. The scientific program featured 15 papers selected among 37 peer-reviewed submissions, grouped into five presentation sessions and one panel discussion, entitled "The Future of Safety-Minded Languages," scheduled in the central days of the conference week, to address topics ranging from runtimes, safety and security, timing verification, programming models, and mixed criticality. The proceedings contained in this volume reflect these contributions (see the table of contents for details).

The conference program also included nine industrial contributions arranged in three industrial presentation sessions. Vendor presentations with accompanying exhibitions completed the core program. Eight tutorials for the equivalent of nine half-day sessions were offered on Monday and Friday. The Friday program included the fourth edition of the Workshop on Challenges and New Approaches for Dependable and Cyber-Physical Systems Engineering (De-CPS), this year focusing on the theme "Transportation of the Future." The proceedings from this part of the conference program will be published, in successive installments, in the *Ada User Journal*, the quarterly magazine of Ada-Europe.

The scientific and industrial submissions originated from 24 countries and 124 distinct authors, from Europe, Asia, North and South America, Australia, and Africa. Thanks to that wealth, the final program was an international digest of contributions from Australia, Austria, Denmark, France, Italy, Portugal, South Korea, Spain, Sweden, Switzerland, UK, and USA.

Each central day of the week opened with a keynote talk focusing on topics of interest to the conference scope. The three keynote talks were:

- "The Laws of Robotics and Autonomous Vehicles May Be Much More Than Three, But Don't Panic… Yet" by Giovanni Battista Gallus, from Array, Italy, who discussed the future European legal framework for the development of autonomous vehicles, especially for programming issues.

- "Behavioral Software Metrics" by Tom Henzinger, from IST, Austria, who showed how the classic satisfaction relation between programs and requirements can be replaced by quantitative preference metrics that measure the "fit" between programs and requirements. Depending on the application, such fitness measures can include aspects of function, performance, resource consumption, and robustness.
- "Dependable Internet of Things" by Kay Römer from TU Graz, Austria, who presented the challenge resulting from the increasing use of wireless networked embedded systems in safety-critical applications, which must be proven to meet strict dependability requirements even under the harshest environmental conditions. The presentation highlighted recent results that improve the dependability of wireless communication and localization, embedded computing, and networked control for the Internet of Things.

The tutorial program covered the following topics:

- "Introduction to SPARK 2014," Peter Chapin, Vermont Technical College
- "Ada on ARM Cortex-M, A Zero-Run-Time Approach," Maciej Sobczak, GE Aviation and Inspirel
- "Software Measurement for Dependable Software Systems," William Bail, The MITRE Corporation
- "Real-Time Parallel Programming with the UpScale SDK," Luis Miguel Pinho, ISEP, and Eduardo Quinones, BSC
- "Using Gnoga for Desktop/Mobile GUI and Web development in Ada," Jean-Pierre Rosen, Adalog
- "Frama-C, a Collaborative Framework for C Code Verification," Julien Signoles, CEA LIST
- "On Beyond ASCII: Characters, Strings, and Ada 2012," Jean-Pierre Rosen, Adalog
- "Modular Open System Architecture for Critical Systems," William Bail, The MITRE Corporation

The industrial program featured the following presentations:

- "Astronomical Ada," Ahlan Marriott, White Elephant GmbH, Switzerland
- "IP Network Stack in Ada 2012 and the Ravenscar Profile," Stephane Carrez, France
- "Hardware-Based Data Protection/Isolation at Runtime in Ada Code for Microcontrollers," German Rivera, USA
- "Automated Testing of SPARK Ada Contracts: Progress and Case Study Report," Simon Daniel, Rolls-Royce plc, UK, and Stuart Matthews, Altran UK, UK
- "Introducing Static Analysis to a Mature Project," Jacob Sparre Andersen, JSA Research & Innovation, Denmark
- "Challenges and Opportunities for Improvements of the Testing Process for Ada based Safety Critical Systems," Guillem Bernat, Rapita Systems, UK
- "Experiences with Ada in the Safety-Critical Communication and Ground Control Systems of the nEUROn UCAV," Luis Pabón, Artemio Jiménez, and José M. Martínez, Airbus Defence & Space, Spain

- "Experience with Use of Model-Driven Code Generation on the ASIM Project," Steen Palm, Terma A/S, Denmark
- "A Time-Triggered Middleware for Safety-Critical Automotive Applications," Ayhan Mehmed, Wilfried Steiner, and Maximilian Rosenblattl, TTTech Computertechnik AG, Austria.

We would like to acknowledge the work of all the people who contributed, with various responsibilities and official functions, to the making of the conference program overall. The success of the conference depends in large part on the quality of the program contents. The authors of the selected contributions are to be thanked first and foremost for that. The members of the Program and Industrial Committees had the difficult task of screening the submissions and selecting the contributions to include in this proceedings volume and in the *Ada User Journal*.

The Organizing Committee put it all together: Wolfgang Kastner (Conference Chair); Jacob Sparre Andersen (Industrial Chair); Ben Brosgol (Tutorial and Workshop Chair); Dirk Craeynest (Publicity Chair); Ahlan Marriott (Exhibition Chair). All of them deserve our gratitude for their effort.

We hope that the attendees enjoyed every element of the conference program at least as much as we did in organizing it.

June 2017   Johann Blieberger
                                                                                  Max Bader

Organization

Conference Chair

Wolfgang Kastner   TU Vienna, Austria

Program Co-chairs

Johann Blieberger   TU Vienna, Austria
Markus Bader   TU Vienna, Austria

Tutorial and Workshop Chair

Ben Brosgol   AdaCore, USA

Industrial Chair

Jacob Sparre Andersen   JSA Consulting, Denmark

Publicity Chair

Dirk Craeynest   Ada-Belgium and KU Leuven, Belgium

Exhibition Chair

Ahlan Marriott   White Elephant, Switzerland

Local Chair

Markus Bader   TU Vienna, Austria

Sponsoring Institutions

AdaCore
Ellidiss Technologies
PTC Developer Tools
RAPITA Systems Ltd.
Vector Software

Program Committee

Mario Aldea   Universidad de Cantabria, Spain
Ted Baker   NSF, USA

Ezio Bartocci	Vienna University of Technology, Austria
Bernd Burgstaller	Yonsei University, South Korea
Juan A. de la Puente	Universidad Politécnica de Madrid, Spain
Lukas Esterle	Vienna University of Technology, Austria
Michael González Harbour	Universidad de Cantabria, Spain
J. Javier Gutiérrez	Universidad de Cantabria, Spain
Jérôme Hugues	ISAE, France
Raimund Kirner	University of Hertfordshire, UK
Wilfried Kubinger	FH Technikum Wien, Austria
Albert Llemosí	Universitat de les Illes Balears, Spain
Kristina Lundkvist	Mälardalen University, Sweden
Franco Mazzanti	ISTI-CNR, Italy
Laurent Pautet	Telecom ParisTech, France
Justus Piater	University of Innsbruck, Austria
Luís Miguel Pinho	CISTER/ISEP, Portugal
Erhard Plödereder	Universität Stuttgart, Germany
Jorge Real	Universitat Politècnica de València, Spain
José Ruiz	AdaCore, France
Sergio Sáez	Universitat Politècnica de València, Spain
Tucker Taft	AdaCore, USA
Theodor Tempelmeier	University of Applied Sciences Rosenheim, Germany
Elena Troubitsyna	Åbo Akademi University, Finland
Santiago Urueña	GMV, Spain
Tullio Vardanega	Università di Padova, Italy
Armin Wasice	University of California at Berkeley, USA
Michael Zillich	Vienna University of Technology, Austria

Industrial Committee

Ian Broster	Rapita Systems, UK
Jørgen Bundgaard	Rambøll Denmark A/S
Dirk Craeynest	Ada-Belgium & KU Leuven, Belgium
Thomas Gruber	Austrian Institute Of Technology (AIT), Austria
Egil Harald Høvik	Kongsberg, Norway
Ismael Lafoz	Airbus Defence and Space, Spain
Björn Lundin	Consafe Logistics, Sweden
Ahlan Marriott	White Elephant, Switzerland
Paolo Panaroni	Intecs, Italy
Paul Parkinson	Wind River, UK
Andreas Richtsfeld	DS Automotion GmbH, Austria
Jean-Pierre Rosen	Adalog, France
Emilio Salazar	GMV, Spain
Jacob Sparre Andersen	JSA Consulting, Denmark
Jean-Loup Terraillon	European Space Agency, The Netherlands
Sergey Tverdyshev	SysGO, Germany

Additional Reviewers

Jorge Garrido Balaguer
Hector Perez
Juan Zamorano

Contents

Runtimes

Evaluating MSRP and MrsP with the Multiprocessor Ravenscar Profile

Jorge Garrido[✉], Juan Zamorano, Alejandro Alonso,
and Juan A. de la Puente

Sistemas de Tiempo Real e Ingeniería de Servicios Telemáticos (STRAST),
Universidad Politécnica de Madrid (UPM), Madrid, Spain
str@dit.upm.es

Abstract. One of the main challenges of developing real-time systems with Ada on multiprocessor platforms is finding an appropriate scheduling policy and locking policy for shared objects. Some modifications of the standard Ceiling_Locking policy have been proposed for multiprocessor architectures, among which MSRP and MrsP have raised most interest. In this paper the possible uses of both policies in full Ada and Ravenscar programs are explored. To this purpose, classical response time analysis is extended in the paper to deal with heterogeneous access costs in multiprocessor systems. A case study has been used to validate the approach, and an extensive test bench for comparing MSRP and MrsP has been run in order to compare the schedulability properties of both methods. The conclusion is that, although MrsP provides a better overall performance, in many practical situations the simpler MSRP protocol provides comparable results when considering heterogeneous access costs, while being compatible with the Ravenscar restrictions.

Keywords: Real-time systems · Multiprocessor systems · Ada Ravenscar profile · Schedulability analysis

1 Introduction

In recent years, the need for using multiprocessor platforms in embedded real-time systems has arisen, mainly due to the increasing requirements of computing power and other resources. This trend has given rise to new research related to scheduling methods and schedulability analysis techniques that can be used in hard real-time multiprocessor systems [7].

One of the main issues in developing multiprocessor real-time systems is resource sharing. Some extensions of single processor protocols, such as the Multiprocessor Priority Ceiling Protocol (MPCP) [14] and its reformulation as the Distributed Priority Ceiling Protocol (DPCP) [15,16], or the Multiprocessor

This work has been partially funded by the Spanish National R&D&I plan (project M2C2, TIN2014-56158-C4-3-P).

J. Blieberger and M. Bader (Eds.): Ada-Europe 2017, LNCS 10300, pp. 3–17, 2017.
DOI: 10.1007/978-3-319-60588-3_1

Stack Resource Policy (MSRP) [9], have been proposed. All of these protocols can be used with partitioned fixed-priorities or EDF scheduling. MSRP, which uses a non-preemptable, busy-wait mechanism (*spin-lock*) to provide a bounded locking time in shared data access, is simpler and more efficient than MPCP, and can be analysed with well-known response-time analysis techniques [2]. However, it should be noted that non-preemption may lead to significant blocking undergone by high priority tasks, thus potentially making access to protected objects inefficient.

Burns and Wellings [6] proposed the Multiprocessor Resource Sharing Protocol (MrsP), identifying and addressing the main properties required for an efficient general purpose lock-based resource sharing protocol. MrsP limits the amount of blocking incurred by high-priority tasks using a novel helping mechanism, thus improving the efficiency of the protocol.

The Ada 2012 standard [1] supports multiprocessing in a flexible way, including mechanisms for a variety of real-time scheduling methods. It also supports multiprocessors under the Ravenscar profile [5,8], with the restriction that tasks are not allowed to migrate from one processor to another. As is well known, the scheduling policy under the profile is fixed-priority (FIFO_Within_Priorities), and the locking policy is Ceiling_Locking.

MSRP can be used to implement Ada protected objects with a fully partitioned structure, as proposed in [4], with only slight changes to prevent preemption in protected operations [12]. This is also compatible with the Ravenscar profile, although the amount of blocking suffered by high-priority tasks may limit the usefulness of the protocol.

MrsP can also be used with Ada, with the constraint that all tasks must be assigned to the same dispatching domain. However, migration between processors in the domain is required to implement the protocol [4]. Task migration is forbidden in the Ravenscar profile, which means that the protocol cannot be used in Ravenscar programs, unless the profile is redefined in a future revision of the language.

It may thus seem that Ravenscar multiprocessor programs are limited in their use of protected objects by being forced to use a less efficient protocol than MrsP. However, considering heterogeneous access costs, i.e. from different processors, and taking into account the common industry trend to implement simple cost-effective solutions to real world problems, the possible drawbacks of using MSRP instead of MrsP may be alleviated.

In order to assess the validity of this claim, we have extended response time analysis techniques [2], to take into account heterogeneous accesses to shared objects, and compare its performance against the previous homogeneous analysis. We have used a real case study of an academic satellite to show the difference between homogeneous and heterogeneous analysis methods. In this case study, an EEPROM memory is used on board for non-volatile data storage. For this memory, the accessing time of writing operations is orders of magnitude longer than that of reading operations. The resulting improvement of the response time analysis when considering the heterogeneity of access costs for this particular case study is discussed. We have also evaluated the performance of MSRP and MrsP using an extensive test bench, with results supporting our previous claim.

The rest of the paper is organized as follows: Sect. 2 reviews the main points of the MSRP and MrsP protocols including the traditional homogeneous response time analysis for the given protocols. The extended timing analysis for heterogeneous access is presented in Sect. 3. Section 4 presents the case study and its results. An overall evaluation of the analysis presented against the homogeneous access cost analysis is presented in Sect. 5 for both MSRP and MrsP. Finally conclusions are provided in Sect. 6.

2   Summary of MSRP and MrsP

The intuition under MSRP and MrsP is to extend the priority ceiling protocol benefits (including a simple response time analysis scheme) to multiprocessor systems. This can only be achieved if concurrent access costs to shared resources are bounded. Both MSRP and MrsP protocols [4,6] accomplish this by forcing that, at most, only one task per processor may be requiring access to a shared resource at any given time. To this purpose, the active priorities of tasks accessing a resource are increased, and the tasks spin-wait until access is granted. In fact, the main difference between the protocols (and then their schedulability analysis) is that, while MSRP performs the access in a non-preemptive way (which is equivalent to increasing the priority of the task to the highest one in the system), MrsP only increases the priority of the accessing task to the local ceiling of the resource on that processor.

For both MSRP and MrsP, access to a shared resources is granted in FIFO order. As concurrent accesses to a resource are bounded to one task per processor, the longest queue a task will have to wait to be granted access to a resource is also bounded, and so is the total access cost to the resource.

As above stated, tasks under MSRP perform the spin-wait and the access to a resource in a non-preemptable way. On the contrary, tasks under MrsP do so only at the local ceiling priority of the accessed resource. As a result, MrsP tasks can be locally preempted while waiting or accessing a resource. This preemption could affect other tasks waiting for accessing the resource in the FIFO queue, specially if the task has already acquired the associated lock. This delay would clearly undermine the protocol schedulability analysis. In order to prevent such situations, MrsP incorporates a novel helping mechanism, by which a locally preempted task execution can be taken over by another task waiting for accessing the resource. As identified in [4], the only practical way to do this is to migrate the locally preempted task to the processor where the waiting task is spinning. There the task resumes the protected execution at the local ceiling priority of the resource on that processor. When the task releases the resource lock, it is migrated back to its host processor, and scheduled with its base priority. A thorough analysis of the migration procedure and costs is out of the scope of this paper.

With these scheduling and locking policies, both protocols maintain the main PCP/SRP properties. In both MSRP and MrsP a task is only locally blocked once per activation and before it starts executing. Then, all resources are locally available and deadlocks are prevented.

Response Time Analysis

Both MSRP and MrsP inherit a scheduling analysis based on the Response Time Analysis (RTA) technique [2]. However, this RTA now needs to account for the FIFO queue to access the resource. For both protocols, let c^j be the maximum execution time for a resource r^j, and $|map(G(r^j))|$ the number of processors from where r^j can be accessed. The cost of accessing the resource (e^j) is bounded by:

$$e^j = |map(G(r^j))|c^j \tag{1}$$

Then, the worst case executing time of a task τ_i can be computed as the sum of its worst case execution time out of shared resources plus the cost of each access to a shared resource as expressed in:

$$C_i = WCET_i + \sum_{r^j \in \mathbf{F}(\tau_i)} n_i e^j \tag{2}$$

where $\mathbf{F}(\tau_i)$ is the set of resources accessed by τ_i and n_i is the number of times the resource r^j is accessed per τ_i activation. Finally, the response time of τ_i under both MSRP and MrsP can be computed as:

$$R_i = C_i + \max(\hat{e}, \hat{b}) + \sum_{\tau_j \in \mathbf{hpl}(i)} \left\lceil \frac{R_i}{T_j} \right\rceil C_j \tag{3}$$

where $\mathbf{hpl}(i)$ is the set of local higher priority tasks, $\hat{b}$ is the maximum non-preemptive execution time induced by the RTOS and $\hat{e}$ is the arrival blocking incurred by the analysed task due to lower priority tasks accessing a shared resource. The calculation of $\hat{e}$ is where the difference of the dynamic increase of priorities of the accessing tasks is reflected. While under MSRP $\hat{e}$ is equal to the highest resource access cost of a local task to a shared resource, under MrsP this is only the access cost of a resource used by a local task with a priority lower than τ_i and a task of equal or higher priority.

For both protocols, it can be derived from Eqs. 1–3 that the response time is highly dependant on the value of e^j. Section 3 presents an approach to tightening the analysis of e^j and thus the overall response time analysis.

3   Response Time Analysis for Heterogeneous Accesses to Shared Resources

As shown before, the MSRP and MrsP original formulation of a shared resource access cost in Eq. 1 assumes constant (homogeneous) access costs. As noted in [6], this is an oversimplification of the task model. Brandenburg [3] gives an intuition on different access costs to resources, which can be used to improve schedulability analysis when there is knowledge on the access patterns from all entities on MSRP systems. For a task model considering heterogeneous access times to a shared resource, we can define the access cost of a resource r^j as:

$$e^j = \sum_{p_k} \hat{c}_k^j \tag{4}$$

where $\hat{c}_k^j$ is the maximum access time to a resource by a task executing on processor p_k. This approach keeps the interpretation of e^j as the worst case access cost for a resource, where the task having the longer access time on each processor is queued for accessing it. However, any system having different higher access times on each processor will benefit from this new analysis.

With this approach, access costs would still be considered equal for all tasks accessing the resource from a given processor. However, the e^j analysis can be tightened even more, up to task level. This is achieved by considering the specific access time to r^j of the task under analysis. Then, the worst case access cost is sum of the worst case costs on other processors, plus the access time of the task itself. Thus, the cost of accessing a resource e^j for a task τ_i is:

$$e_i^j = c_i^j + \sum_{p_k \backslash \mathbf{P}(\tau_i)} \hat{c}_k^j \tag{5}$$

where $\mathbf{P}(\tau_i)$ returns the processor p_k where task τ_i executes.

The value of e_i^j computed for each access of τ_i to r^j. Note that c_i^j is the time required for every such access. Therefore, Eq. 5 is also valid for task models considering tasks accessing shared resources from different interfaces. In this way, each access to the resource may have a different cost within the same task. This will be exploited in the case study presented in Sect. 4.

As the only change to the equations in [2,6] is the way e^j is calculated, the rest of the equations remain valid, including the calculation of R_i (Eq. 3), which is still extremely similar to the original equation for PCP.

Given the notion of c^j in [2,6] as the maximum execution time for a resource, when considering heterogeneous access times for a given resource, other access times need to be equal or lower than c^j. Formally, it means that $\hat{c}_k^j \leq c^j$. As this is the only factor altered in the response time analysis for MrsP, it directly implies that this analysis strictly dominates the one presented in [6].

4   Case Study

Real-Time embedded systems usually experience different access times for shared resources. One common resource with a high difference between access times, depending on the interface used, is non-volatile memories. This kind of devices are characterised by having several magnitude orders of difference between write and read accesses.

UPMSat-2 [13] is a micro-satellite mission which is being developed by several research groups within the UPM and different industrial partners. For non-volatile data storage, the UPMSat-2 On-Board Computer (OBC) relays on two EEPROM memory chips of 1 MB each. This memory is used mainly to store three types of information: executable code, configuration parameters, and telemetry to be sent to the ground segment, including housekeeping and event data.

The EEPROM chips used in the UPMSat-2 require a minimum separation between block writing operations of 15 ms. Due to the Ravenscar profile restrictions [10], this separation is enforced by an active wait within the shared resource. As a consequence, writing access times go necessarily over 15 ms, having found 15 870 µs to be a safe upper bound for the overall access time.

On the contrary, reading operations on EEPROM memories have comparable access times to those of main memories. As a consequence, an upper bound of 575 µs has been adopted for read operations.

As proposed in [13], a dual-core implementation of the UPMSat-2 computer would have the telemetry and telecommand subsystem (TTC) allocated to a dedicated core, in order to maximize the availability of the communication hardware and thus the communications link budget. A critical scheduling situation arises when the satellite is in telemetry transmission mode. Since the radio equipment is half duplex, transmission slots are allocated to both the ground station and satellite system. During telemetry transmission, concurrent tasks accesses to EEPROM memory per task activation are summarized in Table 1.

Table 1. EEPROM memory accesses per task activation.

	Task	Writes	Reads
Core_0	Housekeeping_Task	2	0
	ADCS_Measurement_Task	1	0
	ADCS_Control_Task	1	0
	ADCS_PWM_Task	0	0
Core_1	TMTC_Task	0	1

As TMTC_Task executes by itself on Core_1, only read accesses are performed (for retrieving stored telemetry messages to be sent to ground) on this processor. Consequently, all write accesses are invoked from Core_0.

The analysis of a similar problem for single core platforms was addressed in [17], where it was shown that an equivalent safe task set could be defined to better analyse the response time of these tasks while still complying with the Ravenscar Profile [5]. As explained in [17], tasks are assigned priorities according to a Deadline Monotonic scheme [11]. The only exception are the PWM tasks, which are assigned the highest priorities to provide the tightest possible bound to their response time. As the attitude control system accuracy highly depends on the length of the PWM duty cycle, this priority assignment provides the best possible results. The approach in [17] has also been followed here to define a task set suitable to analyse the system under both the original MrsP formulation and our analysis proposal.

The equivalent task set and the response time results obtained for MrsP using the original, homogeneous analysis technique are shown in Table 2. The results obtained using the heterogeneous analysis are shown in Table 3. These results show an average response time reduction of 34.86%, where higher priority tasks are the most benefited ones with respect to their response times, and lower priority tasks are the most benefited in net time values.

The improvements obtained from the heterogeneous analysis are summarized in Table 4. Higher priority tasks not accessing any shared resource are obviously not affected at all by the kind of analysis. On the contrary, the highest priority task in Core_0 has a response time which is 43.74% lower with the heterogeneous analysis technique than that obtained with original analysis method proposed in [6]. The second lowest priority task on the same processor, which is the last task undergoing blocking, experiments a reduction of 39.79% in its response time. For the lowest priority task in the same processor, the reduction is still 38.05%. Notice also that the task executing by itself on Core_1 has a reduction of 11.61% in its response time.

5   Evaluation

The case study presented in Sect. 4 illustrates how this approach can be of benefit in a real world system. In order to evaluate the difference between MSRP and MrsP with the heterogeneous analysis technique that was introduced in Sect. 3, a study has been carried out on a set of synthetic task sets with different processor configurations, processor utilizations, and timing requirements. The schedulability of each task set has been analysed considering homogeneous and heterogeneous access costs, and it has been compared to an ideal optimal protocol not causing any blocking. A total of 100 000 task sets have been generated for each configuration.

Each task set has been generated using as parameters the number of processors N, the number of shared resources R, which has been set equal to N for this study, and a target utilization U for each processor and the whole system. The utilization of each task has been set to $U_i = f_i \times U$, where f_i is a uniform random variable in an interval $[U_{min}..U_{max}]$.

Task periods are also randomly generated in an interval $[T_{min}..T_{max}]$, and deadlines have been made equal to periods. The worst case execution time for each task is $C_i = U_i \times T_i$.

For each task τ_i and every resource r^j, the probability of the task accessing at least once the resource has been set to $1/R$. Then, the resource execution time for that task was uniformly designated between 0.01% and 10.00% of the overall task execution time. Then, the probability of a task accessing the resource N times on each task activation is calculated so as $P(N) = 1/N^2$. In order to maintain the envisaged task utilization, the accessing times to shared resources were deducted from the task original C value.

Table 2. UPMSat-2 case study original analysis. Tasks are ordered by decreasing priority. All times in ms.

	Task	T	D	C	Write	Read	B	R
Core_0	ADCS_PWM_1	2000	800	0.81				0.810
	ADCS_PWM_2	2000	800	0.81				1.620
	ADCS_PWM_3	2000	800	0.81				2.430
	ADCS_Control_Task	2000	100	4.02	15.870		31.740	69.930
	ADCS_Measurement_1	2000	200	2.73			31.740	72.660
	ADCS_Measurement_2	2000	200	2.73			31.740	75.390
	ADCS_Measurement_3	2000	200	2.73			31.740	78.120
	ADCS_Measurement_4	2000	200	2.73			31.740	80.850
	ADCS_Measurement_5	2000	200	2.73	15.870		31.740	115.320
	Housekeeping_Task	1000	1000	13.71	2×15.870			160.770
Core_1	TMTC_Task	1000	1000	100		15.870		131.740

Table 3. UPMSat-2 case study heterogeneous analysis. Tasks are ordered by decreasing priority. All times in ms.

	Task	T	D	C	Write	Read	B	R
Core_0	ADCS_PWM_1	2000	800	0.81				0.810
	ADCS_PWM_2	2000	800	0.81				1.620
	ADCS_PWM_3	2000	800	0.81				2.430
	ADCS_Control_Task	2000	100	4.02	15.870		16.445	39.340
	ADCS_Measurement_1	2000	200	2.73			16.445	42.070
	ADCS_Measurement_2	2000	200	2.73			16.445	44.800
	ADCS_Measurement_3	2000	200	2.73			16.445	47.530
	ADCS_Measurement_4	2000	200	2.73			16.445	50.260
	ADCS_Measurement_5	2000	200	2.73	15.870		16.445	69.435
	Housekeeping_Task	1000	1000	13.71	2×15.870			99.590
Core_1	TMTC_Task	1000	1000	100		0.575		116.445

Table 4. UPMSat-2 EEPROM memory analysis improvement summary.

Task	Homogeneous	Heterogeneous	Reduction
ADCS_Control	69.930 ms	39.340 ms	43.74%
ADCS_Measurement_5	115.320 ms	69.435 ms	39.79%
Housekeeping	160.770 ms	99.590 ms	30.05%
TMTC	131.740 ms	116.445 ms	11.61%

The experiment was carried out for systems with a configuration of $N = 2, 4, 8$, and 16 processors. For each value of N, the processor utilization U was increased from 0.1 to 0.7 by steps of 0.05. For each configuration, values for U_{min} and U_{max} have been set to $[0.1, 0.2]$, $[0.1, 0.3]$, $[0.1, 0.4]$, $[0.1, 0.5]$, $[0.1, 0.9]$, and

[0.25, 0.75]. The values of T_{min} and T_{max} were kept equal to [100, 10 000] for all the configurations.

The total number of different configurations in the experiment is $318 = 52 \times 6$. For the sake of conciseness, only the most relevant results and comparisons are presented in this paper.

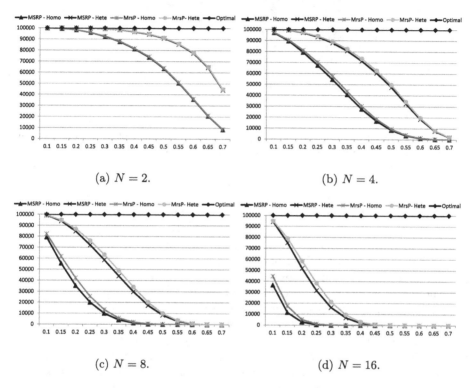

(a) $N = 2$.   (b) $N = 4$.

(c) $N = 8$.   (d) $N = 16$.

Fig. 1. Number of schedulable systems against system utilization. Tasks have an utilization between 0.1 and 0.2 of the total processor utilization.

Figure 1, shows the number of systems schedulable under both homogeneous and heterogeneous analysis for the four different numbers of processors considered, based on the average system utilization. It can be seen that using the heterogeneous analysis technique provides better schedulability as the number of processors increases. It can also be seen that MrsP provides overall better schedulability than MSRP.

Figure 2 describes how this approach gives better results as the number of processors grows, by showing the percentage of schedulable systems under each analysis for a certain configuration. It can be clearly seen that the difference between homogeneous and heterogeneous analysis increases as the number of processors gets larger.

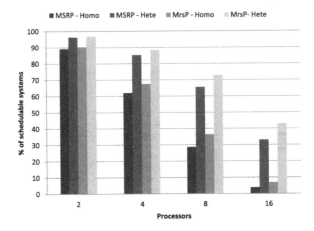

Fig. 2. Number of schedulable systems depending on the number of processors. System utilization: 0.35. Utilization per task [0.1, 0.9] of overall utilization.

Finally, Fig. 3 plots the percentage of extra systems that are schedulable only under heterogeneous access costs analysis. For both protocols, improvement is achieved even for simpler systems (dual core, 10% utilization). For more complex systems, the improvement is exponential on the number of processors, better reflected on systems with higher utilizations.

The improvement is driven by the fact that, the more processors the system has, the longer a queue for a resource can be in the worst case, as there can be more parallel requests. Given that, the more processors from where requests can be issued, the more probable is to have significantly different worst access costs from each processor. As a result, the homogeneous analysis becomes more pessimistic. Therefore, systems with a higher utilization benefit more from heterogeneous analysis. As in these systems the response times tend to be closer to the deadlines, the schedulability analysis is more reactive to changes in computation times.

In order to compare how response times are affected by the proposed approach, specific response times were collected as part of the experiments. In particular, the response time of the highest and lowest priority tasks allocated to the first processor were recorded. Only values from systems deemed schedulable with all the analysis techniques have been considered. For those, the extra response time for each task compared to the optimal scheduling was calculated. Figure 4 shows the overhead for systems with the biggest differences between task utilizations. In the figure, as expected, the highest priority tasks have their worst response times under homogeneous MSRP analysis. With this technique, the highest priority task has to cope with a blocking time equal to the highest access time to a shared resource in the system among those accessed from tasks on its own processor, times the number of processors from where this resource can be accessed. Under MrsP this is improved by only incurring blocking from resources also used by the same highest priority task. However, the blocking time

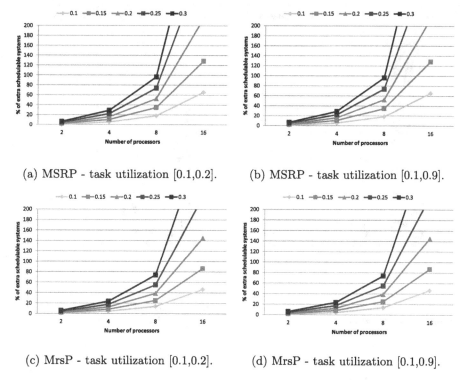

(a) MSRP - task utilization [0.1,0.2].   (b) MSRP - task utilization [0.1,0.9].

(c) MrsP - task utilization [0.1,0.2].   (d) MrsP - task utilization [0.1,0.9].

Fig. 3. Percentage of extra schedulable systems of heterogeneous over homogeneous analysis for increasing system utilizations.

would still be equal to the worst access time to the resource times the number of processors from where this resource can be accessed.

In the same way as in the analysis of schedulable systems, the MSRP heterogeneous analysis provides better results than the homogeneous MrsP. In this case, with MSRP the blocking suffered by the highest priority task is the maximum of the sum of worst accesses per processor of a resource used on its host processor. While this still includes resources not accessed by the higher priority tasks, the variability on different worst access costs among processors gives, on average, better results. Finally, MrsP heterogeneous analysis gives the tighter response times.

Regarding lower priority tasks, results are similar for both protocols and analysis techniques: as the only difference between MSRP and MrsP analysis is the impact of arrival blocking, and the lowest priority tasks are not affected by arrival blocking, the same results are obtained for both protocols. However, there is still an improvement, coming from the self accesses to resources of lowest priority tasks, even for tasks of similar utilizations, as shown in Fig. 5.

It is also worth mentioning that, for the 31 200 000 systems that were analysed in the experiment, there was no system schedulable under the homogeneous

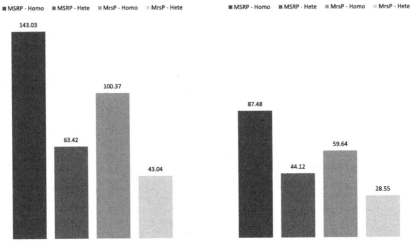

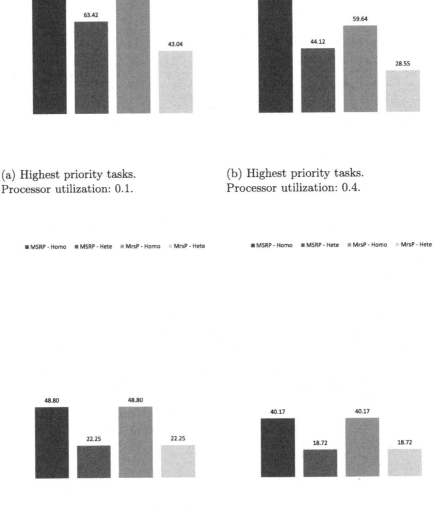

(a) Highest priority tasks.
Processor utilization: 0.1.

(b) Highest priority tasks.
Processor utilization: 0.4.

(c) Lowest priority tasks.
Processor utilization: 0.1.

(d) Lowest priority tasks.
Processor utilization: 0.4.

Fig. 4. Percentage of extra response time over optimal scheduling. Task utilization: [0.1, 0.9] of overall processor utilization. 8 processors.

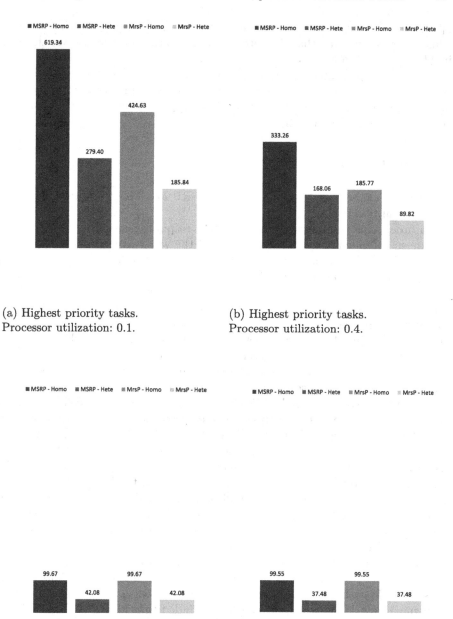

(a) Highest priority tasks.
Processor utilization: 0.1.

(b) Highest priority tasks.
Processor utilization: 0.4.

(c) Lowest priority tasks.
Processor utilization: 0.1.

(d) Lowest priority tasks.
Processor utilization: 0.4.

Fig. 5. Percentage of extra response time over an optimal scheduling. Task utilization: [0.1, 0.2] of overall processor utilization. 8 processors.

approach that was not schedulable under the heterogeneous analysis technique. This confirms our claim that the heterogeneous analysis dominates over the original homogeneous analysis.

The results presented above show that both MSRP and MrsP analysis tend to decrease their efficiency as the number of processors increases. In order to be able to support future generation of many-core processors, an efficient allocation strategy will indeed be required.

6   Conclusions

A thorough analysis of schedulability for MSRP and MrsP protocols has been presented in this paper.

In order to obtain more accurate results, response time analysis techniques have been extended to get a tighter value of the worst-case response times. We have validated the extended analysis technique on a real-life case study, using a tool developed to this purpose. In this case study we have analysed the access costs to an EEPROM memory in the UPMSat-2 satellite considering a dual-core platform. The experiment has shown an overall reduction of a 34.86% in the overall response time over the original homogeneous approach. The enhanced analysis technique thus provides better schedulability, as more tasks can be run on the same platform without missing any deadlines.

In order to achieve a more general assessment, an extensive experiment using randomly generated task sets has been carried out. Schedulability results for different configurations under the MSRP and MrsP protocols, as well as an ideal optimal protocol have been analysed. The experiment shows that the potential extra blocking for high priority tasks imposed by MSRP is not relevant in most situations. The results manifest that the heterogeneous analysis for MSRP consistently shows better results in both schedulability and response times than the MrsP homogeneous access cost analysis. As expected, the heterogeneous access cost analysis for MrsP offers the overall best results. However, this protocol, in its current form, is far from being implemented in high-integrity critical applications, due to the current challenges on measuring the costs of migrating tasks on real platforms.

On the other hand, MSRP is in essence similar to MrsP and provides comparable results in many cases. Since it does not require task migrations, MSRP is compatible with the Ravenscar profile in its present form, and is simpler to implement in Ada. Therefore, it can be concluded that MSRP is a good choice for implementing access locks under the Ravenscar profile, while MrsP would be a sensible choice for full Ada real-time programs.

It should be noted that a slight improvement in real-time analysis techniques, as proposed in the paper, can help programmers to compare locking protocols and adopt the best solution for a given development.

Acknowledgements. The authors would like to acknowledge the fruitful discussion with Guillem Bernat who provided some initial ideas for the paper.

We would also like to acknowledge the helpful comments by anonymous reviewers, which have contributed to improve the quality of the paper.

References

1. ISO/IEC 8652:2012(E): Information Technology – Programming Languages – Ada (2012)
2. Audsley, N.C., Burns, A., Richardson, M., Tindell, K., Wellings, A.: Applying new scheduling theory to static priority preemptive scheduling. Softw. Eng. J. **8**(5), 284–292 (1993)
3. Brandenburg, B.B.: Scheduling and locking in multiprocessor real-time operating systems. Ph.D. thesis, The University of North Carolina at Chapel Hill (2011)
4. Burns, A., Wellings, A.J.: Locking policies for multiprocessor Ada. Ada Lett. **33**(2), 59–65 (2013)
5. Burns, A., Dobbing, B., Vardanega, T.: Guide for the use of the Ada Ravenscar profile in high integrity systems. Ada Lett. **XXIV**, 1–74 (2004)
6. Burns, A., Wellings, A.J.: A schedulability compatible multiprocessor resource sharing protocol-MrsP. In: 2013 25th Euromicro Conference on Real-Time Systems (ECRTS), pp. 282–291. IEEE (2013)
7. Davis, R.I., Burns, A.: A survey of hard real-time scheduling algorithms and schedulability analysis techniques for multiprocessor systems. ACM Computing Surveys **43**(4) (2011)
8. Dobbing, B., Burns, A.: The Ravenscar profile for high-integrity real-time programs. Ada Lett. **XVII**(6), 1–6 (1998). Proceedings of the ACM SIGAda International Conference – SIGAda 1998
9. Gai, P., Lipari, G., Natale, M.D.: Minimizing memory utilization of real-time task sets in single and multi-processor systems-on-a-chip. In: Proceedings of the 22nd IEEE Real-Time Systems Symposium. IEEE Computer Society (2001)
10. Garrido, J., Lacruz, B., Zamorano, J., de la Puente, J.A.: In support of extending the Ravenscar profile. Ada Lett. **36**(1), 63–67 (2016)
11. Leung, J.Y.T., Whitehead, J.: On the complexity of fixed-priority scheduling of periodic real-time tasks. Perform. Eval. **2**(4), 237–250 (1982)
12. Lin, S., Wellings, A.J., Burns, A.: Ada 2012: resource sharing and multiprocessors. Ada Lett. **33**(1), 32–44 (2013)
13. de la Puente, J.A., Zamorano, J., Alonso, A., Garrido, J., Salazar, E., de Miguel, M.A.: Experience in spacecraft on-board software development. Ada User J. **35**(1), 55–60 (2014)
14. Rajkumar, R., Sha, L., Lehoczky, J.P.: Real-time synchronization protocols for multiprocessors. In: IEEE Real-Time Systems Symposium (1988)
15. Rajkumar, R.: Real-time synchronization protocols for shared memory multiprocessors. In: Proceedings of the 10th International Conference on Distributed Computing Systems, pp. 116–123. IEEE (1990)
16. Rajkumar, R.: Synchronization in Real-Time Systems: A priority Inheritance Approach. Kluwer Academic Publishers, Dordrecht (1991)
17. Zamorano, J., Garrido, J.: Schedulability analysis of PWM tasks for the UPMSat-2 ADCS. In: de la Puente, J.A., Vardanega, T. (eds.) Ada-Europe 2015. LNCS, vol. 9111, pp. 85–99. Springer, Cham (2015). doi:10.1007/978-3-319-19584-1_6

Ravenscar-EDF: Comparative Benchmarking of an EDF Variant of a Ravenscar Runtime

Paolo Carletto$^{(\boxtimes)}$ and Tullio Vardanega$^{(\boxtimes)}$

Department of Mathematics, University of Padua, 35121 Padua, Italy
carletto.paolo@gmail.com, tullio.vardanega@math.unipd.it

Abstract. Subsequent to the publication of the seminal work by Liu and Layland in 1973, researchers and practitioners alike started discussing which online scheduling algorithm was to be preferred between FPS and EDF. Results published in 2005 sustained the superiority of EDF, already proven in theory, also from an implementation perspective. With this work, we aim at digging deeper into the roots of those results. To this end, we took the first-ever instance of an Ada Ravenscar runtime, with its FPS scheduler, combined with its IPCP locking policy companion, and developed a variant of it that implements EDF scheduling coupled with DFP locking. In this manner, we were able to transparently attach those two runtime variants to a suite of synthetic benchmarks, which we used to perform an extensive quantitative comparison between those two runtimes, getting to the bottom of where one prevails on the other.

Keywords: Ravenscar profile · Earliest Deadline First · Deadline Floor Protocol · Analysis and development · Performance comparison

1 Introduction

The publication of the seminal work by Liu and Layland [6] back in 1973 sparked a great deal of interest on the question of which online (preemptive) scheduling policy for single-core processors was best. From that moment, the real-time systems community divided between two camps: one supporting Rate Monotonic (RM); the other championing Earliest Deadline First (EDF). From the usage perspective, this confrontation seems to have been won by the RM camp, as the most part of existing technology, whether general-purpose operating systems or real-time kernels implements Fixed Priority Preemptive Scheduling, hence RM. Arguably, this happens because RM is easier to implement on top of runtimes that do not support the notion of timing deadline natively. Implementation is simpler also because a fixed-priority constant value can be assigned per task and simply copied to each recurrent job of it, without the per-job dynamic computation that the deadline driven approach requires. A simplistic technique to implement a deadline-driven scheduler on top of a priority-based runtime directly maps absolute deadlines to the existing priorities. In that manner, any real-time kernel that supports priorities can also support deadline-driven scheduling, at

© Springer International Publishing AG 2017
J. Blieberger and M. Bader (Eds.): Ada-Europe 2017, LNCS 10300, pp. 18–33, 2017.
DOI: 10.1007/978-3-319-60588-3_2

the cost of computing the deadline-to-priority mapping at any job release, and of resolving the conflicts that may arise when multiple deadlines map to the same priority. Some authors [7] suggested that this additional implementation burden and the runtime overhead stemming from dynamic priority management was the prime reason for EDF not being supported in commercial real-time kernels, in spite of it being known that EDF would maximise the total schedulable utilization of the processor [11].

The work we present here illustrates an empirical, quantitative comparison between concrete implementations of the RM and EDF variants of a real-time kernel embedded in the Ada Ravenscar runtime developed by AdaCore for the Leon processor[1] family.

Arguably, our work yields two distinct contributions. First, it makes a very fair comparison as the *sole* elements that change in the systems being confronted are the scheduling operations that implement RM and EDF in the corresponding runtimes. As the application stays unchanged, any performance difference is directly ascribable to the scheduling variant being used. Second, it stresses each system to the limits discussed in the literature [11] using exactly the same, unchanged, application software, as the switch of scheduling policy is completely transparent to it.

On those two premises, we have created a suite of synthetic benchmarks that aims to (and if fact does) single out the conditions under which one policy performs better than the other, to help appreciate why that happens more profoundly – we think – than discussed in [7].

2   The RM-to-EDF Transformation Process

2.1   The Ada Ravenscar Profile

The Ravenscar profile [3,4] is an important asset of the Ada programming language. Especially when used for embedded targets, it allows simple yet flexible real-time systems, fully analysable for their timing feasibility (aka schedulability), to be implemented on a runtime system that is itself lean, small and fast, fit for being engineered to the highest level of integrity. The profile is specified in the Ada standard (since its 2005 revision) via a collection of restrictions on the full language. It is defined to support applications that use a statically-defined set of library-level tasks scheduled by the fixed priority scheme known as "FIFO Within Priorities". The Ada Ravenscar Profile is especially designed for those embedded applications that have tight timing and memory requirements, high-integrity (eg. safety-critical) constraints, and want to dispense with the heavy constraints of traditional cyclic scheduling.

The first-ever Ravenscar runtime to be released to industrial use was produced by AdaCore for the Leon processor family, and named *GNAT-2012-LEON-ELF-BIN*. That technology originated from a fork of the Open Ravenscar Real-Time Kernel (ORK+) developed by the Technical University of Madrid[2].

---

[1] http://www.adacore.com/gnatpro-safety-critical/platforms/erc32/.
[2] http://www.dit.upm.es/~ork/index.html/.

The Leon processor that was targeted by that runtime is a 32-bit CPU microprocessor core, based on the SPARC-V8 RISC architecture and instruction set. It was originally designed by the European Space Research and Technology Centre (ESTEC), part of the European Space Agency (ESA), and subsequently developed, in synthesizable VHDL and maintained by Gaisler Research, now Cobham Gaisler.

An application conforming to the Ada Ravenscar Profile comprises N tasks that are due to execute concurrently on the same processor core. All such tasks are defined to have a period (denoted by the symbol T) that is the minimum time span that elapses between two subsequent releases of it, a relative deadline (D), and a worst-case execution time demand (C). For the system to be feasible, any task τ_i arriving at time t must be able to execute for its maximum computation time (C_i) by its absolute deadline, which falls at time $t + D_i$.

With fixed priority scheduling, each task is assigned a static priority (P), which is attached at release to all of its recurring jobs. For best schedulability results, the task priority is derived from its relative deadline (or equivalently, its rate, when $D = T$). Two tasks with relative deadlines D_i and D_j, such that $D_i < D_j$, will be assigned priorities such that $P_i > P_j$.

Under the Ravenscar Profile, tasks may contend for exclusive access to shared resources that are enclosed within protected objects. To warrant predictable arbitration of such contention, protected objects are assigned a static ceiling priority, and access to the protected object is controlled by the priority ceiling protocol (PCP) [9]. The form of PCP assumed in the Ravenscar Profile is the "immediate" version (IPCP) of it, in which the contending task's priority is raised to the resource ceiling immediately upon access to the resource.

The Ada runtime that we used in this work does not support the 2012 version of the language, and therefore does not allow the user to directly represent relative deadlines in the program code. We circumvented that limitation by providing an ad-hoc API, which is only used during task elaboration and had no impact on our comparative performance evaluation.

To perform our experiment, we modified the original Ravenscar runtime to support Earliest Deadline First for scheduling [2], and the Deadline Floor Protocol [5] for locking. Thanks to the substantial semantic equivalence between FPS with IPCP and EDF with DFP, we were able to compare those two runtime variants, which only differ in a small number of (important) scheduling operations.

2.2   Turning Priorities into Deadlines

Earliest deadline first (EDF) is a dynamic scheduling algorithm that places tasks in a ready queue sorted by absolute deadline in increasing order. Whenever a scheduling event occurs (job completion, job release, synchronization lock released), the task with the shortest absolute deadline is dispatched to execution.

The Deadline Floor Protocol (DFP) used in an EDF-scheduled system when tasks contend for shared resources, is structurally equivalent to the Immediate

Priority Ceiling Protocol (IPCP) used in a system scheduled under fixed priorities. Under the DFP, every resource is assigned a relative deadline equal to the shortest relative deadline of the tasks that may use it. The relative deadline attribute of a shared resource is called its *deadline floor*, a pun to the sought symmetry with the *priority ceiling* defined for all priority ceiling protocols. The key idea in the DFP is that the absolute deadline of a task might be temporarily shortened while accessing a shared resource, increasing its preemption privilege under EDF. Given a task with absolute deadline d that accesses a resource with deadline floor D_F at time t, the absolute deadline of the task becomes $d := min(d, t + D_F)$ while holding the resource.

Given these definitions, a Ravenscar-EDF Profile [1,2] with DFP presents two main differences to the original one:

1. A different Task Dispatching Policy: the default *"FIFO Within Priorities"* scheduling policy is replaced by *"EDF"*, while retaining the logic that jobs with identical deadlines (a much rarer event than having identical priorities) would have FIFO ordering in the ready queue. As a Ravenscar runtime has only one scheduling policy, we changed the fixed priority default to EDF directly inside the source code of the Ravenscar-EDF runtime. Notably, since our EDF system variant works only in an *"EDF"* mode we did not need to follow the Ada standard *"EDF Within Priorities"* scheduling which was designed to allow it to coexist with other dispatching policies;
2. A different Locking Policy for shared resources: the default locking policy, IPCP [9] is replaced by DFP [5], designed for EDF scheduling. As a Ravenscar runtime can only have one locking policy, we changed IPCP to DFP directly in the source code of the Ravenscar-EDF runtime.

To implement the new scheduling model and the new locking policy of the Ravenscar-EDF runtime [2], we had to modify some fundamental data structures in the original runtime; specifically, those related with the handling of tasks and protected objects, as shown in Fig. 1. Let us now illustrate the changes we applied in some detail.

First, we needed to support pragma Relative_Deadline in place of the original pragma Priority, to attach the EDF scheduling attribute to application tasks. The attribute value declared by the user is used at initialization time to set the new Base_Relative_Deadline attribute, added to the Ada Task Control Block, which never changes during program execution. In turn, this value serves to maintain two new task attributes:

1. Active_Relative_Deadline: to represent the task's relative deadline, which the runtime must consider for the purposes of scheduling. The value of this attribute may change because of DFP, which may temporarily lower it when the task acquires a protected object. If this attribute were missing, DFP would overwrite the Base_Relative_Deadline attribute thereby preventing correct restoration of the original base relative deadline of the task when leaving the protected object.

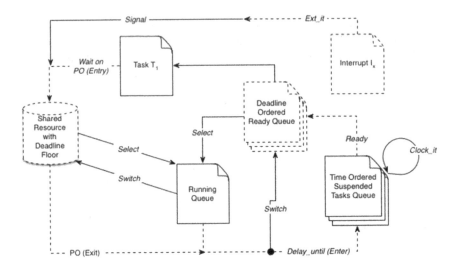

Fig. 1. An outline of the internals of the EDF runtime. Dotted lines represent the data structures that have to be changed to support EDF and DFP.

2. `Active_Absolute_Deadline`: to determine the task position in the ready queue, at every dispatching point. The absolute deadline of a job of τ_i released at time t is $t + D_i$ where D_i is the task's relative deadline.

Next, we had to introduce a new directive `pragma Deadline_Floor` to replace `pragma Priority` for setting the locking attribute of protected objects.

The biggest changes obviously concerned the scheduling policy, which required replacing every priority based criteria in use to manage the ready queue with a new deadline based policy.

This change entailed a full revamp of the queueing system in the runtime. Whereas the original version compared static priority values to determine one task's position in the ready queue, the EDF version compares absolute time values, which are computed at release for every new job. To avoid unduly biasing the evaluation, we chose to retain in the EDF runtime exactly the same linked-list organization that was implemented in the original version. A linked list that needs linear traversal for positioning a task in the ready queue is obviously not the most efficient choice of runtime structure: the FPS solution should rather use an array of per-priority queues; The EDF solution instead a binary tree. Yet, we did not go that way, to make the comparison fair.

In contrast with [2], we decided to retain the `Delay_until` API for the EDF runtime, so that application tasks would have an identical API to invoke across the two runtime variants. Again, this choice may seem to deflect from the Ada standard, but in a Ravenscar-EDF runtime, the EDF semantics of `Delay_until` is very straightforward and allows the application to stay unchanged on the switch of runtime. To this end, we moved to the `Wakeup_Expired_Alarms` procedure the operation of computing the new absolute deadline on task resumption and placing it in the ready queue accordingly, so that Delay_until only had to assert the preemption variable when the running task is taken off the CPU. Notably, this simplification eased our refactoring of interrupt handling.

Further changes were needed to support DFP, but they turned out to be easy because DFP works in exactly the same way as IPCP once the runtime replaces priorities by deadlines. Both the original (IPCP) and the new version (DFP) modify the corresponding attribute of the task that gains access to a protected object (PO). IPCP raises the task's current priority to the priority ceiling of the PO; DFP lowers the relative deadline of the task to the deadline floor of the PO.

To implement DFP, we had to add a new Floor attribute to the Protection record of the PO, which stores the deadline floor attribute assigned to the protected object at declaration. We then added a Caller_Relative_Deadline attribute to store the relative deadline of the task that acquires the PO, to allow restoring the task's original relative deadline on leaving the PO. We changed the Initialize_Protection procedure that is called when pragma Deadline_Floor is encountered by the main program during initialization, to set the value of Floor attribute in the PO. Finally, we changed the Lock and Unlock procedures so that they update the relative deadline of the task on access to the PO and restore the original one on exit, respectively.

2.3   Implementation Challenges

Implementing the changes described in the previous section caused some development problems, which may be worth recalling to illustrate the bottom-up repercussions of top-down pressure of language changes.

First of all, we incurred the circular dependency shown in Fig. 2 when, following the suggestions in [5], we included the package Ada.Deadlines as a dependent of Ada.Real_Time. Using the ''limited with'' clause did not help, since it does not apply to subtypes, which deadlines are in fact.

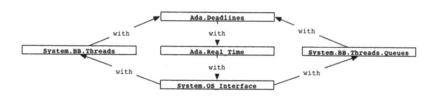

Fig. 2. Circular dependency caused by the introduction of package Ada.Deadlines.

We solved that problem by moving all the relevant contents of Ada.Real_Time into System.BB.Time, so that introducing System.BB.Deadlines as a child unit to it did not cause any visibility issues. Not a clean solution, indeed, though effective for the particular internal organization of the runtime we used.

A much bigger and more fundamental problem we incurred had to do with the handling of interrupts. The crux of it is that interrupt handling intrinsically assumes priorities, which – in principle – do not belong in an EDF system.

In the original Ravenscar runtime (as well as in the Ada standard), interrupts have their own set of priority values, defined by the `Interrupt_Priority` type, at the top of the interrupt range, from 241 to 255 for our processor target. The intent is that interrupt handlers go directly to the top of the ready queue and concur solely with other interrupts as described in the left of Fig. 3. This mechanism is very natural for a priority based system, but it does not fit well in a deadline-based runtime as long as they have no deadline attribute (as reported in the center of Fig. 3).

The solution that we adopted reserves a fictitious position at the top of the ready queue for the current interrupt handler. If an interrupt handler is active, that position is used and the deadline-based part of the queue is frozen. If no interrupt is running, that position is not in use and cannot be contended. We unlock the queue when the handler exits, thereby enabling normal tasks to execute again. This solution does *not* support interrupt nesting, but it could be extended to it by making the top position point to a priority-ordered queue reserved for interrupts. The right part of Fig. 3 shows the reengineering of the ready queue from the original version to the EDF one with support for interrupts.

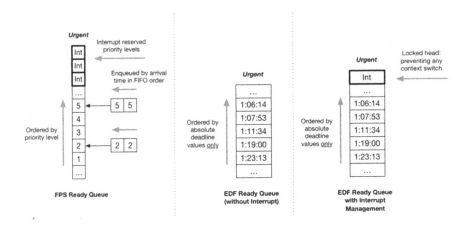

Fig. 3. Different ready queue organizations.

To implement these mechanisms, we changed the `Change_Priority` procedure to use a persistent boolean flag, to tell whether an interrupt handler is running or not. Asserting that variable effectively inhibits context switch and enables interrupt handlers to execute undisturbed.

The `Change_Priority` procedure is called inside `Interrupt_Wrapper`, the container that enables interrupt handlers to execute on their own stack, transparently to normal tasks.

The not-very-elegant nature of the solution that we devised for interrupt handling was one of the two major integration problems that we encountered. The other arose in evaluating the `Default_Relative_Deadline` attribute, which mirrors the `Default_Priority` value of the FPS runtime, assigned to all priority attributes that lack explicit user setting. The FPS attribute is set, arbitrarily, to the value that best approximates the medium point in the standard priority range, excluding the top subrange reserved for interrupts. In our FPS runtime, the chosen value was 120. In a deadline based system, there is no sound value to choose. A small value penalizes urgent tasks that have been set an explicit relative deadline by the user. A large value may penalize the "defaulted" task if it happened to live in a system with many urgent tasks.

Since none of our synthetic tasks had uninitialized deadlines, we were free to arbitrarily set the `Default_Relative_Deadline` attribute value to zero and let it be overwritten by the relative deadline that the program assigned to the task at declaration. A better solution should be defined for general use.

3   Evaluation Benchmark

In keeping with the empirical nature of our experiment, we based our evaluation approach on the generation, categorization and execution of a large number of test scenarios designed to thoroughly stress both runtime variants.

To this end, we defined three types of synthetic tasks - Short, Mid and Long -, each with corresponding magnitude of period P and worst-case execution time C. We then composed those tasks into tasksets with different cardinality (which ranged from 30 to 180 concurrent tasks) and a variety of CPU utilization scenarios between 75% and 125%.

We further duplicated the tasksets into one version with *implicit* deadlines and the other with *constrained* deadlines, using Rate Monotonic or Deadline Monotonic assignments respectively for the FPS benchmarks.

Figure 4 depicts the automation engine that we constructed to generate, build, execute and record the run of 5.438 tasksets. In the first step, the engine composes tasksets, incurring a bound on their maximum cardinality determined by the 4 MB limit of the target processor's limit. Subsequently, it tests their feasibility using Response Time Analysis (RTA) for FPS [10] and the equivalent criterion for EDF. Since those tests are exact and accurate, we were able to have fine-grained control over the worst-case utilization scenarios that we wanted to generate.

For the FPS case, our engine uses a simpler variant of the fine-grained high-accuracy version of the classic RTA equation presented in [12]:

$$R_i^{n+1} = CS1 + C_i + \sum_{j \in hp(i)}^{n} \left\lceil \frac{R_i^n}{T_j} \right\rceil \cdot (CS1 + C_j + CS2) \tag{1}$$

With Eq. 1, a taskset scheduled with FPS, is feasible if and only if $R_i \leq D_i \ \forall i$. Let us briefly recall the meaning of the cost factors that appear in it.

1. $CS1$ is the context switch experienced by task τ_i when it preempts another task on access to the CPU.

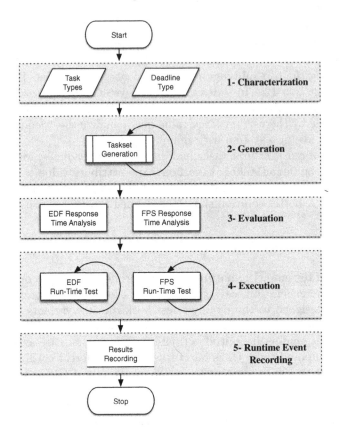

Fig. 4. Automated engine generation and evaluation steps.

2. C_i is the highest computation time demand of task τ_i;
3. T_j is the period of task τ_j;
4. $CS2$ is the dual of $CS1$ and accounts for the cost of cleaning the context up when task τ_j releases the CPU;

The feasibility of the same tasksets was then evaluated for EDF with the quantitative method proposed in [11] for constrained-deadline systems, using Eq. 2:

$$h(t) = \sum_{j=1}^{i} \max \left(0, \left\lfloor \frac{t - D_j}{T_j} \right\rfloor + 1 \right) \cdot (CS1 + C_j + CS2) \tag{2}$$

which stipulates that a taskset is schedulable under EDF if and only if the worst-case CPU load L does not exceed 1:

$$L = \max_{\forall t} \left(\frac{h(t)}{t} \right) \leq 1 \tag{3}$$

The subsequent step was the core part of our automation engine: in it, we compile, build and execute the benchmark tasks for both runtimes, recording each occurrence of 3 events of interest:

- **Regular Completion**: when a task's job completes execution within the assigned deadline;
- **Deadline Missed**: when a task's job completes after its assigned deadline;
- **Preemption**: when the current task is preempted by a newly release job.

We run our benchmarks on an evaluation version of the *TSIM/LEON SPARC simulator*, which limits the longest span of execution to $2^{32} = 4.294.967.296$ clock cycles. To overcome that limitation we used an approach derived from [8], which suggests how to generate bounded hyperperiods using a composition of bases and exponents. As we needed to contain the highest hyperperiod to 2^{32}, we set an artificial upper-bound to $2^7 \cdot 3^6 \cdot 5^3 \cdot 7^3 = 4.000.752.000 < 2^{32}$. Adding this constraint to the taskset generation algorithm, we ensured that all their hyperperiods would fully execute with our simulator. Moreover, using prime numbers as the basis of the calculation, we yielded a sufficient quantity of not harmonic[3] tasksets.

4   Evaluation Results

Citation [7] arguably is the most famous discussion of a structured quantitative performance comparison of EDF vs FPS. Acknowledging it, we decided to follow its same overall logic, setting the following evaluation criteria:

1. **Highest Schedulable Utilization**: Which tasksets achieved the highest schedulable utilization in each runtime variant? How did the corresponding values relate to the theoretical ratios discussed in [11]?
2. **runtime Overhead**: Do the less preemptions and context switches that EDF incurs justify the higher costs of its scheduling operations?
3. **Resilience to Overload Situations**: What happens to EDF and FPS under overload conditions, when the CPU utilization exceeds 100%?
4. **Locking Policy**: How does DFP perform compared to IPCP?

Question 1 reflects the intent to seek empirical evidence in relation to the theoretical results presented in [11]. That work in fact shows that the performance of EDF is 1,44269 better than FPS for Implicit Deadlines, 1,76322 for Constrained Deadlines and 2 for Arbitrary Deadlines.

Table 1 presents the results we obtained in response to criterion 1. Interestingly, they are much less slanted in favour to EDF than they were in [11].

The highest utilization (obtained without incurring deadline misses) reached by our EDF runtime was only 3,72% (first two lines of Table 1) better than achieved by FPS for the same tasksets. As expected in point of theory, EDF prevailed because it generated a lower number of preemptions, which yielded room

---

[3] A task system has harmonic rates if and only if the periods of its tasks are pairwise divisible (for each i, j one has $p_i|p_j$ or $p_j|p_i$ with no remainder.

Table 1. Highest schedulable utilization achieved by EDF over FPS (line 1 & 2) and vice-versa (line 3 & 4). **RC** stands for Regular Completions; **DM** for Deadline Misses; **PR** for Preemptions

Taskset type	Task types	Delta schedulable utilization	Max CPU load	EDF			FPS		
				RC	DM	PR	RC	DM	PR
Constrained	Short & mid	**2,89%**	105,50%	30.714	0	3.637	29.850	415	6.202
Implicit	Mid only	**3,72%**	102,63%	18.691	0	837	18.021	673	2.040
Constrained	All	**0,05%**	104,06%	24.398	0	5.131	24.409	0	5.211
Implicit	All	**5,22%**	100,85%	24.935	953	6.309	26.236	0	5.715

for higher schedulable utilization, but surprisingly less markedly for constrained-deadline tasksets, and more visibly – but still marginally – for implicit-deadline tasksets. In our experiments, tasks' execution times are short enough to be sensitive to the overhead of runtime procedures, making the different complexity of the two runtimes more manifest.

The good relative performance of FPS presented in the bottom half of Table 1 can be explained in two ways, depending on the type of experiment that yielded it: when the number of preemptions spared by EDF with respect to FPS is small, then the marginal gain in schedulable CPU utilization also becomes small; conversely, when a taskset overloads the CPU, EDF may "blow up" and cause an inordinate number of vacuous preemptions, many of which lead to deadline miss.

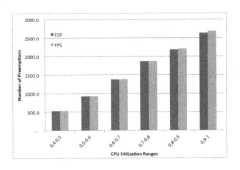

Fig. 5. Average number of preemptions in both runtimes with utilization ≤100%.

The different preemption behaviour of the two runtimes leads to Question 2. As the cost of individual context switch operations is nearly the same (ca. 2,389 CPU cycles) in both runtimes, answering that question required considering the cumulative cost incurred in the respective executions. Figure 5 shows the average benefit gained by EDF from lesser recourse to preemption for schedulable utilizations under 100%. The total quantity of CPU time that the application tasks could earn from that benefit in a hyperperiod scarcely exceeded 120000 CPU cycles, very little indeed, considering that the smallest (short) tasks in our experiments run for 750000 cycles. This quantity however must be considered with care, since it is an average value, which balances out best- and worst-case situations, where the two runtimes may perform rather differently.

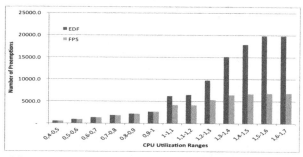

(a) Total preemptions in the full utilization spectrum.

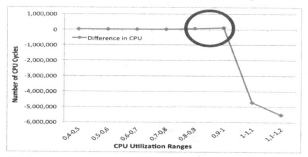

(b) Average cumulative differences in clock cycles over a full hyperperiod for CPU loads that increase from 0 to severe overload situations.

Fig. 6. Effect of differences in average number of preemptions for varying CPU loads.

When the CPU utilization exceeds 100%, the prevalence of EDF over FPS inverts radically: EDF incurs a much greater number of preemptions (cf. Fig. 6a), for a massive loss of application performance, which shadows to the modest gain achieved near 100%. Figure 6b contrasts the gain to the loss.

Question 3 delves deeper into the issue of what happens under overload conditions. Figure 7 plots the graph of dispersion for EDF and FPS, which helps highlight the greater resilience of FPS. When FPS operates in overload conditions in fact, the number of completed executions, deadline misses and preemptions are linear to one another (cf. Fig. 7b). This happens because only tasks with lower priorities (the "long" ones) are delayed indefinitely, without this affecting those with higher priority. EDF, instead, has a radically different behavior: beyond 100% utilization, its performance immediately starts to deteriorate and

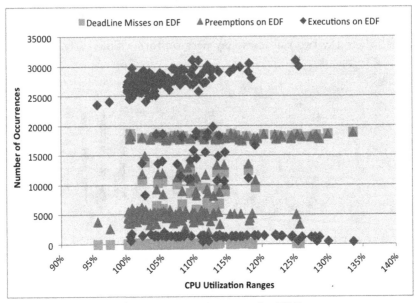

(a) Overload conditions under EDF.

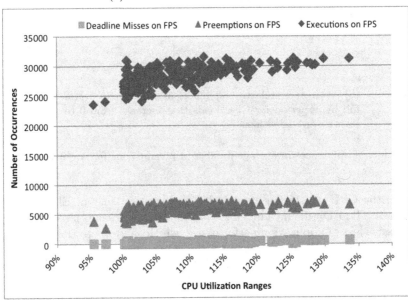

(b) Same taskset, same overload conditions but different behavior under FPS.

Fig. 7. Overload conditions under EDF and FPS.

two kinds of extreme behavior emerge, with a blurred zone in between them as shown in Fig. 7a. When the overload condition is transient (or rather the excess load is modest), EDF still allows a high number of completed executions (higher darkest diamonds in Fig. 7a) with a low number of misses and a relative small number of preemptions (respectively lower darker triangles and squares in the same graph). When the overload conditions are more marked, they generate a sort of domino effect, which causes the number of preemptions and misses to increase dramatically (higher darker triangles and squares), while the number of completed executions drops equally fast (lower darkest diamonds in Fig. 7a).

We should clarify that the utilization factor computed in accord with [11] represents the highest CPU load that the system incurs during a hyperperiod. This value may be much higher than the average load that we were able to measure at run time. Hence, a very high max CPU load does not necessarily mean an unsustainable situation, but can rather be seen as a transient overload that both runtime variants can possibly cope with.

Question 4 reports a quantitative comparison between the two locking policies we implemented in our runtime variants. From our implementation, we learned that they are extremely close to one another in terms of runtime overhead.

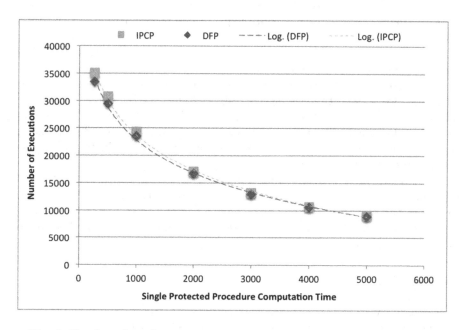

Fig. 8. Number of regular execution completions incurred in the experiment.

To tell the performance differences between them, we made a number of runs of tasksets comprised of only one task whose sole activity was to seize a PO and execute a protected procedure in it, varying its computation time from small to large. With this setting, we counted how many task executions each runtime was able to complete with the longest run of the simulator, without incurring deadline misses. Comparing the results, we saw that the applications running with IPCP completed more executions than with DFP. This difference decreases with a logarithmic converging progression as the computation time of the protected procedure increases (cf. Fig. 8). This result shows that DFP incurs more cumulative overhead than IPCP, evidently due to the need to read the clock in checking absolute deadlines.

5   Conclusions

In the past, the real-time systems community studied in earnest the relative benefits of EDF and FPS, with an eye to their use in industrial systems. Most of those studies where theoretical in nature, that is, they concentrated on the respective feasibility equations, showing that, in point of theory, EDF warranted much better performance.

In this work, we built an experimental framework where an EDF variant of an Ada Ravenscar runtime was developed and exposed to a quantitative comparison with the FPS original.

An interesting trait of our EDF runtime variant is that it changes the behavior of the smallest possible set of runtime primitives needed to support deadline-driven scheduling, without changing the API provided to the application. In that manner, we only had to build one (large) single set of benchmark applications and transparently bind them to the desired runtime.

Overall, our tests confirmed the theoretical conclusions reached by earlier works. Yet, we showed that the actual gain of EDF over FPS is far lower than anticipated even for CPU loads very close to 100%, where EDF was due to reap the best of its benefit. We also studied the behavior of EDF vs FPS scheduling under overload situations, where we experimentally observed the fragility of the former and contrasted to the resilience of the latter.

We hope to have provided milestone technology for the further study of this topic. Thanks to the high performance, modularity, and predictability of our Ravenscar runtimes, there is now room for further deeper investigations of how EDF (with DFP, which we also added to our implementation) behaves in comparison to FPS (with IPCP).

References

1. Burns, A.: A deadline-floor inheritance protocol for EDF scheduled real-time systems with resource sharing. Technical report YCS- 2012-476, Department of Computer Science, University of York, UK (2012)
2. Burns, A.: An EDF runtime profile based on Ravenscar. Ada Lett **XXXII**(1), 24–31 (2013)
3. Burns, A.: The Ravenscar profile ACM. Ada Lett. **XIX**(4), 49–52 (1999)
4. Burns, A., Dobbing, B., Romanski, G.: The Ravenscar tasking profile for high integrity real-time programs. In: Asplund, L. (ed.) Ada-Europe 1998. LNCS, vol. 1411, pp. 263–275. Springer, Heidelberg (1998). doi:10.1007/BFb0055011

5. Burns, A., Wellings, A.: The deadline floor protocol and Ada. ACM SIGAda Ada Lett. **36**(1), 29–34 (2016)
6. Liu, L., Layland, J.W.: Scheduling algorithms for multiprogramming in a hard real-time environment. J. ACM **20**(1), 46–61 (1973)
7. Buttazzo, G.: Rate monotonic vs EDF: judgment day. Real Time Syst. **29**, 5–26 (2005)
8. Goossens, J., Macq, C.: Limitation of the hyperperiod in real-time periodic task set generation. In: Proceedings of the RTS Embedded System (RTS 2001), pp. 133–147 (2001)
9. Sha, L., Rajkumar, R., Lehoczky, J.: Priority inheritance protocols: an approach to real-time synchronisation. IEEE Trans. Comput. **39**, 1175–1185 (1990)
10. Audsley, N., Burns, A., Richardson, M., Tindell, K., Wellings, A.J.: Applying new scheduling theory to static priority pre-emptive scheduling. Softw. Eng. J. **8**(5), 284–292 (1993). doi:10.1049/sej.1993.0034
11. Davis, R., Baruah, S., Rothvoss, T., Burns, A.: Quantifying the sub-optimality of uniprocessor fixed priority pre-emptive scheduling for sporadic tasksets with arbitrary deadlines. In: RTNS 2009, Paris, ECE, 26–27 October 2009
12. Vardanega, T., Zamorano, J., De La Puente, A.J.: On the dynamic semantics and the timing behavior of Ravenscar kernels. Real Time Syst. **29**, 59–89 (2005)

Safety and Security

Sanitizing Sensitive Data: How to Get It Right (or at Least Less Wrong…)

Roderick Chapman[✉]

Protean Code Limited, Bath, UK
rod@proteancode.com

Abstract. Coding standards and guidance for secure programming call for sensitive data to be "sanitized" before being de-allocated. This paper considers what this really means in technical terms, why it is actually rather difficult to achieve, and how such a requirement can be realistically implemented and verified, concentrating on the facilities offered by Ada and SPARK. The paper closes with a proposed policy and coding standard that can be applied and adapted to other projects.

Keywords: Security · Sanitization · SPARK · Verification · Volatile · Optimization · Proof

1 The Problem

Secure systems must be built to resist attack by increasingly sophisticated adversaries. An attacker might be able to observe or provoke a system into "leaking" or revealing secret data, such as cryptographic keys, the plaintext of passwords and so on. A well-documented example is where an intruder manages to read the operating system page file or a core dump of a running (or deliberately terminated) process in order to gain access to unsanitized sensitive data.

Several coding standards and guidance documents exist that call for sensitive data to be *sanitized* when no longer needed, but offer little advice on how this is to be achieved or verified, especially given the complexity of programming languages and hardware. This paper considers this problem in detail and describes the key technical challenges, before going on to consider the facilities offered by Ada and SPARK that can meet these demands, based on experience gained from a recent project.

1.1 Why Is Sanitizing Data Hard?

Sanitizing sensitive data might seem simple at first: just overwrite the data with zeros and carry on, right? A less trivial analysis reveals important questions, including:

- How do we define "sensitive"? What objects in the program are "sensitive" and how are they identified?
- Imagine that we have two variables A and B which are defined to be "sensitive." We declare and initialize a local variable C with an initial value derived from some function that combines A and B. Is C "sensitive"? Does C need to be sanitized?

© Springer International Publishing AG 2017
J. Blieberger and M. Bader (Eds.): Ada-Europe 2017, LNCS 10300, pp. 37–52, 2017.
DOI: 10.1007/978-3-319-60588-3_3

- Can constant objects be sensitive? If so, how are they to be sanitized?
- Exactly *when* should sanitization be performed, relating to the scope and lifetime of data objects which is, in turn, intricately entwined with a particular programming language's model of how data should be organized and (de-)allocated?
- Compiler optimization might remove a sanitizing assignment if the assignment is seen to be redundant or "dead" by the optimizer. How can this be prevented?
- How do we verify that sanitization really has been performed correctly, to the satisfaction of ourselves, our customers, and regulators?

1.2   Standards, Guidance and Problems

There are several (possibly far too many) sets of guidance or coding rules for secure systems that call for sensitive data to be sanitized as soon as it is no longer needed, so that (for example) a subsequent buffer over-read will not find any useful data. This section considers an incomplete set of these, and tries to point out problems in meeting their advice.

GCHQ. The UK's national technical authority for secure software, GCHQ, offers a short (but thankfully unclassified) "Guidance Note" on secure coding [1]. It offers some generic advice, but mainly consists of coding rules for C and C++. A need to avoid copying sensitive data is mentioned (to avoid a copy existing even if the original is sanitized), with two paragraphs specifically on sanitization:

> "Sanitise all variables that contain sensitive data (such as cryptovariables and unencrypted data) by overwriting with zeroes once they are no longer needed. This includes all copies of the data: call-by-value functions (as found in C) implicitly copy the value of their parameters, so their parameters should always be sanitised before the function exits. At protective markings higher than Restricted, sanitisation may require multiple overwrites or verification, or both." [1, para 58].

and

> "The sanitisation is needed because errors may result in the disclosure of a block of memory, therefore the risk of that memory containing anything useful needs to be minimised. The size of the data is not a factor: even single bytes need to be sanitised, since in some cases a difference of 8 bits could have a significant impact on the practicality of an attack. On the other hand, the lifetime of data may be a factor: if a variable can be shown to be overwritten shortly afterwards, it may be acceptable not to sanitise it, provided it is sanitised when it is no longer needed. 'Shortly' is not defined more precisely, since it will depend on the situation..." [1, para 59].

This is well-meaning, but offers little in the way of real technical detail of how sanitization is to be achieved or verified. The failure to define "shortly afterwards" is also disappointing.

CERT Coding Standards. The CERT at CMU has produced coding guidance for secure software development, covering C, C++, Java and Perl to date, with several tool vendors claiming compliance. The CERT C Coding Standard [2] provides some advice on sanitization:

- Recommendation 08 (Memory Management), Item 06 is titled "Ensure that sensitive data is not written out to disk" which mostly covers the problem of an operating system "paging out" sensitive data to a disk or an application doing a "core dump" which writes the state of a process to a disk file, potentially revealing the state of sensitive data. These are valid concerns, relevant to any application running on an operating system that supports paging and so on, so not really a "C language issue" per-se, since these problems could affect code written in any language.
- Recommendation 48 (Miscellaneous), Item 06 is titled "Beware of compiler optimizations" and covers the problem of a compiler removing a sanitizing assignment. It goes on to recommend using "optimization safe" C functions such as memset_s(), C's "volatile" qualifier (more of which later…) or operating-system specific functions that are designed to sanitize memory.

Both of these recommendations appear to presume the existence of some sort of operating system (and possibly a "disk"), but what if we're programming an embedded "bare metal" system with no OS at all? How can we sanitize data properly in such an environment?

ISO SC22/WG23 Technical Report 24772. The ISO's SC22 Working Group 23 has produced Technical Report 24772 entitled "Guidance to avoiding vulnerabilities in programming languages through language selection and use." [3] The TR recognizes sanitization as an avoidance mechanism for some vulnerabilities, but does not go into specific details. The language-specific annexes for Ada, C and SPARK offer no additional advice.

Common Weakness Enumeration (CWE). Mitre's CWE [4] includes CWE-14 "Compiler Removal of Code to Clear Buffers" which identifies the risk of removal of sanitizing assignments by optimizing compilers. It advocates the use of volatile objects and suggests "configure your compiler so that it does not remove dead stores."

Cryptography Coding Standard. The Cryptography Coding Standard is "a set of coding rules to prevent the most common weaknesses in software cryptographic implementations" [5]. Their coding rules touch on sanitization in a number of places:

- Coding Rule 5 "Prevent compiler interference with security critical operations" mentions the problem of compilers removing sanitizing assignments, and how even a call to C's standard "memset" function can be optimized away in some cases. It offers the rather vague advice to "Look at the assembly code produced and check that all instructions are there" which hardly seems practical for anything but trivial code. It also recommends "consider disabling compiler optimizations that can eliminate or weaken security checks" but again this seems impractical – modern compilers have *hundreds* of optimization switches, which makes it almost impossible to "know" which set of them will or won't "interfere" with security. Finally, rule 5 does point out that the 2011 C standard does include a new "memset_s" function, a call to which is explicitly *not* allowed to be optimized.
- Coding Rule 11 "Clean memory of secret data" looks promising, recommending that code should "Clear all variables containing secret data before they go out of

scope." It points out the existence of a SecureZeroMemory function in the Win32 API for this purpose. It also offers a portable C function that can be used to overwrite memory that works "for non-buggy compilers" [sic].

1.3 Technical Issues

Having seen that the standards and guidance documents offer well-meaning but imprecise advice, we now turn to a selection of more detailed technical problems.

Unwanted Compiler Optimization. Several of the guidance documents cited above refer to this problem, so it warrants more attention here.

Modern implementations of computer architectures feature a marked difference between the access time of CPU registers, data cache(s), and main memory, sometimes by many orders of magnitude. In short, DRAM access times have not kept pace with CPU clock rates, so the penalty for a "register miss" or a "cache miss" is pronounced. Modern compilers therefore devote significant effort in several, related classes of optimization [6], including:

1. Common sub-expression elimination and partial redundancy elimination. These prevent semantically equivalent expressions from being evaluated more than once.
2. Register allocation and tracking, so that variables and the values of expressions are stored in CPU registers as much as possible.
3. Dead-load and dead-store elimination.

   These improve average-case performance, but create some issues for sanitization:

- Guidance calls for the "memory" occupied by a sensitive variable to be overwritten "before the variable goes out of scope", but what does that mean if the variable only ever exists in an internal CPU register and there is no "memory" allocated for it at all?
- A final sanitizing assignment needs to occur just before a variable "goes out of scope", so is (by definition) a "dead store" in the eyes of an optimizer, so might be removed, on the assumption that once a variable has gone out of scope it can't be accessed any more. This creates a conflict in the compiler: we (the programmers) want dead stores to be retained for one or more particular variables, but the compiler is trying its hardest to remove them in the interests of improving performance of the generated code.

Derived Values and Copies. In his thorough analysis "Zeroing buffers is insufficient" [7], Percival points out several more pernicious technical issues with a simple "write zeros into memory" approach. Specifically, he points out:

- Sanitizing the *one* memory block where a variable is stored is not good enough. Compilers implicitly make copies of data into registers or implicitly-declared and initialized local variables, so these might also contain a copy of some sensitive information that needs to be sanitized. In the worst case, a compiler might evaluate the value of a sensitive variable into a CPU register *and* spill that register into an implicitly allocated temporary variable on the stack. There is no way to portably sanitize such temporary variables in C or Ada, since those variables do not appear in the source code.

- If a sensitive piece of data is left in a CPU register, you *cannot* assume that that CPU register will be re-used and the data over-written "quickly". Percival points out that some CPU registers (such as the SSE registers on x86) are rarely used, and some registers are specifically designed for cryptographic algorithms such as AES – the problem being that you carefully use a "special" register to hold an AES key (for example), but then that register is not used for anything else in your program, so the key value persists and is never overwritten. Secondly, some CPUs such as x86 can implement register renaming, which further complicates matters.

A related problem is that of derived values. As pointed out in Sect. 1.1, if two sensitive variables A and B are combined in some way to get a value in variable C, should C be considered to be sensitive and therefore needing sanitization? The answer is "it depends"... on the exact operation used to derive C, the nature of A and B, and so on. It is far from simple to suggest a generic one-size-fits-all policy for such variables.

By-Copy Parameter Passing. If a subprogram parameter is passed by copy, then the value of the actual parameter is copied into the storage associated with the formal parameter (which might be stack memory or a CPU register). If the actual is sensitive, then so is the formal parameter. In Ada, this is particularly problematic, since "in" mode parameters are constant and so cannot be assigned to at all, and the choice between by-copy and by-reference passing can be unspecified for some types.

CPU Data Caching and Memory Hierarchy. Anyone that has programmed a device-driver on a "bare metal" target will know that the presence of a "write" instruction does *not* guarantee that the data actually reaches the target hardware device at all, or in the order indicated in the source code. Modern CPUs have multiple levels of data caching, which may be in "write back" mode, so an instruction to write a particular word of memory might not actually reach the main memory device until the offending data cache line is flushed or invalidated. Secondly, modern CPUs can execute instructions out-of-order and re-order memory accesses in rather unexpected ways, which can complicate matters further.

Some operating systems offer functions that are specifically designed to securely sanitize memory, such as Win32's SecureZeroMemory function. We presume these functions take care of any required flushing of caches, paged-out data and so on.

On bare-metal targets, we might turn off all data caching or insist on "write through" mode, but this may be Draconian, since disabling all caching for all stack-allocated data would incur a potentially huge performance penalty. Some CPUs might allow special instructions to flush particular cache lines and so-called "memory fence" instructions that instruct the CPU to pause until all queued memory accesses are complete. These techniques are valid (and indeed may be absolutely necessary), but require recourse to obviously non-portable assembly language programming at some level.

The recent 2011 editions of both the C [8] and C++ [9] languages have been extended to define an abstract "memory model" for these languages, plus support in the standard library for atomic types and fence operations, both of which may offer mechanisms that support sanitization more portably.

1.4   An Example – How It Can Go Wrong in Ada

This section closes with a short (and somewhat contrived) example of how sanitization can fail in Ada. In the remainder of the paper, all examples have been compiled with the GPL 2016 Edition of GNAT for 32-bit x86 running on Windows 7 Pro.

Consider a simple procedure GK that takes three seed values A, B, and C, and produces a derived key value K from them. For example:

```
subtype Word32 is Interfaces.Unsigned_32;
procedure GK (A, B, C : in      Word32;
              K        :     out Word32);
```

The body of GK combines A, B, and C using a local, temporary variable T which we have decided is sensitive and needs to be sanitized with a final assignment, thus:

```
procedure GK
   (A, B, C : in      Word32;
    K        :     out Word32)
is
   T : Word32;
begin
   T := A xor B; -- line 15
   T := T xor C;
   K := T;

   -- Now sanitize T
   T := 0; -- line 20
end GK;
```

To see what's going on, we'll compile with both "-g" and "-fverbose-asm" flags. We'll also enable all warnings with "-gnatwa" and "-Wall" as we would on any real project. Compiling GK does yield a warning:

```
p1.adb:20:07: warning: useless assignment to "T", value never
referenced
```

which hints at trouble ahead. Compiling with –O0 (little or no optimization) yields the following assembly language for lines 15 through 20 of GK:

```
movl    8(%ebp), %eax    # a, tmp88    LINE 15
xorl    12(%ebp), %eax # b, tmp87
movl    %eax, -12(%ebp)  # tmp87, t
movl    16(%ebp), %eax # c, tmp89    LINE 16
xorl    %eax, -12(%ebp)  # tmp89, t
movl    -12(%ebp), %eax  # t, tmp90    LINE 17
movl    %eax, -16(%ebp)  # tmp90, k
movl    $0, -12(%ebp)    #, t LINE 20
```

so we can see the final assignment to T on line 20 has indeed been generated as a single "movl" instruction.

Turning on the optimizer at level "−O1" reveals a different story. For the same fragment of code, we get:

```
movl    16(%ebp),  %eax # c, c
xorl    12(%ebp),  %eax # b, D.3010
xorl     8(%ebp),  %eax # a, k
```

and that's all. The local variable T is not allocated at all on the stack – it has completely disappeared, in fact, with the intermediate results left in the CPU register EAX. Our well-intended attempt to sanitize T has been discarded by the compiler, but then again, T has disappeared entirely, so is this sufficient? What about the intermediate value left in EAX – is that overwritten "soon" by the calling subprogram perhaps?

2 Sanitization – Constraints and Goals

In developing the coding standard for a recent project, we had to meet both CESG's guidance for sanitization [1], but also the constraints imposed by the wider demands of the project, including the runtime environment, compilers, features of the target platform and its operating system and so on.

In searching for the most general solution, we tried to respect the following constraints:

1. The approach to sanitization should minimize dependence on predefined library units and the use of language features that require substantial support from the Ada runtime library. In particular, for our project, we required compatibility with GNAT's "Zero Footprint" (ZFP) runtime library.
2. The approach should not depend on any operating system facilities, and so can be deployed on a "bare metal" target system.
3. The approach should be compatible with the SPARK language (either SPARK 2005 [10] or SPARK 2014 [11, 12]) and verification tools.

Secondly, what does a "good" approach to sanitization look like? In developing these guidelines for Ada, we tried to respect the following goals:

1. Any proposed approach should be *portable* in that it should not depend on non-standard behavior from the compiler, and should not rely on particular *unspecified* or *implementation-defined* choices made by a compiler.
2. Our approach should permit compiler optimizations to be enabled at all levels, with sufficient confidence that sanitization code would be preserved and implemented correctly.
3. Our approach must prevent (as far as is possible) explicit or implicit copying or assignment of sensitive values. This also affects parameter passing, since a "by-copy" formal parameter involves assignment.
4. Our approach should facilitate (or at least not obstruct) verification with the SPARK toolset.

5. Our approach should meet or exceed the demands of the various regulatory standards, such as [1]. Furthermore, we should be able to explain and justify our approach to those regulators so that we can convince them that it actually works.

3 Sanitization Mechanisms in Ada

Having considered the scope of this problem, this section turns to the language-based mechanisms that are available in Ada. Knowing what mechanisms are available can then lead to a policy that can be adopted for a particular project.

3.1 Volatile

Ada, C and C++ all include a facility to mark an object as "Volatile", meaning that the compiler must respect the exact sequence of reads and writes to such an object that are indicated in the source code. Ada goes further, allowing Volatile *types* as well as objects. The Ada RM [13] offers a clear implementation requirement (Ada 2012 RM, C.6(20)):

"The external effect of a program…is defined to include each read and update of a volatile or atomic object. The implementation shall not generate any memory reads or updates of atomic or volatile objects other than those specified by the program."

Let's see what happens to our example procedure GK with the declaration of T changed as follows:

```
T : Word32 with Volatile;
```

With that in place, we should be able to turn the optimizer "up to 11" (well…3) and compile with "−O3". Firstly, the warning from the front-end about the useless assignment to T disappears, which is a good sign. The generated code for lines 15–20 is:

```
movl    12(%ebp), %eax # b, b  LINE 15
xorl     8(%ebp), %eax # a, D.3014
movl    %eax, -12(%ebp) # D.3014, t
movl    -12(%ebp), %eax # t, D.3015   LINE 16
xorl    16(%ebp), %eax # c, D.3014
movl    %eax, -12(%ebp) # D.3014, t
movl    -12(%ebp), %eax # t, k  LINE 17
movl    $0, -12(%ebp)    # t  LINE 20
```

so we see that *all* the reads and writes of T have been preserved, including the final sanitizing assignment.

At first glance, this appears to be a perfect match, at least when it comes to preventing the optimization of sanitizing assignments. Unfortunately, it's not that simple for several reasons:

1. Volatile prevents optimization of *all* reads and writes to an object, but we only require that the *final* sanitizing assignment is preserved, so use of Volatile might have a serious but unnecessary impact on the performance of the generated code.
2. SPARK 2014 (release 16.0.2) only permits library level objects to be declared Volatile. Local variables may not be Volatile.
3. Most seriously and worryingly, Regehr and Eide [14] have shown that compilers can mis-compile Volatile and *do* optimize away reads and writes when they shouldn't. Regehr and Eide only tested 13 compilers and their work dates from 2008 so we hope compilers have improved since then. Their tests were based on analysis of C programs, but their concerns are real, especially since their results include those for 9 builds of GCC, which shares its back-end (and optimization code) with GNAT.

So, despite its initial good looks, the use of Volatile is not a panacea for data sanitization. Secondly, it does not address the need to restrict assignment and copying of sensitive data objects at all.

3.2 Controlled Types

Ada's "Controlled Types" offer a tempting approach to supply a "Finalize" procedure that sanitizes an object. At first glance, this seems attractive, but there are several serious problems:

- Controlled types require significant support from the Ada runtime library which conflicts with our requirement for compatibility with the ZFP runtime.
- They are not permitted by SPARK.
- Their semantics and implementation are notoriously difficult to understand [15, 16].

In light of these problems, controlled types were rejected without further investigation.

3.3 Limited Types

Ada's limited types are particularly attractive for holding sensitive data. Firstly, the programmer can have complete control over exactly what set of operations are available to clients. Secondly, and by default, assignment is not defined for limited types, so we can control both copying and creation of derived values. Finally, an explicitly limited record type is defined to be a *by-reference* type (RM 6.2(7)) so we can be sure that all formal parameters of such a type will be passed by reference, not by copy.

3.4 By-Reference Types

Where the use of a limited record type is not appropriate or practical, there are still other means of forcing a type to be a "by-reference" type in Ada, which will, at least, prevent copying by parameter passing where we don't want it. RM C.6 (18) tells us that if any sub-component of a type is Atomic or Volatile, then the type is defined to be a by-reference type. Additionally, RM 6.2(5) specifies that all tagged types are by-reference. Thus we can force by-reference passing for even a simple scalar type by wrapping it in a tagged record or a record which has a single Atomic or Volatile component. For example, instead of declaring a formal "in" mode parameter of type Boolean, we might declare:

```
type Sensitive_Boolean is tagged record
   F : Boolean;
end record;
```

or

```
type Sensitive_Boolean is record
   F : Boolean with Volatile;
end record;
```

to ensure by-reference parameter passing. There are pros and cons to both approaches. The Volatile field has no space overhead and makes the field volatile, but is not compatible with SPARK 2014 at the time of writing. The tagged record is allowed by SPARK, but imposes some space overhead by adding an implicit tag field to the record.

Using GNAT, it is also possible to *verify* the parameter passing mechanism using the "–gnatRm" flag.

3.5   Pragma Inspection_Point

This little-used (and little-understood perhaps) pragma has particular relevance to this problem. Inspection_Point was introduced in Ada 95 as part of the RM's Safety and Security Annex H. It is designed to specify a list of objects that must be *inspectable* at a particular point in a program. A pragmatic interpretation means that the listed objects are supposed to be stored in memory at the inspection point so that their values can be seen by external means, such as a logic analyser, a JTAG probe, a real-time debugger or similar. From the point of view of optimization, the Ada RM is clear:

'The implementation is not allowed to perform "dead store elimination" on the last assignment to a variable prior to a point where the variable is inspectable. Thus an inspection point has the effect of an implicit read of each of its inspectable objects.' (Ada RM H3.2 (9)).

This seems ideal for our needs – if a final, sanitizing assignment to a sensitive object is immediately followed by a pragma Inspection_Point for that object, then that final assignment should not be optimized away. This provides much finer control than pragma Volatile. For the curious, GNAT actually implements pragma Inspection_Point by generating a dummy volatile read to each of the objects specified in the pragma. See the file gcc-interface/trans.c in the GNAT sources for details [17] and search the file for "Inspection_Point".

Returning to our simple example, we revert to declaring T as a normal (non-volatile) local variable, but now follow the final assignment with an Inspection_Point, thus:

```
-- Now sanitize T
T := 0; -- line 20
pragma Inspection_Point (T);
```

The generated code at –O1 is:

```
# 21 "p3.adb" 1
# inspection point: t is in $0  #
# 0 "" 2
movl 12(%ebp), %eax  # b, b
xorl 16(%ebp), %eax  # c, D.3010
.loc 1 16 0
xorl 8(%ebp), %eax   # a, k
```

which is interesting. Again, the variable T has been entirely eliminated, but commentary has been added that "t is in $0" since T does not have an accessible address in memory at all.

3.6   No_Inline and Sanitizing Operations

Having identified the problems with Volatile objects, Regehr and Eide go on to recommend that all reads and writes of a volatile variable should be performed by a subprogram call that can never be inlined, since inlined code has the potential to be optimized away during the compilation of any calling units. They demonstrate how this works well for C, and the equivalent mechanism exists for Ada with the GNAT-defined pragma No_Inline.

Combining this idea with the use of a limited private type for sensitive data yields the following pattern for a sensitive abstract data type:

```
package Sensitive is
   type T is limited private; -- so no assignment

   procedure Sanitize (X : out T);
   pragma No_Inline (Sanitize);
private
   type T is limited record -- so by-reference
      F : … -- and so on…
   end record;
end Sensitive;
```

The body of Sensitive.Sanitize might depend on the target platform and operating system, so we recommend implementing it as a separate subunit of package Sensitive to allow for alternative implementations to be chosen at build-time. Let's imagine that the field F of type T is of type Word32. In that case, a suitable implementation for a bare-metal/ZFP target might be:

```
separate (Sensitive)
procedure Sanitize (X : out T) is
begin
   X.F := 0;
   pragma Inspection_Point (X);
end Sanitize;
```

At −O3, the generated code for the assignment statement and the pragma is:

```
movl    8(%ebp), %eax # x, x
movl    $0, (%eax)   #, x_2(D)->f
# 6 "sensitive-sanitize.adb" 1
# inspection point: x address is in %eax # x
# 0 "" 2
```

We can also check the parameter passing mechanism using −gnatRm which yields:

```
procedure sanitize declared at sensitive.ads:5:14
   convention : Ada
   x : passed by reference
```

4 Verification and SPARK

The SPARK toolset offers two major forms of static verification—information-flow analysis and proof of user-defined contracts. This section briefly considers the interplay between sanitization and these forms of verification.

4.1 Information Flow Analysis

As expected, both the SPARK 2005 and SPARK 2014 tools will reliably report that a final sanitizing assignment to a local variable is *ineffective*, meaning that the assignment has no influence on the final value of any exported variable of the subprogram under analysis. This is perfectly correct and reasonable. At first, such errors being reported might seem an annoyance, we can turn this to our advantage using pragma Warnings to document the expectation and need for the sanitization. For our earlier example, we would add:

```
pragma Warnings (Off, "unused assignment",
                 Reason => "Sanitization");
T := 0;
pragma Inspection_Point (T);
```

4.2 Proof

At first glance, it might be possible to prove that sanitization of variables has been performed, but closer inspection reveals two main issues:

- The final value of a *local* variable cannot be asserted in the post-condition of the subprogram that declares it, owing to its very local-ness. It would be possible to assert the value of a sanitized library-level variable.
- Writing an assertion regarding the *value* of a sensitive variable means that we need to decide on a (constant) value that should be used. The naive approach of "zero all bits" might not be appropriate, since "all zeros" might not be a valid value. SPARK and Ada have no "memset" or similar, so we need to be able to write an assignment statement which is legal and itself free from runtime errors.

5 A Policy for Sanitization

In light of the difficulties described above, and the facilities offered by Ada and SPARK, and our experience on one project, we would offer the following policy for sanitization of sensitive data for future work.

5.1 Identification and Naming of Sensitive Variables

A project must document a clear policy for what exactly is and isn't considered to be a "sensitive" object. This is clearly project- and application-specific. In cryptographic applications, for example, sensitive data might include cryptographic keys, single-use random "nonce" values, and initialization vectors for encryption algorithms.

The definition of "sensitive" may also have to consider the visibility and lifetime of the objects—local variables and library level states might have to be treated very differently, for example.

Having chosen a policy for deciding which states are sensitive, we propose a naming convention as follows:

- The names of *types* used for sensitive data should be prefixed with "Sensitive_".
- The names of *variables* that are sensitive should have the suffix "_SAN" meaning that such variables should be sanitized.
- The name of a formal subprogram parameter that *might* be associated with a sensitive actual parameter shall also have the suffix "_SAN".
- Sensitive *constants* are not permitted.

5.2 Types and Patterns for Sensitive Data

- By-reference types should be used for all sensitive data.
- Preferably, and if possible, a limited type should be used for sensitive data to forbid assignment. In this case:
  - A "Sanitize" procedure should be supplied, as shown in Sect. 3.6, which has a No_Inline pragma applied to it.

- The body of such a "Sanitize" procedure should be a separate subunit to allow for multiple implementations for different platforms and operating systems.
- The body of "Sanitize" shall include a pragma Inspection_Point immediately following the final assignment to the formal parameter. Note that the presence of the pragma is sufficient to suppress the "useless assignment" warning illustrated in Sect. 1.4. This is useful for verification, since presence of this warning is a strong indication that the programmer has forgotten to add the pragma.

- If a limited type is not possible, then a Sanitize procedure shall still be supplied for any sensitive type, implemented as above. In this case, code review checklists must include a check that assignment is not used for objects of such types.
- For SPARK code, a pragma Warnings shall always precede a final sanitizing assignment (or the call to a Sanitize procedure) to document the need for the sanitization and to suppress the information-flow warning.

5.3   Compiler Switches and Analysis

- All code should be compiled with "-gnatwa" to ensure that the "useless assignment" warning is generated. This should be expected for sanitizing assignment, but suppressed with pragma Inspection_Point.
- The "-gnatRm" switch should be used to verify that the compiler has chosen by-reference parameter passing mechanism for all sensitive formal parameters. This is easy if the naming convention above has also been followed.
- Analysis of the generated assembly language should be performed using the "-g" and "-fverbose-asm" flags to verify that the inspection points are present and correct.
- Additional analysis of the generated code might be required to verify that cache manipulation instructions and memory fences are as required.

6   Related and Further Work

Several authors have called for compilers to help automate sanitization via some sort of special compilation switch ("-fsanitize_local_data" perhaps?). This could go further than source-based techniques since the compiler could arrange to sanitize *all* local states, derived variables, temporaries, and CPU registers for example. How a compiler designer would convince others of the correctness of such an approach remains unknown.

A compiler switch seems a rather blunt instrument though. Sanitizing *all* local data might produce an unacceptable performance overhead, so we return to the idea of how objects in a program can be marked as sensitive and therefore requiring sanitization. We might imagine a new "Sensitive" aspect in Ada 2012 that can be applied to types and/or objects, rather like Volatile.

A standardized Ada binding to the C11 "stdatomic" library might be a useful exercise to supply portable access to memory fence operations.

Another compiler-related issue is that of link-time optimization (LTO). This style of optimization has appeared recently in compilers like GCC [18] and LLVM [19]. Studies are needed to verify that sanitization code is preserved in the presence of LTO.

There has been significant interest in the verification of compilers, particularly owing to the CompCert effort [20, 21]. The proof of CompCert covers the correct compilation of Volatile objects, which could carry over to the correctness of sanitizing assignments and inspection points.

The problem of sensitive derived variables could be addressed through more advanced information flow analysis. If a tool like GNATProve, for example, knew that variables A and B were sensitive, then could it automatically infer that C (derived from A and B) were also sensitive? This can also be seen as a variant of the taint analysis embodied in languages like Ruby and Perl.

7 Conclusions

Sanitization of sensitive data remains a thorny issue: standards call for it to be done, but offer little advice on how it should be achieved in practice or verified. This paper has illustrated some of the problems and shown how they can be addressed in Ada and SPARK and developed into a policy, coding standard, and verification strategy for a particular project.

Acknowledgements. The author would like to thank Robert Seacord, Florian Schanda, Bill Ellis and the conference reviewers for their comments on earlier drafts of this paper.

References

1. CESG. Coding Requirements and Guidance (IA Developers' Note 6), CESG, Issue 1.1, October 2015. www.ncsc.gov.uk/guidance/coding-requirements-and-guidance-ia-developers-note-6
2. US CERT. SEI CERT C Coding Standard. www.securecoding.cert.org/confluence/display/c/SEI+CERT+C+Coding+Standard
3. ISO/SC22/WG23. Information Technology — Programming Languages — Guidance to avoiding vulnerabilities in programming languages through language selection and use. TR 24772 (2013). http://www.open-std.org/JTC1/SC22/WG23/
4. Mitre Corp. Common Weakness Enumeration (CWE). http://cwe.mitre.org/
5. Cryptography Coding Standard Project. cryptocoding.net/index.php/Cryptography_Coding_Standard
6. Aho, A.V., Lam, M.S., Sethi, R., Ullman, J.D.: Compilers: Principles, Techniques and Tools, 2nd edn. Pearson, Upper Saddle River (2013). ISBN 978-1292024349
7. Percival, C.: Zeroing Buffers is Insufficient. www.daemonology.net/blog/2014-09-06-zeroing-buffers-is-insufficient.html
8. Programming Langauges – C. ISO/IEC 9899:2011 (2011). http://www.open-std.org/jtc1/sc22/wg14/www/standards.html

9. Programming Langauges – C++. ISO/IEC 14822:2011 (2011). http://www.open-std.org/JTC1/SC22/WG21/docs/standards.html

10. Barnes, J.: With Altran Praxis. SPARK: The Proven Approach to High-Integrity Software (2012). ISBN: 978-0-9572905-0-1

11. McCormick, J.W., Chapin, P.C.: Building High-Integrity Applications with SPARK. Cambridge University Press, Cambridge (2015). ISBN 978-1-107-04073-1

12. SPARK 2014 Community Site. www.spark-2014.org

13. Consolidated Ada 2012 Language Reference Manual. ISO/IEC 8652:2012/Cor 1:2016 (2016). www.ada-auth.org/standards/ada12_w_tc1.html

14. Regehr, J., Eide, E.: Volatiles are miscompiled and what to do about it. In: Proceedings of the Eighth ACM and IEEE International Conference on Embedded Software (EMSOFT), Atlanta, Georgia, October 2008. doi:10.1145/1450058.1450093, www.cs.utah.edu/~regehr/papers/emsoft08-preprint.pdf

15. Comar, C., Dismukes, G., Gasperoni, F. The GNAT implementation of controlled types. In: Proceedings of Tri-Ada 1994, Baltimore. ACM Press (1994). doi:10.1145/376503.376724

16. Kirtchev, H.: A new robust and efficient implementation of controlled types in the GNAT compiler. In: Proceedings of High-Integrity Language Technology 2012, ACM SIGAda Letters, vol. 32, issue. 3 pp. 43–50 (2012). doi:10.1145/2402676.2402693

17. GNAT sources at gcc.gnu.org. gcc.gnu.org/viewcvs/gcc/trunk/gcc/ada/gcc-interface/trans.c

18. GCC Online Documentation. Chap. 24 – Link Time Optimization. https://gcc.gnu.org/onlinedocs/gccint/LTO.html

19. LLVM Compiler Infrastructure. Link Time Optimization: Design and Implementation. http://llvm.org/docs/LinkTimeOptimization.html

20. Leroy, X.: Formal verification of a realistic compiler. Commun. ACM, **52**(7), (2009). doi:10.1145/1538788.1538814

21. Kang, J., Kim, Y., Hur, C-K., Dreyer, D., Vafeiadis, V.: Lightweight verification of separate compilation. In: Proceedings of the 43rd Annual ACM SIGPLAN-SIGACT Symposium on Principles of Programming Languages (POPL) 2016, pp. 178–190. ACM Press. doi:10.1145/2837614.2837642

Enforcing Timeliness and Safety
in Mission-Critical Systems

António Casimiro[✉], Inês Gouveia, and José Rufino

LaSIGE, Faculdade de Ciências, Universidade de Lisboa, Lisbon, Portugal
{casim,jmrufino}@ciencias.ulisboa.pt, igouveia@lasige.di.fc.ul.pt

Abstract. Advances in sensor, microprocessor and communication technologies have been fostering new applications of cyber-physical systems, often involving complex interactions between distributed autonomous components and the operation in harsh or uncertain contexts. This has led to new concerns regarding performance, safety and security, while ensuring timeliness requirements are met. To conciliate uncertainty with the required predictability, hybrid system architectures have been proposed, which separate the system in two parts: one that behaves in a best-effort way, depending on the context, and another that behaves as predictably as needed, providing critical services for a safe and secure operation. In this paper we address the problem of verifying the correct provisioning of critical functions at runtime in such hybrid architectures. We consider, in particular, the KARYON hybrid architecture and its Safety Kernel. We also consider a hardware-based non-intrusive runtime verification approach, describing how it is applied to verify Safety Kernel software functions. Finally, we experimentally evaluate the performance of two distinct Safety Kernel implementations and discuss the feasibility issues to incorporate non-intrusive runtime verification.

Keywords: Real-time and embedded systems · Software architectures · Architecture hybridization · Reliability and safety · Runtime verification

1 Introduction and Motivation

Advances in sensor, microprocessor and communication technologies have been fostering new applications of cyber-physical systems, often involving complex interactions between distributed autonomous components and the operation in harsh or uncertain contexts. A good example can be found in the automotive domain, where car makers strive to increase the autonomy of vehicles, exploiting existing technologies to make them more intelligent. While the state of the art

This work was partially supported by FCT, through funding of LaSIGE Research Unit, ref. UID/CEC/00408/2013. This work integrates the activities of COST Action IC1402 - Runtime Verification beyond Monitoring (ARVI), supported by COST (European Cooperation in Science and Technology).

J. Blieberger and M. Bader (Eds.): Ada-Europe 2017, LNCS 10300, pp. 53–69, 2017.
DOI: 10.1007/978-3-319-60588-3_4

approach consists in using information collected from local sensors to feed control loops, future cars will be connected to other cars and to the infrastructure, and will cooperate for information exchange. Connectivity introduces additional security risks and, given that it is enabled by wireless networks, also introduces temporal uncertainties that conflict with real-time requirements. Additionally, processing huge amounts of incoming data will require complex processing solutions, which favor uncertainty, not predictability.

A particular challenge is to conciliate uncertainty with the required predictability, for which hybrid system architectures have been proposed. For instance, Simplex [21] considers that a control system can be composed of a controller executing in a complex subsystem, and a simple but reliable controller that is used when the complex controller malfunctions, being deployed in a separate part of the system, to be protected from potential faults in the complex subsystem.

In the scope of the KARYON project [6], we proposed the KARYON hybrid system architecture [7] to build safe cooperative systems with improved performance. This software architecture encompasses application components that execute in a complex part of the system and a Safety Kernel (SK) that, along with critical application components, should be implemented separately and should be verified to execute in a timely and reliable way. The role of the SK is to monitor the behavior of complex software components and trigger the necessary adjustments or reconfiguration actions in the complex part of the system, as needed to satisfy a set of predefined safety requirements. Note that an SK software instance will exist in each node of a distributed system (e.g., on each car) and hence the paper focuses only on a single node and not on the distribution aspects of the safety critical application or function.

In this paper we address the problem of how to verify in runtime that fundamental properties of the KARYON SK are satisfied. In fact, while it is possible to use several dependability techniques, such as the replication of software components or software verification, to enforce the required properties and raise confidence that they will be secured, these are costly and there is always a probability that, due to an accidental or even intentional fault, a property no longer holds. For example, an SK function might not complete its execution within a required temporal bound or it might produce an erroneous value. Runtime verification adds another layer of protection that is fundamental for safety assurance.

We propose a hardware-based non-intrusive runtime verification approach, which is able to detect the violation of well-defined SK properties in runtime. We describe the approach and how it is applied to verify concrete properties of the SK. We also provide experimental results that illustrate the performance of the SK implemented in two platforms, complemented with a discussion on feasibility issues relative to the incorporation of non-intrusive runtime verification.

The paper is structured as follows. Section 2 briefly reviews the KARYON hybrid architecture, describing the role of the SK. Then, Sect. 3 provides details on the SK design, important for explaining, in Sect. 4, how the runtime verification approach is applied to secure design assumptions. Relevant details of the

SK implementation and a comparative evaluation of the SK operation in two different platforms is provided in Sect. 5. Sections 6 and 7 respectively address related work and conclude the paper.

2 Hybrid Architectures

Hybrid distributed system models and architectural hybridization [24] can be explored as a baseline design principle to address a trade-off between performance and timeliness or safety or even security. In essence, hybrid distributed system models assume that different parts of the system are characterized by different properties (for instance, each part having different timeliness properties or different integrity levels with respect to some assumed failure modes), and architectural hybridization explicitly separates system functions or components into these different parts, as needed to ensure that each component enjoys the properties provided by the part of the system in which it is allocated.

When considering the temporal domain, a system with a hybrid architecture is structured in at least two parts: one that encompasses all complex components, whose temporal behavior cannot be fully predicted or is hard to enforce, and another part that usually contains simple but critical components that execute in a predictable way. Such nice properties, like timely execution, must be enforced by design and in the implementation. For instance, dedicated hardware may be used to execute critical components, ensuring that they are temporally isolated and shielded from failures in the complex part, and that interactions between the two parts are done through a well-defined interface that preserves the properties of the part containing critical components.

The architectural hybridization concept was explored in the context of the KARYON project, which defined a generic architectural pattern for the

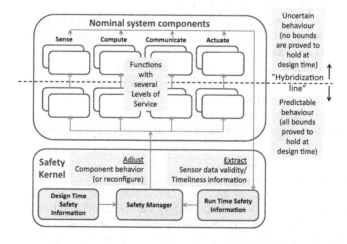

Fig. 1. The KARYON hybrid architectural pattern.

development of sensor-based autonomous and cooperative systems [7]. This architectural pattern is shown in Fig. 1.

The several components that constitute the autonomous system and perform the cooperative functions are considered the *nominal system components*. These include *sensors, actuators, computation* and *communication* components. Each of these components can be used to support multiple functions. Each function can be provided with several *levels of service* (LoS), depending on the components that are being used and/or the *performance level* of each component. For instance, a function to detect obstacles ahead of a vehicle may be realized with a higher LoS if implemented using a camera sensor and an associated video processing component that is able to identify the kind of obstacle, but it may also be provided with a lower LoS by using just the information provided by a distance sensor. While it might not always be possible to execute a function at a higher LoS, namely when some needed complex component is failing to execute its function timely enough, it is assumed that it can always be executed at the lowest LoS, given that in this case it is ensured that all the involved components (considered critical ones) execute in a timely way. The hybridization line separates the system in two parts: the one where no temporal bounds can be assumed, and the predictable part, which contains critical components that are expected to execute timely and reliably (by design and implementation).

The architectural pattern is based on a Safety Kernel that is responsible for maintaining the system safe, despite the possible occurrence of faults affecting components above the hybridization line. Safety conditions are determined at design time. For each function, it is necessary to determine the safety rules that must hold to allow the function to be executed with a given LoS, that is, using a certain combination of components. For instance, the obstacle detection function can only be run at the highest LoS if the video processing component is able to timely process a video frame and provide results with good quality (which may not be possible in bad lighting conditions). The role of the Safety Kernel is hence to continuously extract information about the timeliness and quality (or validity) of sensor and processed data, use this information to verify which safety rules are satisfied, and adjust the system configuration at runtime so that all the functions are executed with the highest LoS that still secures safety.

To perform its task, the Safety Kernel includes: a Safety Manager component, a repository containing Design Time Safety Information, and a repository that is continuously updated with Runtime Safety Information. We highlight the fact that these components are located below the hybridization line. This is necessary because the Safety Kernel, as a critical component, must behave in a reliable and timely way.

3   Safety Kernel Design

Figure 2 provides an overview of the Safety Kernel functional components and the data flows between them. At startup the *eXtensible Markup Language (XML) Parser* reads a local configuration file, builds a *Safety Rules* repository and initializes *Runtime Safety Information* (RSI) structures, which will be continuously updated in runtime with the relevant safety-related information. The configuration file provides the safety rules and also *unit* definitions, expressed in XML. A unit represents a Safety Kernel input (collected data), output (adjustment data – typically a component performance level, PL) or locally calculated values (for instance, the acceptable LoS for some function). Each unit has a unique identifier that is used in the XML specification of the safety rules.

A safety rule is a boolean expression involving combinations of static values (bounds) and unit identifiers. A safety rule is meaningful for a specific LoS of some function. For instance, consider that a nominal system (e.g., an autonomous vehicle control system) is designed to perform some function F (e.g., keep a safe front distance value to any front object), and this function can be performed in two different ways (e.g., using different sensors), one way providing a higher LoS, (e.g., LoS2, allowing a smaller safety distance but requiring sensor data with high validity, possibly not achievable in some situations), and a default way providing a baseline LoS (LoS1, imposing a higher safety distance, proved to be enough even when the validity of sensor data cannot be the highest one). In this case, a safety rule would be necessary to specify the conditions for function F to be safely executed in LoS 2. If the condition (a single one, in this example) was the validity of sensor data, V_{Sens}, to be greater that 70, the safety rule would be expressed as: $F(LoS2) \rightarrow V_{Sens} > 70$.

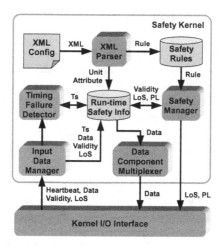

Fig. 2. Safety Kernel components. (Color figure online)

The *Input Data Manager* receives data inputs from the external (nominal system) components and updates the RSI.

The *Timing Failure Detector* (TFD) is responsible for checking if certain data inputs have been received from external components within predefined temporal bounds. This TFD executes periodically, during each execution round of the Safety Kernel. When the TFD detects a timing failure (i.e., when some expected data is not timely produced at the Safety Kernel interface), it stores this information in the RSI unit corresponding to the untimely data. In this paper, as detailed in Sect. 4, we propose a design that moves into hardware a significant part of the TFD operation: the detection of timing failures.

The *Data Component Multiplexer* (DCM) selects, from two or more data inputs (collected from nominal components), one that is forwarded to its output. This is useful, for instance, when a function can be realized using one of several components that provide the same data (e.g., a front distance value), but with different timeliness or different validity. The Data Component Multiplexer selects, among the input values, the one that should be forwarded to the output (and hence nominal system), according to the permitted LoS for that function.

Finally, the *Safety Manager* is the central component as it evaluates at runtime if safety rules are satisfied given the RSI data.

4   Securing Design Assumptions Through Non-intrusive Runtime Verification

The timeliness, safety and security guarantees of Safety Kernel correct operation can be strongly enhanced through runtime verification, being of particular relevance the verification whether the design assumptions specified for the Safety Kernel are being strictly met or, somehow, have been violated.

4.1   Observer Entity

Runtime verification (RV) obtains and analyses data from the execution of a system to detect and possibly react to behaviours, either satisfying or violating a given specification. The classical approach to runtime verification implies the instrumentation of system software components, such as the Safety Kernel. Small components, which are not part of the functional system, acting as *observers*, are added to monitor and assess the state of the system in runtime.

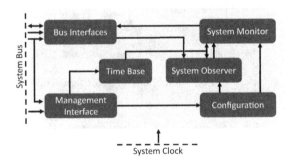

Fig. 3. Observer Entity architecture

The usage of reconfigurable logic supporting versatile FPGA-based computing platform designs enables non-intrusive approaches to runtime verification [16]. *Non-Intrusive Runtime Verification* (NIRV), provides *high flexibility*, meaning instrumentation with software-based probes is not required, although it may be used; *configurability*, which can be performed statically (offline) or dynamically, while the system is executing; *adaptability*, in the sense it is able to accommodate over time a set of different system-level, application-related and even mission-specific event observations; *independence* and *isolation*, in the sense that being supported directly in hardware, the accomplishment of runtime verification actions does not disturb nor introduce any overhead in the execution of system software components, Safety Kernel included. Similarly, the execution of software components does not ill affect the timeliness and effectiveness of runtime verification actions.

The Observer Entity is plugged to the platform where the SK software components execute, and comprises the hardware modules depicted in Fig. 3: *Bus Interfaces*, capturing all physical bus activity, such as bus transfers or interrupts; *Management Interface*, enabling observer entity configuration; *Configuration*, storing the patterns of the events to be detected; the *System Observer* itself, detecting events of interest based on the set configurations; *Time Base*, which allows to time stamp events of interest, to establish its occurrence rate or to register its inter-arrival time and even to check if application-level and/or system-specific time bounds are being fulfilled; *System Monitor*, which detects possible violations to the specified system behaviour. As soon as a deviation from the specified behaviour is detected, a notification is issued.

4.2   Safety Kernel Design Assumptions and Timeliness Analysis

Let us define T_{SK} as the period of the Safety Kernel process. This process must be completed within its period, thus defining the relative deadline, D_{SK}:

$$D_{SK} = T_{SK} \tag{1}$$

The Safety Kernel process is powered by two threads: a Listener Thread, assuming the role of *Input Data Manager* (depicted in yellow in Fig. 2), is activated for every incoming packet; a Periodic Thread, identified as *Timing Failure Detector* in Fig. 2, runs once every Safety Kernel period. Given that $C_{listener\_thread}$ and $C_{periodic\_thread}$ represent the worst-case execution time, respectively for the Listener and Periodic threads, and that $N_{packets}$ represents the maximum total number of input packets received during a single T_{SK} period, one will have the following timing constraint:

$$N_{packets} \times C_{listener\_thread} + C_{periodic\_thread} \leq D_{SK} \tag{2}$$

As illustrated in Fig. 2, there are different types of incoming packets, namely: heartbeat, data validity, multicomponent data or cooperative level of service. In the design of the Safety Kernel we assume the number of packet types is upper bounded by PKT_TYP. The worst-case execution time for a single activation of the Listener Thread, $C_{listener\_thread}$, corresponds to the longest worst-case processing time of a packet, out of the worst-case packet processing times for each packet type, $C_{pkt\_processing}(typ)$. We also take into consideration the worst-case processing time necessary to read a packet from the corresponding interface (whose location is well known and statically defined), either through (memory-mapped) I/O ports and/or network interfaces, represented by $C_{pkt\_reading}$. The maximum value of $C_{listener\_thread}$ can be expressed as:

$$C_{listener\_thread} = C_{pkt\_reading} + max_{typ=1}^{PKT\_TYP}\{C_{pkt\_processing}(typ)\} \quad (3)$$

In contrast with the Listener Thread, the Periodic Thread runs only once per SK period executing three functions in sequence and in the following order: a residual software part of the original TFD (Fig. 2), that we name herein Timing Failure Detector Service Function (TFD_SF), the Safety Manager (SM) and the Data Component Multiplexer (DCM). The Periodic Thread worst-case execution time, $C_{periodic\_thread}$, is therefore given by:

$$C_{periodic\_thread} = C_{TFD\_SF} + C_{SM} + C_{DCM} \quad (4)$$

The DCM function scans the unit[1] array to find out the component data value to be forwarded and has a worst-case execution time given by C_{DCM}. The Safety Manager is a more complex function as it evaluates for each unit the safety rules and determines the new level of service or performance level. Given the number of items (e.g., number of units, number of safety rules per unit, etc.) to be processed by the Safety Manager is bounded by design, its execution time is assumed to not exceed the upper bounded given by C_{SM}. The Timing Failure Detector Service Function is much simpler: it scans the unit array to find out if there are updates (e.g., heartbeat, data validity,...) untimely received and analyses them: a minimum number of required successes and a maximum number of tolerated failures (both configured at the Safety Kernel, per input unit), have to be observed in a row to prevent instability and to steadily declare the corresponding input unit as "timely" or "non-timely", respectively. This function executes within a time that does not exceed C_{TFD_SF}, being $C_{TFD\_SF} < C_{TFD}$, the worst-case execution time of the original Timing Failure Detector entirely implemented in software.

4.3   Runtime Monitoring of Safety Kernel Operation

Let us define $t_{SK\_begin,j}$ and $t_{SK\_end,j}$, as the real-time instants where the jth instance (job) of the Safety Kernel process begins and ends, respectively. Additionally, we define $n_{pkt,j}$ as the actual number of packets received within the duration of the jth job of the SK process, i.e. during the interval:

---

[1] A unit corresponds to a Safety Kernel information structure, concerning input (collected data), output (adjustment data) or locally calculated values. The term unit is coined from the Safety Kernel XML configuration file (Sect.3).

$$\delta_{SK,j} = t_{SK\_end,j} - t_{SK\_begin,j} \tag{5}$$

Thus, one will have the following RV value and timing constraints:

$$\forall_{j\in\mathbb{N}} \quad 0 \le n_{pkt,j} \le N_{packets} \tag{6}$$

$$\forall_{j\in\mathbb{N}} \quad 0 \le \delta_{SK,j} \le D_{SK} \tag{7}$$

Verifying that no more than $N_{packets}$ are received during each T_{SK} period, as given by Expression (6), implies: initializing an Observer Entity counting monitor with the $N_{packets}$ value each time an instance of the SK process is started; the value of the counter is decremented by one whenever a packet is received; if it reaches a value smaller than zero, a violation is signalled. Detecting when an instance of the SK process begins is achieved by configuring the address of its first instruction as an event of interest and linking it to the counting monitor.

Verifying the timeliness of an SK job implies the use of a timeliness monitor, a specialization of a counting monitor, which is initialized with the job relative deadline, as specified by Expression (7); the time counter is decrement by one at each system clock tick; if the time counter reaches a value smaller than zero, a timeliness violation is signalled; the time counter is stopped/restarted when an SK job is completed. Detecting when an SK job begins and when it ends is achieved by configuring, respectively, the address of its first and last instructions as events of interest, which will trigger the relevant (re)start/stop actions at the timeliness monitor.

The timing failure detection capabilities of the original Safety Kernel TFD design, described in Sect. 3, are herein moved to hardware and fully integrated in the Observer Entity. A timeliness monitor is instantiated for each relevant data input, being (re)started whenever a data input packet (e.g., heartbeat, data validity,...) is received by the Listener Thread. If it expires, a timing failure has been detected and it will be signalled to the Timing Failure Detection Service Function. For better integration with the software functions the signalling of timing failures is made through globally accessible memory variables.

The role of the TFD, implemented either in hardware or in software, is to detect untimely behaviours of components in the nominal system, allowing the Safety Kernel to act before any harmful effect becomes externally visible, e.g. by changing the LoS or the PL (see Fig. 2). Violation of Safety Kernel design assumptions is a more severe situation, calling for some form of exception handling that hopefully will bring the system into a safe state. Since, in general, these situations were unforeseen in the design of the system, no guarantees can be provided that the adequate corrective actions (if any) are taken[2].

---

[2] Most probably, there will be little to do anyway, if the design violation happens during a mission critical phase, such as the landing of a planetary probe. However, that does not necessarily imply the failure of the mission. For example: multiple (overload) alarms, occurring during the descendent flight of the first Moon landing, were advisedly discarded by the Apollo 11 lander crew.

5   Safety Kernel Implementation and Evaluation

For the implementation of the Safety Kernel, a suitable hardware/software platform must be selected. The functional elements to be provided by the hardware
platform include: Processing Unit, providing the computing resources; Read-
Only Memory (ROM), to store the Safety Kernel software code and the safety
rules; Random Access Memory (RAM), supporting the Safety Kernel execution; Input/Output (I/O) Interface, to enable the exchange of data between
the Safety Kernel and the nominal system components. The software platform should include fundamental real-time operating system support concerning: process/thread management and scheduling; input/output management and
access, e.g. through device drivers.

5.1   Hardware Platforms and Software Implementation

In KARYON, the fulfillment of the requirements was achieved by using a development board containing a reconfigurable logic device (FPGA), together with
Intellectual Property (IP) cores from a System-on-a-Chip (SoC) library [1], mapping the functional elements into the reconfigurable logic device. The selected
development board (shown on the left, in Fig. 4) was a Trenz TE-0600, comprised
of: Xilinx Spartan-6 FPGA; 256 MiB[3] of RAM memory; Ethernet physical interface; Flash ROM and an Secure Digital (SD) card physical interface.

The Flash ROM (not shown in Fig. 4) serves as non-volatile storage for the
Safety Kernel, whilst the SD Card interface supports the Safety Rules, written offline to an SD card. The FPGA supports the mapping of the controller
mechanisms for these memory interfaces, together with the processing unit and
Ethernet controller.

The functional elements implemented in the FPGA (shown on the right, in
Fig. 4) were provided by the GRLIB SoC library [1], which encompasses IP cores
providing I/O functions, such as Ethernet and serial interfaces, together with the
remaining components needed to implement a fully-fledged embedded computer,
e.g. memory and interrupt controllers. The processing unit was implemented by
the LEON3 soft-processor, a SPARCv8 architecture commonly used in avionics
applications by the European space industry.

Furthermore, this hardware platform is able to support all the resources
required by the runtime verification techniques proposed in Sect. 4.3. Since the
Observer Entity is essentially composed of a few counting blocks, its complexity
is much lower than any other component in the FPGA (right side of Fig. 4) and
therefore uses only a small fraction of the occupied FPGA resources.

As software platform, we used the RTEMS real-time operating system [15]
installed on the Trenz TE-0600 hardware board. After initialization, when the
configuration file is processed, two concurrent POSIX threads are used to execute the Safety Kernel functions detailed and analysed in Sect. 4.2: the Listener

---

[3] This corresponds to the prefixes for binary multiples defined in the IEC 60027-2
standard specification [10].

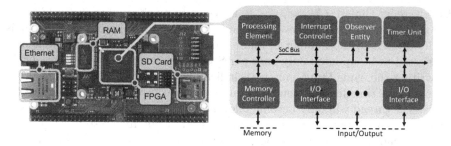

Fig. 4. Hardware platform for the Safety Kernel implementation.

Thread, which handles incoming information to update the runtime safety information repository; the Periodic Thread, which is triggered every T_{SK} time units (e.g., milliseconds), where T_{SK} is the Safety Kernel execution period. This value can be changed in the XML configuration file.

To evaluate the concrete impact of using soft-processor cores, a fully-fledged software-based implementation of the Safety Kernel was deployed on an alternative platform, composed of a real-time Linux environment on a Raspberry Pi Model B Revision 2.0, with a ARM11 processor at 700 Mhz [22]. Integration of non-intrusive runtime verification mechanisms was not possible in this platform, since the SoC present in the current versions of Raspberry Pi does not include the ARM CoreSight facilities [3], indispensable to secure non-intrusiveness of system observation in ARM-based platforms. The unavailability of reconfigurable logic devices on the simple Raspberry Pi platform also precludes the implementation in hardware of SK TFD functions. A Safety Kernel entirely implemented in software had to be used on the Raspberry Pi platform [22].

5.2   Performance Evaluation

To properly configure the Observer Entity it is necessary to know the Safety Kernel execution period, T_{SK}. Moreover, from a practical perspective, it is also important to know if T_{SK} is sufficiently small so that the Safety Kernel can be used in a given application. In fact, this period corresponds to the maximum latency of timing failure detection and also to the time it may take for the Safety Kernel to trigger a system reconfiguration.

Therefore, we performed a set of experiments to evaluate the achievable values for T_{SK} and illustrate the feasibility of the approach. According to Expressions (1) and (2), T_{SK} depends on the worst-case execution time of two threads. The main thread involves the execution of the Timing Failure Detection (TFD) component, the Safety Manager (SM) and the Data Component Multiplexer (DCM). Given that the verification of safety rules is a complex task, the worst-case execution time of this periodic thread, $C_{periodic\_thread}$, can possibly be high. On the other hand, the Input Data Manager task is very simple, just requiring a input unit to be updated, which means that the worst-case execution time of the listener thread, $C_{listener\_thread}$, is typically much smaller. Even knowing that the listener thread wakes up several times per SK period, this number is usually limited to the number of input units. In fact, each different input unit is expected to be updated only once per SK period because there is no point in overwriting the same input unit with indications on the validity of data or on the execution timeliness of some nominal system component. The overhead of the listener thread will only become relevant in systems in which the number of different input units is high. If, for some reason, a nominal system component starts to send more packets to the SK and waking up the listener thread more times than expected, the constraint specified in Expression 6 will be violated and this will be detected by the Observer entity.

Given the above, we focused our experiments on the evaluation of the Periodic Thread response time, which in this particular case is equal to the Periodic Thread execution time, upper bounded by $C_{periodic\_thread}$.

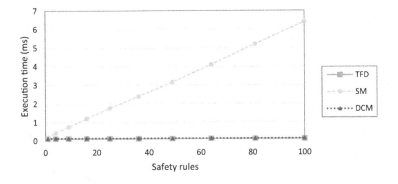

Fig. 5. Periodic thread execution time on the LEON3 soft-processor.

The first experiment was done using the SK implementation on the LEON3 soft-processor, as described in Sect. 5.1. To measure the execution time of SK components, we instrumented the SK code using start/stop timer functions provided by the underlying operating system (RTEMS or Linux), whose temporal interference on the SK execution is very small and can be neglected. Note that this instrumentation, despite intrusive, was necessary only for evaluation purposes and is fully independent from the Observer Entity, whose runtime verification mechanisms are still non-intrusive. The objective of the experiment was to determine the influence of the number of safety rules on the execution time of the periodic thread. Therefore, we created SK configuration files implying the construction of a number of safety rules varying between 1 and 100. As explained in Sect. 3, a safety rule is a Boolean expression whose value evaluates to true or false depending on input data received by the SK (through the Input Data Manager task). The safety rules we used in the evaluation involve one input unit, one output unit and a single comparison. The complexity of the safety rules evaluation algorithm stems from the need to parse a tree-like data structure, initialized at startup time and containing the input and output units, as well as the logical operations and bounds. The details of this data structure and the executed algorithm are out of the scope of this paper and can be found in [26]. For each configuration we measured the contribution of each of the three executed components (TFD, SM and DCM) for the overall execution time. The experiments were repeated 100 times and the average values were collected (the standard deviations are very small, in the order of a few microseconds, and therefore we do not show them).

The results of the first experiment are show in Fig. 5. They clearly show that both the TFD and DCM components have a constant execution time, independent of the number of rules to be checked. On the other hand, the SM component execution time increases linearly with the number of safety rules. Therefore, it is possible to conclude that the SK execution time is mainly and linearly dependent on the number of safety rules, that is, on complexity of the application. However, the absolute value, which reaches 6 ms for 100 safety rules, is significant. In systems requiring a reaction time of less than 60 ms, at most 1000 rules would be acceptable, which seems limited. The reason for such high execution time is fundamentally due to the fact that the SK is running on a soft-processor infrastructure.

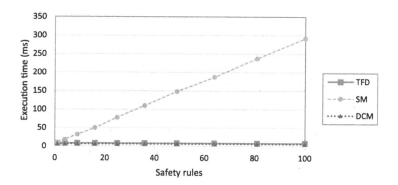

Fig. 6. Periodic thread execution time on a Raspberry PI.

To understand the concrete impact of using a soft-processor, we performed a second experiment by deploying the SK on a real-time Linux/Raspberry Pi platform. The same experiments were performed and yielded the results shown in Fig. 6.

The most important observation is the significant reduction of the execution time, as expected. Instead of 6 ms, processing 100 safety rules takes no more than 300 μs, which is 20 times less. The approach seems thus feasible for most applications, provided that a reasonably good processor is used.

5.3   Effectiveness and Feasibility Analysis

The Safety Manager has, in general, a worst-case execution time, T_{SM}, which largely exceeds those of the Timing Failure Detector, either of the entirely software-based solution, T_{TFD}, or of the hardware/software co-design introduced in Sect. 4, T_{TFD_SF}. Since, $T_{TFD\_SF} < T_{TFD} << T_{SM}$, the performance improvement due to a smaller T_{TFD_SF} value is not significant in terms of the overall Safety Kernel operation. Methods to reduce the value of T_{SM}, allowing a significant performance improvement, will be addressed in future work.

At this point, the main benefit provided by the non-intrusive runtime verification mechanisms is to secure the Safety Kernel design assumptions. Instead of resorting to classical code instrumentation, which is inherently intrusive, our approach relies on independent, isolated and non-intrusive runtime verification mechanisms, easily integrated in reconfigurable logic supporting soft-processors (e.g., LEON3), such as the Trenz TE-0600 platform (see Sect. 5.1). Integration of non-intrusive runtime verification mechanisms in platforms based on ARM processors is dependent on the availability of ARM CoreSight facilities [3].

Detecting a violation of SK design assumptions may significantly contribute to enhance the overall system dependability. For some usages, a special-purpose exception handler could be programmed within the SK context to activate existing safeguard functions, e.g. for the safe stop of a terrestrial/maritime unmanned autonomous vehicle. In general, such functions may not exist (cf. Sect. 4.3).

6   Related Work

A novel perspective on distributed systems' architecture was settled by the notion of hybridization in [23, 25]. The concept of architectural hybridization and its diverse advantages were further discussed in [24]. System parts with distinct synchronism [25] or security [8] properties can take advantage of hybrid distributed system model approaches. Hybrid system modeling has also been previously applied to autonomous control systems [2]. The hybrid nature of systems was also acknowledged in [14], which developed a component-based generic platform for embedded real-time systems.

Both offline and online runtime verification (RV) approaches have been previously studied, with online RV receiving increased attention due to its many benefits regarding safety and performance [4]. Furthermore, non-intrusive runtime monitoring has been previously applied in embedded systems [17, 27] and, more specifically, in safety critical environments [11], presenting an RV architecture for monitoring safety critical embedded systems using an external bus monitor connected to the target system. A novel System Health Management technique was introduced in [18] which empowers both real-time assessment of the system status with respect to temporal-logic-based specifications and supports statistical reasoning to estimate its health at runtime. Configurable non-intrusive event-based frameworks for runtime monitoring have been developed within the embedded systems' scope [13], employing a minimally intrusive method for dynamic monitoring. Additionally, the RV concept has been applied to cyber-physical systems [28], autonomous systems [5], avionic systems [19,20] and to an AUTOSAR-like real-time operating system, aiming the automotive domain [9]. [12] describes a runtime monitoring approach for autonomous vehicle systems requiring no code instrumentation by observing the network state.

7 Conclusion

This paper addressed the problem of hardware-based non-intrusive runtime verification, considering its application on a system with a hybrid architecture. Hybridization allows separating the system in at least two parts, making strong assumptions (on the temporal and/or security domains) only for one of the parts, typically a small one. It is thus important not only to verify in design time that these strong assumptions are effectively satisfied, but also to verify them in runtime, particularly when the operational conditions cannot be fully anticipated.

We described an approach for non-intrusive runtime verification and explained how it is applied in a concrete case: to verify a set of assumptions underlying the design of a Safety Kernel, also described in the paper. The approach was used to verify timing assumptions and also assumptions on the maximum number of events occurring in a time interval.

Finally, the paper also provided experimental results to illustrate the performance that might be expected from two implementations of a Safety Kernel: one running on a soft-processor and another running on a real ARM processor. The results show that with a hardware processor it is possible to use a Safety Kernel in complex applications. On the other hand, we described some feasibility constraints for applying our verification approach on ARM processors. We plan to address these constraints in future work in order to take full advantage of the proposed non-intrusive verification approach.

References

1. Aeroflex Gaisler, A.B., Goteborg, Sweden: GRLIB IP Library User's Manual, April 2014
2. Antsaklis, P.J., Stiver, J.A., Lemmon, M.: Hybrid system modeling and autonomous control systems. In: Grossman, R.L., Nerode, A., Ravn, A.P., Rischel, H. (eds.) HS 1991–1992. LNCS, vol. 736, pp. 366–392. Springer, Heidelberg (1993). doi:10.1007/3-540-57318-6_37
3. ARM: ARM CoreSight Architecture Specification, 2.0 edn., September 2013
4. Backasch, R., Hochberger, C., Weiss, A., Leucker, M., Lasslop, R.: Runtime verification for multicore SoC with high-quality trace data. ACM Trans. Design Autom. Electron. Syst. (TODAES) 18(2), 18 (2013)
5. Callow, G., Watson, G., Kalawsky, R.: System modelling for run-time verification and validation of autonomous systems. In: Proceeding of 5th International Conference on System of Systems Engineering, Loughborough, UK, pp. 1–7, June 2010
6. Casimiro, A., Kaiser, J., Schiller, E.M., Costa, P., Parizi, J., Johansson, R., Librino, R.: The KARYON project: predictable and safe coordination in cooperative vehicular systems. In: Proceeding of 43rd Annual IEEE/IFIP Conference on Dependable Systems and Networks Workshop (DSN-W), pp. 1–12. IEEE (2013)

7. Casimiro, A., Rufino, J., Pinto, R.C., Vial, E., Schiller, E.M., Morales-Ponce, O., Petig, T.: A kernel-based architecture for safe cooperative vehicular functions. In: Proceeding of 9th IEEE International Symposium on Industrial Embedded Systems (SIES), pp. 228–237, June 2014

8. Correia, M., Veríssimo, P., Neves, N.F.: The design of a COTS real-time distributed security kernel. In: Bondavalli, A., Thevenod-Fosse, P. (eds.) EDCC 2002. LNCS, vol. 2485, pp. 234–252. Springer, Heidelberg (2002). doi:10.1007/3-540-36080-8_21

9. Cotard, S., Faucou, S., Bechennec, J.L., Queudet, A., Trinquet, Y.: A data flow monitoring service based on runtime verification for AUTOSAR. In: Proceeding of 14th International Conference on High Performance Computing and Communications. IEEE, Liverpool, UK, June 2012

10. IEC Standards: IEC 60027-2: Letter symbols to be used in electrical technology Part 2: telecommunications and electronics, August 2005

11. Kane, A.: Runtime monitoring for safety-critical embedded systems. Ph.D. thesis, Carnegie Mellon University, USA, February 2015

12. Kane, A., Chowdhury, O., Datta, A., Koopman, P.: A case study on runtime monitoring of an autonomous research vehicle (ARV) system. In: Proceeding of 15th International Conference on Runtime Verification, Vienna, Austria, pp. 102–117, September 2015

13. Lee, J.C., Lysecky, R.: System-level observation framework for non-intrusive runtime monitoring of embedded systems. ACM Trans. Design Autom. Electron. Syst. **20**, 42 (2015)

14. Obermaisser, R., Kopetz, H.: Genesys: A candidate for an ARTEMIS cross-domain reference architecture for embedded systems, September 2009

15. On-Line Applications Research Corporation: RTEMS C User's Guide, 4.9.4 edn. (2010)

16. Pinto, R.C., Rufino, J.: Towards non-invasive run-time verification of real-time systems. In: Proceeding of 26th Euromicro Conference on Real-Time Systems - WIP Session, Madrid, Spain, pp. 25–28, July 2014

17. Reinbacher, T., Fugger, M., Brauer, J.: Runtime verification of embedded real-time systems. Formal Methods Syst. Design **24**(3), 203–239 (2014)

18. Reinbacher, T., Rozier, K.Y., Schumann, J.: Temporal-logic based runtime observer pairs for system health management of real-time systems. In: Ábrahám, E., Havelund, K. (eds.) TACAS 2014. LNCS, vol. 8413, pp. 357–372. Springer, Heidelberg (2014). doi:10.1007/978-3-642-54862-8_24

19. Rufino, J., Gouveia, I.: Timeliness runtime verification and adaptation in avionic systems. In: Proceeding of 12th workshop on Operating Systems Platforms for Embedded Real-Time applications (OSPERT), Toulouse, France, July 2016

20. Rufino, J.: Towards integration of adaptability and non-intrusive runtime verification in avionic systems. SIGBED Rev. **13**(1), 60–65 (2016). (Special Issue on 5th Embedded Operating Systems Workshop)

21. Sha, L.: Using simplicity to control complexity. IEEE Software **18**(4), 20–28 (2001)

22. Upton, E., Halfacree, G.: Raspberry Pi User Guide. Wiley, New York (2012)

23. Veríssimo, P.: Uncertainty and predictability: can they be reconciled? In: Schiper, A., Shvartsman, A.A., Weatherspoon, H., Zhao, B.Y. (eds.) Future Directions in DC 2002. LNCS, vol. 2584, pp. 108–113. Springer, Heidelberg (2003). doi:10.1007/3-540-37795-6_20

24. Verissimo, P.: Travelling through wormholes: a new look at distributed systems models. SIGACT News **37**(1), 66–81 (2006)

25. Verissimo, P., Casimiro, A.: The timely computing base model and architecture. IEEE Trans. Comput. **51**(8), 916–930 (2002)

26. Vial, E., Casimiro, A.: Evaluation of safety rules in a safety kernel-based architecture. In: Bondavalli, A., Ceccarelli, A., Ortmeier, F. (eds.) SAFE-COMP 2014. LNCS, vol. 8696, pp. 27–35. Springer, Cham (2014). doi:10.1007/978-3-319-10557-4_5

27. Watterson, C., Heffernan, D.: Runtime verification and monitoring of embedded systems. IET Software **1**(5), 172–179 (2007)

28. Zheng, X., Julien, C., Podorozhny, R., Cassez, F.: BraceAssertion: runtime verification of cyber-physical systems. In: Proceeding of 15th IEEE Real-Time and Embedded Technology and Applications Symposium, pp. 298–306, October 2015

Timing Verification

Supporting Nested Resources in MrsP

Jorge Garrido[1]([✉]), Shuai Zhao[2], Alan Burns[2], and Andy Wellings[2]

[1] Sistemas de Tiempo Real e Ingeniería de Servicios Telemáticos (STRAST),
Universidad Politécnica de Madrid (UPM), Madrid, Spain
`str@dit.upm.es`
[2] Department of Computer Science, University of York, York, England

Abstract. The original MrsP proposal presented a new multiprocessor resource sharing protocol based on the properties and behaviour of the Priority Ceiling Protocol, supported by a novel helping mechanism. While this approach proved to be as simple and elegant as the single processor protocol, the implications with regard to nested resources was identified as requiring further clarification. In this work we present a complete approach to nested resources behaviour and analysis for the MrsP protocol.

1 Introduction

Both the increasing requirements in terms of computation power and the decreasing availability of single processor platforms have given rise to the need for safe, analysable real-time multiprocessor systems. While providing more execution units increases the overall computation power, it also increases the complexity of the required scheduling protocols with regard to shared resources and task communication management.

Single core approaches benefited from the inherent serialization on access requests imposed by the existence of only one processor. Multicore approaches to shared resources have explored different ways of providing a bound on the time it takes to gain access to such resources. One of the main approaches is to use spin-locks. Following this approach, a task requesting access to a resource places the request on a queue and spin-waits at a certain priority until the access request is satisfied. If the synchronisation protocol does not allow higher priority tasks to preempt tasks accessing shared resources then higher priority tasks may suffer unnecessary blockings. Alternatively, if access requests can be preempted, then a mechanism has to be defined to ensure progress on the locked resource if other tasks are blocked by a resource held by a locally preempted task. This last approach is the one followed by the Multiprocessor Resource Sharing Protocol (MrsP) [4]. In this protocol a helping mechanism is defined, by which locally preempted tasks can migrate to other processors to make progress provided that a task is actively waiting on that processor to access the locked resource.

In this paper we analyse the life cycle of a task with regard to the MrsP shared resource protocol and define a set of rules supporting a fine grained analysis for preemptive, FIFO spin-lock controlled, nested resources.

J. Blieberger and M. Bader (Eds.): Ada-Europe 2017, LNCS 10300, pp. 73–86, 2017.
DOI: 10.1007/978-3-319-60588-3_5

2   Related Work

Despite the academic interest in multiprocessor real-time systems, many proposals are oblivious to, or explicitly ban, task communication and synchronization. Among the work on shared-memory synchronization protocols for multiprocessors real-time systems published up to date, few publications address the analysis of nested resources as required by the complex paradigms of synchronization required by modern real-time systems.

A common approach to supporting nested resources has been to group resources together. In this approach, of which FMLP [2] is a notable example, nested resources are locked and released as a whole. This unfortunately seriously undermining the concurrency of the system, thereby reducing schedulability.

The first proposal for fine-grained analysis was proposed in [10]; forcing a strict order on locks and releases (locking operations are not allowed after a release has been performed on the nesting). An extension of this work is the Real-time Nested Locking Protocol (RNLP) [12,13] which limits the concurrency on nested resource accesses by means of a token mechanism and provides a set of request satisfaction mechanisms aiming for optimality under different system configurations.

Recent work has provided a fully fine-grained blocking bound for nested non-preemptive FIFO spin locks under partitioned fixed-priority scheduling [1]. This is achieved using a novel graph abstraction of the blocking interaction among tasks and resources for which, given a set of invariants stating graph properties, an Integer Linear Programming (ILP) approach is used to find a subgraph yielding a safe worst-case blocking value.

It is also worth to mention SPEPP [11] as a relevant protocol introducing the notion of a helping mechanism, fundamental to MrsP formulation. This helping mechanism was also used in M-BWI [7,8] to deal with the issue of tasks running out of budget while holding a resource in systems ruled by execution-time servers.

Despite the fact that MrsP was recently proposed, it has been effectively implemented [6] in Litmus [5] and RTEMS [9]. Its implementability in Ada is discussed in [3], where a prototype outside-kernel implementation is presented.

3   System and Task Model

The baseline of the current work is the MrsP proposal [4]. In this work a protocol to provide a safe upper bound to resources shared among tasks potentially executing on different processors is presented. In this work, the general *sporadic task model* is considered, under fully partitioned systems. Deadlines are unconstrained, but there can not be more than one active job of a task at a time. As such, the terms task and job are used interchangeably in this paper. Resources are required to be accessed under mutual exclusion. Preemptive fixed-priority scheduling is assumed.

Tasks are related to resources by means of different functions: $G(r^j)$ is the set of tasks that access directly a resource r^j, and $F(\tau_i)$ returns the set of resources used by task τ_i; function *map* returns the set of processors where the argument entities execute, and $\|$ returns the size of a set. If all tasks that access a resource execute on the same processor then the resource is deemed to be *locally accessed*, otherwise it is contended for *globally*.

MrsP, in general, follows the rules of the Priority Ceiling Protocol (PCP): resources are given a Local Ceiling Priority on each processor which is equal to the highest priority of any local task that accessing the resource. Tasks, when attempting to access a resource, rise their active priority to that Ceiling Priority. Authors in [4] claim to inherit four fundamental properties from PCP:

- A job is blocked at most once during its execution.
- This blocking takes place prior to the job actually executing.
- Once a job starts executing, all the resources it needs are (locally) available.
- Deadlocks are prevented.

The scheduling analysis for MrsP keeps the form of Response-Time Analysis (RTA) as in the PCP case, defined in the following equation:

$$R_i = C_i + max\{\hat{e}, \hat{b}\} + \sum_{\tau_j \in \mathbf{hpl}(i)} \left\lceil \frac{R_i}{T_j} \right\rceil C_j \tag{1}$$

where R_i is the worst-case response-time of task τ_i, $\hat{e}$ is the maximum arrival blocking due to local lower priority tasks accessing shared resources, and $\hat{b}$ is the maximum non-preemptive execution time caused by the underlying OS/kernel. C_i is decomposed into the Worst Case Execution Time (WCET) of the task outside its use of shared resources plus the cost of accessing (e) each shared resource r up to n times during each activation:

$$C_i = WCET_i + \sum_{r^j \in \mathbf{F}(\tau_i)} n_i e^j \tag{2}$$

Finally, e is calculated as the cost of each individual access, c^j, multiplied by the number of processors from where the resource can be accessed (this is the maximum length of the FIFO queue):

$$e^j = |map(G(r^j))|c^j \tag{3}$$

This safe upper bound to the access cost is based on two properties of MrsP:

- Only one task per processor can be accessing a resource at any given time. This is directly inherited from PCP.
- A helping mechanism, proposed in [4], by which tasks spin-waiting to access a resource can take over the execution of tasks locally preempted while holding the required resource.

Since the helping mechanism is the most relevant and novel feature in [4], and highly influences the behaviour of the system, it will be further explained in the rest of this section.

Figure 1 represents the different logical states in which a task can be with regard to MrsP controlled resources:

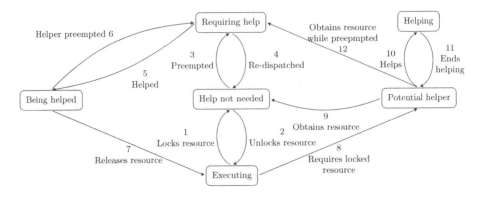

Fig. 1. Task state diagram of helping mechanism without nested resources.

- *Executing*: A task that does not require any resource to make progress.
- *Help not needed*: A task is making progress with a locked resource while being dispatched on its host processor by means of its active priority.
- *Requiring help*: A task holding a global resource that is unable to make progress (as it has been locally preempted) from its host processor.
- *Being helped*: A task that holds a global resource and has migrated to another processor in order to make progress.
- *Potential helper*: A task that requests an already allocated resource, and is spin-waiting for it.
- *Helping*: A task that was spin-waiting and pulled a requiring-help task to make progress on its processor in order to help it to release the requested resource.

Every task initially holds no resource, so its in the *executing* state. At a certain point, a task can request access to a global shared resource. As part of the process of this request, it increases its active priority to the Local Ceiling Priority of the resource. If the resource is free, it will lock the resource (transition, or tran, 1). Otherwise it will be spin-waiting blocked by this resource until access is granted to the resource (tran 8).

Transition 1, locking the resource, moves the task to the *help not needed* state. While in this state, the task can: finish the access to the resource and release its associated lock (tran 2), or be locally preempted while accessing the resource (tran 3).

If a task is locally preempted while holding a lock, it is considered to *requiring help* to make progress on the resource. While it remains in the *requiring help* state, no progress is possible. If no other task requires the locked resource, while being preempted, then this preemption time is just local interference, and the *requiring help* task will, at some point (when the preempting job terminates), be re-dispatched at its host processor due to its active priority (tran 4).

However, if at some point while being preempted, another task requests access (or was already spin-waiting) to the resource, this task will help the preempted one (tran 5 for the preempted task). This transition, in practice, implies a migration to the helper host processor, with the active priority updated to the Local Ceiling Priority of the held resource on that processor. Then, the task will make progress (*being helped*) until it releases the resource, migrating back to its host processor with its base priority (tran 7), or until it is preempted again on the helping processor, *requiring help* (tran 6) again until it is re-dispatched on its own processor or is helped again.

Tasks blocked by a locked resource are *potential helpers*. Their request is added to a FIFO queue and will be served when all requests in front have been satisfied. This can happen when the task is actually spin-waiting for the resource (tran 9), immediately making progress on the resource, or when the task is locally preempted. As it would hold a resource without making progress due to being locally preempted on its host processor, it would be considered to be *requiring help* (tran 12).

If, while being a *potential helper* due to being blocked by a locked resource, the holder of that resource is locally preempted and thus *requires help*, the helping mechanism is fired. This, in practice means that the *potential helper* task pulls the *requiring help* task to its host processor and lends it its active priority, to execute on its behalf (tran 10). The *helping* procedure ends when the helped task releases the held resource or it is preempted on the helping processor (tran 11).

Thus, for a task to be helped, there should be both a task *requiring help* and a *potential helper* for the same resource. The helping mechanism begins with transition 5 for the *requiring help* and transition 10 for the *potential helper*. Equivalently, the helping mechanism ends with a helped task transitioning by 6 or 7, and a helper doing transition 11.

While these behaviours deal adequately with non-nested resources requests, systems including nested resources require a more specific approach. The full description and definition of such an approach is the main contribution of this paper.

4   Nested Resources

The system model and analysis presented in [4] and briefly summarized in Sect. 3 can not, by themselves, be transferred to a system with nested resources. Equation 3 only reflects direct accesses from tasks to resources. In [4], a new term, $V(r^j)$ was proposed as a function returning the set of resources accessing the resource r^j. Based on that definition, the following equation for calculating the cost of accessing a nested resource was proposed:

$$e^j = (|V(r^j)| + |map(G(r^j))|)c^j \tag{4}$$

Equation 4 now defines the maximum queue length for accessing the resource as the number of processors from where the resource can be directly accessed plus the number of outer resources from where the resource can be accessed. While this interpretation of the queue length is correct, the value of e^j does not necessarily represent a safe upper bound for a resource that requires accessing inner resources to complete its execution. The reason for this is that the analysis fails to account for the possible transitive blocking while accessing that inner resources (r^k). That is, a task (or outer resource) attempting to access resource r^k may find it already locked, and be unable to make progress. We shall produce a correct version of this equation in Sect. 4.2.

Another issue raised when considering nested resources in MrsP is local blocking. For non-nested resources, it is proven that, following PCP behaviour, a task can only be blocked once, and only before it actually gets to execute. This property is necessary to maintain the $max\{\hat{e}, \hat{b}\}$ factor for the local blocking in Eq. 1. However, the helping mechanism proposed in [4], together with nested resources, could lead, if no measures are taken, to situations in which higher priority tasks can be blocked more than once after beginning their execution. Due to the helping mechanism, a task holding a resource and locally preempted can be migrated to another processor, in order to make progress, While migrated, it might lock an inner local resource with a higher priority. If the active priority of the task is raised then, on return to the host processor it would preempt a higher base priority task thus causing further delayed local blocking. For this reason the active priority of a migrated task is not raised in this situation.

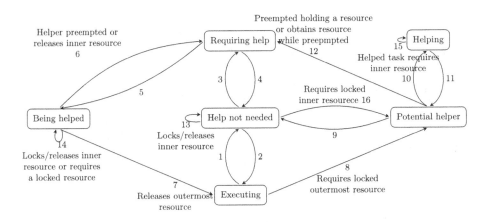

Fig. 2. Task state diagram of helping mechanism with nested resources.

4.1 Desired Nested Resource Behaviour

In this work we propose a complete approach to global nested shared resources, providing a safe upper bound access cost for nested resources as well as a dynamic priority assignment scheme preserving PCP properties. Figure 2 depicts the different logic states of tasks under MrsP, when considering nested resources. While the states remain the same, new transitions arise and some existing ones are now triggered by new events.

Tasks still begin *executing* without any shared resource, and transitions 1 and 8 are triggered when the task requires the outermost resource of a nested call, raising the active priority to the ceiling of that outermost resource. If the access request is satisfied immediately, the task executes without requiring any help. While executing in the *help not needed* state all locks and releases update the active priority of the task (tran 13) as in PCP. If a lock request finds a resource already locked, the task updates its priority to the local Ceiling Priority of the resource and becomes a *potential helper* for that resource (tran 16).

As with the non nested case, the task can, while executing not being helped, be locally preempted and thus *require help* to make progress (tran 3). If at some point while *requiring help*, another task is spin-waiting for one of the resources locked by this preempted task, it will be helped by the spinning task. However, in the nested case, the helper may be helping not due to requesting the innermost locked resource, but due to requesting any of the resources held by the preempted task.

A task, when migrated to be helped (tran 5), is granted the priority of the helper task. While *being helped*, a task is allowed to lock and release further resources (tran 14), but these actions *do not change the priority of the helper*, and thus the priority at which the helped task is executing while *being helped*.

As with the non nested case, a task can, while *being helped*, release its outermost locked shared resource and migrate back to its host processor with its base priority (tran 7). Similarly, a task can leave the *being helped* state to *requiring help* (tran 6). In the nested case, this transition can be triggered by both the task being preempted on the helping processor, and by releasing of the required nested resource by the helping task. In this latter case, the task *being helped* still holds other resources, and still *requires help* to make progress.

Any task finding a required resource already remotely locked while *executing* or in *help not needed* state becomes a *potential helper* for that resource (trans 8 and 16). While being a *potential helper* a task can be preempted. In this case, if the task holds a resource, it *requires help* to make progress on that resource (tran 12).

Potential helpers are ready to help tasks *requiring help*, holding their required resource (tran 10). A task while *being helped* may require a locked inner resource. In this situation, the task is still considered to be helped (tran 14) and spin-waits for locked resource. If the third task holding that inner resource is also *requiring help*, the helping task is ultimately blocked by this third task not making progress. As such, the helper task will also help the third task migrating it to its host processor, and giving it its active priority, executing instead of the task that was *being helped* before (tran 15). This transitive help is maintained until the third task releases the inner resource required by the original helped task.

The helping mechanism can end (tran 11) due to the same two reasons as in the non nested case: the resource required being released or the helper task being locally preempted, with the same implications as in the non nested case.

4.2   Updated Analysis and Properties

In this subsection we propose an analysis in which a safe upper bound can be obtained for the access cost to a resource including any of the inner resources required by this resource. To provide such analysis, we require a strict irreflexive partial order on the resource nesting. This not only prevents deadlocks, but also provides an end to the recursion in the analysis, as at least there has to be one resource in the system not requiring any other resource to complete its execution. Given this, the access cost for a nested resource is now defined as follows:

$$e^j = (|V(r^j)| + |map(G(r^j))|) * (c^j + \sum_{r^k \in U(r^j)} n_j^k e^k) \qquad (5)$$

where $U(r^j)$ is the set of inner resources directly accessed by r^j and n_j^k is the number of times an inner resource r^k is accessed on each access to r^j.

In Eq. 5, the length of the queue is as in [4], where PCP limits the number of concurrent access attempts to a resource to one at a time per processor $(|map(G(r^j))|)$ and the mutual exclusion nature of shared resources under MrsP ensures that only one access attempt can be performed at a time from any outer resource, giving the total number $|V(r^j)|$. Note this queue length may be pessimistic, but our objective here is to provide sufficient analysis.

For the cost of the access itself, now we do not only consider the cost of the accessed resource itself but the cost of accessing all the nested resources. So e^j now represents the full cost for a task accessing nested resources via r^j as an outermost resource, or the cost for outer resources accessing e^j and all its inner resources.

This way of calculating the e value for nested resources now includes the possible transitive blocking on each access. As each access is not considered isolated, but includes the cost of inner resources queues (which are the source of transitive blocking), now Eq. 5 provides a safe upper bound.

Considering the extra blocking a task may suffer due to the helping mechanism, in this proposal we require that a task does not update (increase or decrease) its host active priority while being helped. This way, lower priority tasks can not benefit from the helping mechanism to increase their priority while migrated, with the undesired side effect of causing extra blocking to local higher priority tasks. In turn, tasks are dispatched on their host processor with the priority they had when they were locally preempted. We will refer to this priority as the *Leaving Priority* for the rest of the paper. Migrated tasks *do* update their active priorities when they are re-dispatched on their host processor.

Example. To illustrate the approach, the example for nested resources analysis presented in [4] is now revisited. Consider a system with four tasks, $\tau_1, \ldots, \tau_4$, executing on four different processors $p_1, \ldots, p_4$, and two resources, r^1 and r^2, with execution times c^1 and c^2 respectively. Tasks τ_1 and τ_2 access r^1 directly, and τ_3 and τ_4 access r^2 directly. In addition r^1 accesses r^2, so, for example, when τ_1 accesses r^1 it will, while holding r^1 also access r^2 (Table 1).

Table 1. Task allocation and resource usage.

Task	Processor	$F(\tau_i)$	Resource	$G(r^i)$	$V(r^i)$	$map(G(r^i))$
τ_1	p_1	r^1, r^2	r^1	τ_1, τ_2	$\emptyset$	p_1, p_2
τ_2	p_2	r^1, r^2	r^2	τ_3, τ_4	r^1	p_3, p_4
τ_3	p_3	r^2				
τ_4	p_4	r^2				

As presented in Sect. 4.2, the nested resource analysis proposed is solved by iteration from inner to outer resources. In this example, we have one inner resource, r^2, and one outer resource, r^1. The accessing cost of the inner resource is (following Eq. 5):

$$e^2 = (1 + 2) * (c^2) = 3c^2$$

Then we can calculate the cost of accessing the nesting of resources via r^1, as we know the cost of accessing all its inner resources (r^2):

$$e^1 = (0 + 2) * (c^1 + e^2) = 2(c^1 + e^2) = 2(c^1 + 3c^2)$$

Now e^1 is a safe upper bound, including transitive blocking, for the access to r^1 and all its required inner resources. We note an incorrect answer is given for this example in [4].

4.3   Improved Nested Helping Analysis

With the current definition of local and global resources ceiling priorities, there are situations in which the analysis can benefit from other priority assignments. Specifically, resources accessed only by tasks allocated to the same processor via outer global resources receive a pessimistic analysis. This pessimism can be reduced and in some cases eliminated by a combination of a particular priority assignment (giving global resources encapsulating a call to an inner local resource the ceiling priority of this inner local resource) and the definition of an equivalent task set reflecting the behaviour of the system with that particular assignment of priorities.

Consider a system comprising a specific processor P_1 with a task set including, among others (irrelevant for the example) the following tasks: tasks τ_1, τ_2, τ_3 with lowest priorities on P_1, and τ_{10} with the highest priority on P_1. On this processor, there is a set of local resources r_l^1, r_l^2, r_l^3, which are only accessed by tasks τ_1, τ_2, τ_3 and τ_{10}. Task τ_{10} accesses the local resources directly, while τ_1, τ_2, and τ_3 do so via a global resource, different for each of them. These resources are accessed only from tasks from P_1 and another processor, but accesses from the other processor do not generate accesses to r_l^1, r_l^2 and r_l^3. The relevant information for the example is summarized in Table 2.

Given the analysis presented in Table 2, the access cost for the highest priority task τ_{10} of each local resource would be (considering execution times of global resources c_g and local resources c_l): $r_l = 2c_l$, being the total access cost

Table 2. Task allocation and resource usage without improvement.

Task	Processor	$F(\tau_i)$	Resource	$G(r^i)$	$V(r^i)$	$map(G(r^i))$
τ_{10}	P_1	r_l^1, r_l^2, r_l^3	r^1	τ_1, τ_1'	$\emptyset$	P_1, P_2
τ_3	P_1	$r^3 \rightarrow r_l^3$	r^2	τ_2, τ_2'	$\emptyset$	P_1, P_3
τ_2	P_1	$r^2 \rightarrow r_l^2$	r^3	τ_3, τ_3'	$\emptyset$	P_1, P_4
τ_1	P_1	$r^1 \rightarrow r_l^1$	r_l^1	τ_{10}	r^1	P_1
			r_l^2	τ_{10}	r^2	P_1
			r_l^3	τ_{10}	r^3	P_1

for the three resources $r_l^{1,2,3} = 3 \cdot 2c_l$. This analysis assumes that the higher priority task may have to wait for the lower priority tasks on each access to the local resources. This is due to the access of the lower priority tasks via a global resource. If this was not the case, r_l^1, r_l^2 and r_l^3 would be pure local resources and be completely ruled by PCP. As the lower priority tasks can be preempted while holding the global resources, and each of them can migrate to a different processor to make progress, the three of them can access their respective local resource concurrent with τ_{10} while being helped remotely. In this case, the helping mechanism produces a high blocking time for a high priority task accessing directly to local shared resources. This clearly contradicts the aim and intuition behind PCP and MrsP.

This problem can be addressed by reducing the concurrency of the lower priority tasks. If r_l^1, r_l^2 and r_l^3 are given the same local Ceiling Priority then only one of the three tasks τ_1, τ_2, or τ_3 can gain access to their outer resource. As a result only one can be helped, and only one can gain access to the inner resource while migrated. The impact on τ_{10} is reduced to a single block.

5   Definitions

The detailed approach for MrsP systems supporting nested resources is now presented as a set of rules, lemmas, properties and theorems. Those from PCP and non nested MrsP are assumed and hold unless overridden by those presented here.

Rule 1. Resources under MrsP nest following a strict irreflexive partial order.
Rule 2. A task being helped executes on the helper processor with the helper active priority.
Rule 3. The helping mechanism can be initiated due to the helper task requesting access to any of the resources held by the helped task.
Rule 4. The helping mechanism is transitive, *i.e.* a helper task shall help the locally preempted task ultimately preventing it from making progress.

Property 1. A task holding one or more resources, that is not being blocked accessing another resource, will make progress if there is a task spin-waiting due to being blocked by any of the resources held.

This is the fundamental novel property from MrsP that we wanted to move to nested resources, as it provides the safe upper bound expressed by Eq. 5.

Rule 5. Task only modify their active priority when they are dispatched in their host processor, not being help.

Tasks can lock and release resources whenever they are executing. If they do so while not being helped, the active priority of the task is modified according to PCP rules. If they do so while being helped, there is no modification of active priorities of any the helping or the helped task. The helped task will update its active priority according to the resources held when it is dispatched again on its host processor when its leaving priority is the highest among the tasks eligible to execute.

Rule 6. The helping mechanism shall also be conducted between tasks allocated to the same host processor.

Rule 7. Tasks remain notionally eligible to be dispatched (at their leaving priority) on their host processor while being helped.

By considering tasks being helped and executing on another processor as eligible for dispatching on their host processor, lower priority tasks are prevented from executing when a higher priority task would be executing instead.

Lemma 1. A task is only allowed to begin its execution if all higher base priority tasks allocated on that processor are completed.

Proof. If no task is migrated, then all uncompleted tasks are ready to execute on that processor. Following PCP rules, the task dispatched is the one with higher active priority. For a task that has not locked any resource, all higher base priority task have higher active priorities. As a task can not have locked any resource before actually executing, it is proven. If a higher base priority has migrated, its leaving priority is at least equal to its base priority. Then, following Rule 7 the higher priority task would be eligible to execute against any lower base priority task not holding any resource.   □

Lemma 2. A task can only make progress by being helped if there is a pending task on the same host processor with higher base priority than its active priority.

Proof. A task having a lower priority than the base priority of another task, will keep having a lower priority unless it locks a resource. Given PCP rules and Rule 7, the lower priority task can not be dispatched on its host processor with that lower priority until the higher base priority task is completed. Until then, it can only lock another resource while making progress because of helping. Due to Rule 5, this will not increase its active priority, this will keep it below the higher base priority of the pending task. As a result, a task can not be executed if not being helped while there are higher base priorities pending tasks.   □

Corollary 1. Tasks with lower active priorities than pending tasks with higher base priorities can not increase their active priority.

Proof. Proven during proof of Lemma 2.   □

Lemma 3. Each task can suffer at most a single local block per activation, and this blocking occurs before the task actually executes.

Proof. Lemma 3 in [4] proves this property for MrsP without nested resources, based on the properties of PCP. For nested resources, as tasks are not allowed to increase their priority while migrated, no task can preempt an already higher base priority task.

A higher priority task may require more than one resource already locked by lower priority tasks. However, due to PCP rules, only one task could have locked such resource on its host processor and increase its priority preventing the higher priority task to execute (arrival blocking). The other tasks only could have locked resources required by the higher priority task while migrated. As tasks are dispatched on their host processor by their leaving priority, no further arrival blocking is possible due to lower priority tasks.   □

Lemma 4. Nested MrsP does not suffer from deadlocks.

Proof. The source of deadlock in nested resources systems is when two or more resources requiring each other prevents any progress to be made. By Rule 1 forcing irreflexive partial order, circular dependencies and thus deadlock due to them are avoided.   □

Lemma 5. A safe upper bound to the number of concurrent access attempts to a resource r^j is given by $|V(r^j)| + |map(G(r^j))|$.

Proof. The number of direct accesses is safely bound by $|map(G(r^j))|$ as all direct accesses from tasks are outermost accesses, and thus are all dealt while not being help (and migrated), so this directly inherits all PCP properties. As only one request can be generated at a time from each processor, there is an upper bound on the number of processors from where the resource can be accessed. As shared resources have mutual exclusion, only one task can be requesting its inner resource at a time. The number of concurrent requests from outer resources is thus bounded to the number of such resources, i.e. $|V(r^j)|$.   □

Lemma 6. The cost of each individual access (e') to a resource r^j is bounded by $e'^j = c^j + \sum_{r_k \in U(r_j)} n_j^k e^k$.

Proof. As a consequence of Rule 1, there is at least one terminal resource r^t in the system not accessing any inner resource, i.e. $U(r^t) = \emptyset$. For such a resource, its individual access cost is:

$$e'^t = c^t$$

From Lemma 5, if we simplify the queue of a resource as $q^j = |V(r^j)| + |map(G(r^j))|$ then the total access cost to e^t is:

$$e^t = q^t c^t \Rightarrow e^t = q^t e'^t$$

For the set of resources accessing the terminal resource, $\mathbf{V}(r^t)$, the individual access cost can be expressed as the execution time of the resource plus the access cost to its inner resource r^t as:

$$e'^{t+1} = c^{t+1} + n^t_{t+1}(q^t * c^t)$$

then substituting e^t:

$$e'^{t+1} = c^{t+1} + n^t_{t+1}e^t \Rightarrow e^{t+1} = q^{t+1}(c^{t+1} + n^t_{t+1}e^t)$$

By the common method of recursion proving, it can be demonstrated[1] that this recursion holds for an arbitrary level k of nesting, where:

$$e'^k = c^k + n^{k-1}_k e^{k-1}$$

This can be directly applied to resources sequentially requiring more than one different independent inner resources:

$$e'^k = c^k + \sum_{r^{k-1} \in \mathbf{U}(r^k)} n^{k-1}_k e^{k-1}$$

Theorem 1. Equation 5 is a safe upper bound to the cost of accessing a MrsP shared resource and its required inner resources.

Proof. By construction if Lemma 5 gives a safe upper bound on the number of possible concurrent accesses to a resource r^j and Lemma 6 reflects a safe upper bound on the cost of each individual access to r^j and its required inner resources, then Eq. 5 is a safe upper bound to the cost of accessing r^j.   □

6   Conclusions

MrsP is a resource control protocol providing a safe upper bound on the contention for global shared resources on multiprocessor systems. In this paper we have provided a detailed approach to nested resource access under the MrsP protocol. By implementing local PCP control on each processor, the number of concurrent accesses to a global resource is bounded to at most one per processor on systems not considering nested resource access. By defining a helping mechanism by which busy waiting tasks can undertake progress inside shared resources on behalf of locally preempted tasks, the total access cost to a resource is effectively bounded. Based on this global resource control scheme, the PCP Response Time Analysis can be used to analyse MrsP systems incorporating its specific resource access cost analysis.

The approach presented in this paper defines a complete fine grained approach to nested resources for MrsP systems. The potential shortcomings of the

---

[1] The complete proof can be found at http://www.dit.upm.es/~jgarrido/mrsp/ae17-appendix.pdf.

helping mechanism when used in nested resources systems are addressed specifically. In particular, we have clarified under which circumstances tasks are eligible to help and to be helped. We have also defined how active priorities are updated under our MrsP nested resources approach. Future work will consider analysis that uses more detailed knowledge about resource usage to reduce the pessimism within the analysis presented in this paper.

Acknowledgment. This work has been partially funded by the Spanish National R&D&I plan (project M2C2, TIN2014-56158-C4-3-P).

References

1. Biondi, A., Brandenburg, B.B., Wieder, A.: A blocking bound for nested FIFO spin locks, pp. 291–302 (2016)
2. Block, A., Leontyev, H., Brandenburg, B.B., Anderson, J.H.: A flexible real-time locking protocol for multiprocessors. In: 13th IEEE International Conference on Embedded and Real-Time Computing Systems and Applications (RTCSA), pp. 47–56. IEEE (2007)
3. Burns, A., Wellings, A.: Locking policies for multiprocessor Ada. ACM SIGAda Ada Lett. **33**(2), 59–65 (2013)
4. Burns, A., Wellings, A.J.: A schedulability compatible multiprocessor resource sharing protocol - MrsP. In: 25th Euromicro Conference on Real-Time Systems (ECRTS), pp. 282–291. IEEE (2013)
5. Calandrino, J.M., Leontyev, H., Block, A., Devi, U.C., Anderson, J.H.: LITMUS^RT: a testbed for empirically comparing real-time multiprocessor schedulers. In: 27th IEEE International Real-Time Systems Symposium, RTSS, pp. 111–126. IEEE (2006)
6. Catellani, S., Bonato, L., Huber, S., Mezzetti, E.: Challenges in the implementation of MrsP. In: de la Puente, J.A., Vardanega, T. (eds.) Ada-Europe 2015. LNCS, vol. 9111, pp. 179–195. Springer, Cham (2015). doi:10.1007/978-3-319-19584-1_12
7. Faggioli, D., Lipari, G., Cucinotta, T.: The multiprocessor bandwidth inheritance protocol. In: 22nd Euromicro Conference on Real-Time Systems (ECRTS), pp. 90–99. IEEE (2010)
8. Lipari, G., Lamastra, G., Abeni, L.: Task synchronization in reservation-based real-time systems. IEEE Trans. Comput. **53**(12), 1591–1601 (2004)
9. RTEMS, C Users guide-edition 4.6. 5, for RTEMS 4.6. 5. On-Line Applications Research Corporation (OAR) 30 (2003). http://www.1tems.com
10. Takada, H., Sakamura, K.: Real-time scalability of nested spin locks. In: Second International Workshop on Real-Time Computing Systems and Applications, Proceedings, pp. 160–167. IEEE (1995)
11. Takada, H., Sakamura, K.: A novel approach to multiprogrammed multiprocessor synchronization for real-time kernels. In: The 18th IEEE Real-Time Systems Symposium, Proceedings, pp. 134–143. IEEE (1997)
12. Ward, B.C., Anderson, J.H.: Supporting nested locking in multiprocessor real-time systems. In: 24th Euromicro Conference on Real-Time Systems, pp. 223–232. IEEE (2012)
13. Ward, B.C., Anderson, J.H.: Multi-resource real-time reader/writer locks for multiprocessors. In: IEEE 28th International Parallel and Distributed Processing Symposium, pp. 177–186. IEEE (2014)

Predicting Worst-Case Execution Time Trends in Long-Lived Real-Time Systems

Xiaotian Dai and Alan Burns[✉]

Department of Computer Science, University of York, York, UK
{xd656,alan.burns}@york.ac.uk

Abstract. In some long-lived real-time systems, it is not uncommon to see that the execution times of some tasks may exhibit trends. For hard and firm real-time systems, it is important to ensure these trends will not jeopardize the system. In this paper, we first introduce the notion of dynamic worst-case execution time (dWCET), which forms a new perspective that could help a system to predict potential timing failures and optimize resource allocations. We then have a comprehensive review of trend prediction methods. In the evaluation, we make a comparative study of dWCET trend prediction. Four prediction methods, combined with three data selection processes, are applied in an evaluation framework. The result shows the importance of applying data preprocessing and suggests that non-parametric estimators perform better than parametric methods.

Keywords: Worst-case execution time · Trend prediction · Linear regression · Extreme value theory · Support vector regression

1 Introduction

Worst-case execution times (WCETs) are widely used in verifying the schedulability of a real-time system [18]. For current practice, it is often assumed that the WCET is a fixed value during the whole system life. However, we want to point out that for some long-lived systems, the WCET is not constant but may be gradually increasing with system duration. One reason is that many real-world applications are highly data-dependent, while the size of input data naturally grows up with time. Another cause of increased worst-case execution times is gradually degrading hardware, e.g., decreased maximum operation frequency of a power-aware system due to degraded thermal performance. The influence of these effects could be minimal in a short period, but if being examined in a large time-scale, e.g., days, months or years, the impact on task execution times would be observable. In this work, we extend the constant WCET perspective and assume some WCETs are varying with time, which are denoted as dynamic WCETs (dWCET).

Traditional real-time applications that are deployed in a predictable environment should have a small variation of dWCET, assuming the system is designed

© Springer International Publishing AG 2017
J. Blieberger and M. Bader (Eds.): Ada-Europe 2017, LNCS 10300, pp. 87–101, 2017.
DOI: 10.1007/978-3-319-60588-3_6

well against increased amount of data and has regular maintenance of its hardware. As new systems and architectures are emerging that have larger uncertainties and more interactions with the environment, these applications have more significant dWCET variations which we are concerned with in this work. Some of these systems include autonomous vehicles, space systems, cloud services, self-adaptive systems, machines that learn from their environment, etc.

Systems are often designed with a limited tolerance of worst-case execution times. To design a long-lived and reliable system, it is important to observe the variation of dWCET and predict if the WCET assumption will be violated. More specifically, if one WCET has a trend that would potentially cause a timing fault in the future, it should be addressed earlier to make the system achieve a graceful degradation. Exploring execution time trends could also benefit task scheduling. A scheduler should not be 'short-sighted'. If a scheduler can predict future execution behaviors, it would be possible for it to allocate resources more optimally, and to reduce the number of unnecessary reallocation/redistribution actions. It is interesting to see how adaptive control, as well as dynamic scheduling methods, e.g., feedback scheduling [7,15], could be applied in an integrated framework.

Overall, the objectives of identifying trends are: **(1)** To understand the characteristics and influential variables of worst-case execution times; **(2)** To make future predictions of execution time based on the identified trend model; **(3)** To use the information of dWCET for enhanced feedback scheduling; **(4)** To make the system aware of potential timing failures earlier to take corresponding reactions, e.g., adjusting scheduler parameters, terminating less critical tasks or invoking a system reconfiguration.

The focus of this paper is on the first two objectives, which the authors think are fundamental to understanding dWCET. The content is organized as follows: a general review of trend identification methods is introduced in Sect. 2. Notations and symbols used in this article then follow. In Sect. 4, a comparative experiment that compares four representative trend identification methods is made. Finally, we analyze our experiment result and make recommendations and draw conclusions.

2   Potential Approaches

The question of the presence of a trend in a time-series has been extensively studied in business, economic and environmental studies [16]. For these applications, the variable of interest is measured or calculated at an approximately constant rate, and the resultant time sequence data can be analyzed by statistical methods to test the existence of a trend. Many descriptive and model-based approaches have been used to detect trends, which range from correlation analysis, time-series modelling, regression analysis and non-parametric statistical methods [4].

An important non-parametric statistical test is Kendall's tau, which is widely used as a test of trend existence [20]. In the work of Sen in 1968 [11], a slope estimator based on Kendall's tau, known as Theil-Sen estimator is designed, which is a non-parametric estimator that takes the median of all possible slopes of pairwise observations. This estimator is claimed to be statistically robust and unbiased [1]. The use of Kendall's test and Theil-Sen estimator in extreme precipitation can be found in [6]. Another statistical test for trend detection is Spearman's Partial Rank Correlation (SPRC) [8]. It is similar to Kendall's tau as it measures the relationship between two variables but differs in the interpretation of the correlation result. In our work, we use Theil-Sen estimator as one of the methods for its simplicity and effectiveness.

In Visser and Molenaar's work [17], a structural time-series model is proposed which has a stochastic/deterministic trend and regression coefficients. The stochastic trend is described as an Autoregressive Integrated Moving Average (ARIMA) process, and the overall trend-regression model is estimated by a Kalman Filter (KF). However, it is a challenge for KF to make a long-term prediction in the presence of uncertainty.

One method that can address long-term trends is regression analysis, which is a class of model-based statistical approaches for estimating the relationship between dependent and independent variables. Linear models with a trend and a seasonal component are often applied in prediction and forecasting of time series data, where the parameters are often estimated with an ordinary least square (OLS) estimator. However, for the OLS estimator, residuals of the time series are required to follow a normal distribution [11], which is not always valid. Reinsel and Tiao [10] use linear regression models to estimate trends with a correlated noise that is modelled by an autoregressive process. In their model, additional explanatory variables are used in the analysis to improve the prediction precision. Linear regression is applied by Tiao in the detection of trends in stratospheric ozone data using time series models with autoregressive noise [16]. We will use OLS estimator as the second method in our comparison.

Predicting trends are also of great interest in modelling and explaining the variation in rare and extreme events. Detecting long-term trends in the frequency of extreme events is studied in [3]. In this study, Frei and Schär modelled the counts of extreme events based on a binomial distribution and used logistic regression to estimate trends. Several methods of detecting the change of intensity in the extreme values are reviewed in [13]. A common way to model extreme events is to use generalized extreme value (GEV) distributions [6,20], which was first introduced by Fisher and Tippett in their study in 1928 [2]. The extreme value distribution is generally applied on block maxima, e.g., annual or monthly maximums in a time series.

One drawback of using block maxima is that only one data point in each block is used in the analysis. Alternative data preprocessing approaches include Peak-over-threshold (POT) and r-largest methods, which use relatively more data points to train a model or fit a distribution. The POT is used in [12] to study extreme precipitation in Ethiopia. In their study, the location parameter of the EV distribution is represented by a monthly constant and a yearly trend. A similar model is also applied in [13], in which the parameters of the extreme distribution are estimated by the maximum likelihood that is considered separately for each month. We will study GEV and explore both block maxima and r-largest as methods of data selection.

Machine learning is also an active research field for trend detection. Neural Networks has been widely used for time series modelling and forecasting [5,9,19]. However, few practical guidelines exist for building a time series Neural Network model, in terms of the number of input nodes and hidden layers, etc. Support vector regression (SVR) is another data-driven machine learning method. It belongs to the non-parametric regression class and is firmly grounded in the background of statistical learning theory. It is extremely flexible because few assumptions are imposed upon the mean function of the distribution, and it is capable of revealing non-linear relationships between variables. However, non-parametric techniques are relatively more computationally intensive. A description of SVR and its mathematical details are given in [14]. SVR is a rapidly developing field of research in Machine Learning, and it has potentials as a method of trend prediction. Hence we will use it as the fourth method.

3   Problem Formulation: Predicting WCET Trend

As noted, trend prediction is a well-studied area in other application domains, e.g., stock market prediction, sales estimation, etc. However, to the authors' best knowledge, there are few studies on trend analysis of worst-case execution times in the context of real-time scheduling. It is hard to say whether the results obtained from other domains can also be applied to worst-case execution times due to the unique characteristics that WCET exhibits, which include:

1. **It is not directly measurable.** Unlike physical and financial indices which can be measured from sensors or statistics, measuring the maximum execution time in a short period can only produce a high-water mark. This mark could be smaller than the actual WCET if the worst-case execution scenario (including the worst-case execution path, worst-case input data, and the worst-case cache/memory condition) is not encountered during the window.
2. **The factors that contribute to a WCET trend are less realized, studied and understood.** This work claims a new perspective of WCET, which breaks the conventional assumption that WCET is static. The increment in the size of input data, more frequently extreme events and degrading hardware performance could all change the temporal behaviour of a program. However, the influence of these factors and what impacts they have on WCETs remain largely unknown.
3. **Complexity of estimating WCET.** It is realized by the computing community that the interactions in a computer system would increase exponentially as the number of entities increases. As real-time systems are generally becoming more complicated in both software and hardware, the difficulty of static or measurement-based WCET estimation will increase significantly.

By doing this initial study, we hope to get some insights into dynamic WCET. Specifically, the purpose of this work is to see if one can apply existing trend prediction techniques in the context of predicting WCET and if there are any techniques that perform better than the others. Two data selection methods (block maxima and r-largest) are also considered to see if the performance could be improved compared with using raw data. We also introduce notions of predicted failure point, reaction time of control and reaction deadline to help improve the decision-making process of when to take corrective action against a potential timing failure. The rest of this paper will explain the experiment and the result obtained.

3.1 The Dataset

In this experiment, we use controlled synthetic data that is injected with different magnitude of trends. The model we used for generating the baseline data is abstracted from an application which has four major execution paths according to its operating states. We assume a deterministic trend, if it exists, is only in the worst-case execution path. It is notable that the trend may also exist in less critical paths, but as the execution time of the path increases, that path will eventually overwhelm and become the worst-case path. It should also be pointed out that there are different types of a trend: (i) Linear deterministic trend (LDT), (ii) Linear stochastic trend (LST), (iii) Non-linear deterministic trend (NDT), and (iv) Non-linear stochastic trend (NST). For this work, we focus on type (i) LDT, because other types can be decomposed and approximated by a set of linear trends.

To generate execution time observations, we applied a Markov model with an estimated state-transition matrix to simulate the correlation between consecutive samples. To introduce variations in the data, we added corrupting white noise to represent the non-determinisms of run-time execution, i.e., cache misses, branch predictions and waiting for hardware resources. It is notable that the objective here is not for precise modelling of execution time, but is to explore the patterns behind execution times that are varying as the system runs. Hence we didn't include every factor that would affect WCET in the generation process. Overall, we have 50 datasets which are divided into five groups for our evaluation.

3.2 Compared Methods

In our comparative study, we include four representative trend prediction methods that are mentioned in Sect. 2, which can be further categorized into parametric and non-parametric statistics:

– *Ordinary Linear Regression* [OLR] (parametric)
– *Kendall's tau* and *Theil-Sen Estimator* [TSE] (non-parametric)
– *Support Vector Regression* [SVR] (non-parametric)
– *Extreme Value Distribution* [EVD] (parametric)

Note the difference between parametric and non-parametric methods is whether a distribution is explicitly or implicitly assumed in the process of modelling. As the type of dataset we focused on is less studied in the literature, our experiment is implemented more in an exploratory way. We conducted a comparative study between the listed methods, as well as different data preprocessing approaches for selecting the training data.

The objective of a prediction is to estimate the influence of a trend in the future, i.e., predicting a potential failure point where the execution time will eventually exceed a safe upper bound due to the existence of a trend. In order to evaluate the prediction precision, we define the *Hypothetical Failure Point* (HFP) as the theoretically time point after which the system will fail the system's temporal requirements. We also define *Estimated Failure Point* (EFP) as the estimated HFP that is predicted by trend prediction algorithms. Due to page limitations, we can not give details of each individual method. For more information, please refer to the references provided in Sect. 2.

4   Evaluation

To make comparisons, we implemented the aforementioned trend identification algorithms in MATLAB©R2015a. Two categories of dataset were generated, and each dataset consists of multiple samples that are generated by the models described earlier. In the following sections, we will first introduce symbols that we used in this experiment, followed by experiment setup and evaluation metrics.

Note a single experiment, with one algorithm and one dataset, will give rise to a large number of predictions – as the system moves from start-up to the failure point (end of the dataset). Some of these predictions may be good, others not. Hence the set of predictions need to be analyzed together to give an overall estimate of the quality of the algorithm in that experiment. We assume that the controlled system can take corrective action if the failure point, H, is identified within a relative deadline, D. But taking action too early is not useful so there is a maximum reaction-time R defined.

4.1   Symbols and Notations

A diagram that shows the important terms and notations is given in Fig. 1. The symbols and notations we used in this experiment are listed below:

- t: the current (discrete) time; we assume t is equally spaced in time and there are no observations between two successive time points t_{n-1} and t_n.
- C_{ub}: the upper bound of task execution time. During run-time if the worst-case execution time C_m exceeds this bound, i.e., $C_m > C_{ub}$, a system failure will occur.
- k: the actual deterministic trend that is ejected while generating a dataset. We use $\hat{k}(t)$ to represent the trend magnitude that is estimated at time t.
- H: H is the *Hypothetical Failure Point* (HFP), which is defined as the expected time of failure. If $k > 0$, H can be directly estimated by $H = (C_{ub} - C_{m_0})/k$, where C_{m_0} is the initial WCET. For datasets that have $k = 0$ (i.e. no trend), we make $H = \infty$.

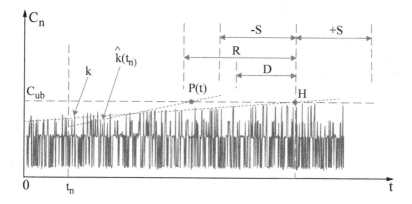

Fig. 1. Representation of important notations and regions

- R: the reaction time, which is defined as the earliest time that a system should make actions before a failure happens. If a control action is made earlier than $(H - R)$, we have a false positive.
- D: D is the deadline before which any control action should have been made. If any action is made in the interval $(H - R, H - D]$, we say that this estimator behaves correctly and mark the action as a true positive. Otherwise, we have a false negative if no action is made.
- $P(t)$: is a prediction of H made at time t; We have $P(t) \to \infty$ if no trend or a negative trend is found. In practice we make $P(t) = t + B$, if $P(t) \geq t + B$, where B is a boundary. This boundary indicates that the failure is too far away to be concerned now.
- S: the satisfactory region deviated from H that is used to evaluate the goodness of $P(t)$. If $H - S \leq P(t) \leq H + S$, we say the estimation is satisfactory.

During run-time, the system will continuously estimate a failure point and will only make a control action if the estimated failure point will be reached soon. Specifically, an action is taken if $P(t) < t + R$, or more accurately if the prediction is run every T time, then an action is made based on the criterion $P(t) < t + R - T$. The use of confidence intervals is not involved in this work, and each action is made independently. To evaluate the effectiveness of each algorithm, we associate positives and negatives with whether an action is taken when it should be. We have a logic table shown in Table 1.

Table 1. Definition of positives and negatives

$t \in$	$[0, H - R)$	$[H - R, H - D)$	$[H - D, H)$
Action made	False positive	True positive	True positive
No action	True negative	False negative	False negative

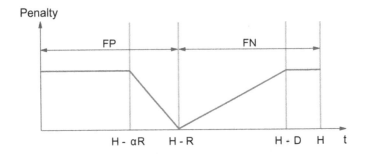

Fig. 2. Penalties that are given to false positives/negatives

In reality, we found the numbers of false positives/negatives cannot provide enough information of the goodness of an algorithm, e.g., a false control action made close to the reaction region is at least better than the one made far earlier. Hence we introduce a penalty function (shown in Fig. 2). The penalty of false positives is decreased when the time is approaching the response region $(H - R)$, and the penalty of false negatives is increasing from $(H - R)$ to the deadline $(H - D)$. The coefficient α defines the tolerance of early actions. When $t > H - D$, any false negative will score a higher penalty, as the deadline is already missed in this case.

4.2   Experiment Setup

In general, we have two groups of synthetic time-series data: **(A)** trend-free; **(B)** with a trend. We use the same initial worst-case execution time in both groups, and in group B we have five distinct magnitudes of trends that are gradually increasing from 1% to 4%. For each value of trend we independently generated 10 datasets, so overall we have 50 datasets. Each dataset is generated until the point where a failure would happen, which is directly calculated from the actual trend. The size of the trend-free dataset is made the same as data with 1% trend. A full list of the datasets is shown in Table 2.

Table 2. A table of generated datasets

Group	Subgroup	Dataset index	Data size	Increasing trend
A	A1	1–10	5,000	0%
B	B1	11–20	5,000	1%
	B2	21–30	2,500	2%
	B3	31–40	1,667	3%
	B4	41–50	1,250	4%

For each dataset in the table, we take the following evaluation steps:

1. Define a sampling window W, and start to make the first estimation at time $t = W$.
2. Apply data selection process for samplings from $(t-W)$ to t. Fit pre-processed time series data with each trend analysis method to generate trend models.
3. Use the models to estimate the system failure point $P(t)$. Make a (dummy) control action if $P(t)$ satisfies $P(t) - t \leq R$.
4. Make an evaluation of each estimation, including prediction error, valid/invalid of the estimation and the property of the action if is made. A cumulative penalty is added if a false positive/negative is presented.
5. Move to $t = t + M$ and repeat from step 2 until all data points are processed, where M is the step size. M controls the fraction of new data that is not overlapped in the training set. For example, if $M = 0.2W$, at each step 20% new data will be added into the analysis.

To evaluate the quality of an estimation, we can use the knowledge of the actual failure time H. We define the failure estimation error at time t as: $e_h(t) = H - P(t)$. If $|e_h(t)| \leq S$, the estimation is satisfactory (valid). Otherwise, we recognize it as invalid. A smaller prediction error represents a better estimation, and an ideal predictor would have $e_h = 0$. In practice, we want to have a predictor that would give a positive error (earlier) rather than a negative error (later), as in the former case, it gives more time for the system to process and make a reaction.

In addition to failure estimation error, we also have trend estimation error, which is calculated as: $e_k(t) = k - \hat{k}(t)$. Note that e_k and e_h are correlated, but e_k is more intuitive in evaluation of the precision of estimated slopes. To study the absolute performance of each algorithm, we introduce a baseline algorithm: the *Ideal Predictor* (IDP), which has the foresight to know the HFP and associated time regions. For IDP, we have $\forall t : e_k(t) = 0$ and $\forall t : e_h(t) = 0$.

4.3   Results

Following the experiment steps that we defined earlier, we evaluated all combinations of trend identification and preprocessing methods. To have a understanding of advantages and disadvantages of different methods, we have overall three evaluations that focus on different aspects of the results obtained from the previous experiment.

Impact of Data Preprocessing. Data preprocessing is an important procedure in processing time-series data. In this evaluation, we compared the raw data (*-raw*) with two data preprocessing methods: block maxima (*-max*) and r-largest (*-r*) value, which are both schemes used in extreme value analysis. For each method i, preprocessing method j and dataset κ, we obtained the mean of estimated trend error $\bar{e}_k^{i,j,\kappa}$ of all evaluations over that dataset:

$$\bar{e}_k^{i,j,\kappa} = \frac{1}{N_\kappa} \sum_{n=1}^{N_\kappa} e_k^{i,j,\kappa}(W + n * M)$$

$$= \frac{1}{N_\kappa} \sum_{n=1}^{N_\kappa} (k - \hat{k}^{i,j,\kappa}(W + n * M)) \tag{1}$$

where W is the sampling window, M is the step size and N_κ is the number of evaluations made over dataset κ. In our case, datasets with different magnitude of trends have different sizes. Hence N_κ of each subgroup is distinct, which can be calculated from:

$$N_\kappa = floor((\text{size\_of}(\kappa) - W)/M) + 1. \tag{2}$$

We group $\bar{e}_k^{i,j,\kappa}$ by $\{i, j\}$, and plot them out as box plots in Fig. 3. We have overall 12 box blots (4 identification $\times$ 3 preprocessing methods), and each box plot consists of 50 data points that comes from all datasets. From Fig. 3, we could clearly see that results using *raw* data have the worst performance, i.e., *olr-raw, tse-raw, svr-raw* and *evd-raw*. Compared with the other two methods *max* and *r*, methods using *raw* have a significant larger median and variance of mean errors. This is reasonable because if raw data is used in the training set, the extreme values that have trends in them will be overwhelmed by the data points with no trend. Actually as what we observed during the experiment, $\hat{k}$ is approximately 0 for all raw-based methods, i.e., no trend is identified.

If we further compare block-maxima and r-largest, we can see that even considering outliers, block-maxima still performs much better than r-largest across all four methods. To measure the improvement, we make pairwise comparisons for each identification method with block-maxima and r-largest. Specifically, we compare minimum, median, mean, maximum and standard deviation across all -*max* and -*r* methods. The result is shown in Table 3 (all numbers in the table are multiplied by 1×10^3).

From the table, we can see the minimal errors are roughly the same, except *svr-max* which has slightly larger error. If we look at *olr-max* and *olr-r*, we can

Table 3. Mean error of $\hat{k}$ for block maxima and r-largest

	Minimum	Median	Mean	Maximum	σ
olr-max	−1.91	4.16	6.31	27.64	7.21
olr-r	−2.07	7.68	10.59	32.10	9.31
tse-max	−1.12	2.23	3.07	17.45	3.27
tse-r	−1.15	9.14	9.91	26.00	7.72
svr-max	−5.24	0.15	1.60	25.65	5.71
svr-r	−1.00	9.65	12.72	44.36	12.74
evd-max	−1.46	1.60	3.40	23.47	4.75
evd-r	−0.45	5.34	6.86	30.20	6.77

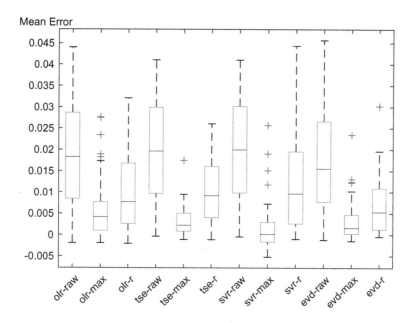

Fig. 3. Distribution of mean trend errors $\hat{k}$ of considered prediction methods

see that *olr-r* has 85% larger median, 69% larger mean and 16% larger maximal error. For *tse-max* and *tse-r*, these values are 310%, 223% and 49%. *svr-max* outperformed *svr-r* with 69.5% improvement in mean and 1.87×10^{-2} less in maxima. Considering the original trend is in a magnitude of 1×10^{-2} (from 1% to 4%), this is a significant improvement. Finally for *evd-max* and *evd-r*, a similar conclusion is obtained: *evd-max* is about 100% better than *evd-r* in terms of mean error, and 6.73×10^{-3} less in maxima.

As a conclusion, compared with using raw data, data preprocessing can significantly improve identification performance. It can be seen that, for our particular dataset and block size, block maxima performs the best.

Impact of Variations in Dataset. As part of our evaluation, we studied the impact that the magnitude of trend would have on the performance of our methods. In our datasets, we have five subgroups, each of which has a distinct trend ranging from 0% to 4%. We plot the mean trend errors of each method as an individual line across all datasets in Fig. 4. The x axis represents the index of the dataset, and the y axis is the mean trend estimation error for all predictions in that dataset. From the figure we can see that mean errors tend to be increased when the magnitude of trend is increased. This can be clearly seen from the peaks of mean errors in each subgroup. We can also see that in each subgroup of dataset, there exists a large variation between individual datasets. This suggests that the estimation error is highly correlated to the magnitude and characteristics of the trend.

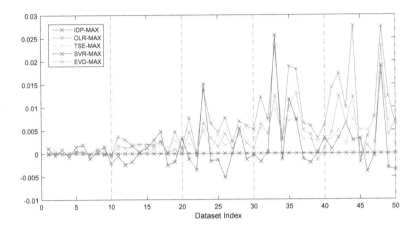

Fig. 4. Estimated trend error of each dataset. All methods use block maxima for data preprocessing. Subgroups are separated by dashed lines.

As a conclusion, estimation error is data sensitive. With the magnitude of trend increases, the error will be increased proportionally. All of these methods are sensitive to the actual characteristic of a dataset. From Fig. 4, we can see different methods have very similar patterns in terms of peaks and troughs. This indicates that although these methods are sensitive to datasets, but as the way they vary is similar and the same dataset is used across all methods, the characteristics of the dataset will not break the fairness of this comparison. However, a large number of datasets should be used to average the variations across datasets so the actual performance can be revealed.

Comparison of Identification Methods. In this evaluation, we will compare trend identification methods with only block maxima, as it performed the best among all data preprocessing methods. To compare the effectiveness of a trend identification method, one important index is the ability to detect a trend. In our work, this is measured by two factors: the validation of an estimation, and the positiveness of a related control action. A diagram that shows the relative performance is shown in Fig. 5. Each bar plot shows a different metric of all four methods, plus the Ideal Predictor (IDP), separated by dataset subgroups. For plots of valid and true positives, data is normalized to [0, 1] by IDP, while for plots of invalid and false positive/negative, data is normalized by the worst method.

From the valid/invalid plots in the figure, we can see that *tse-max* and *svr-max* are the two best methods. OLR has the largest number of invalids for dataset groups B1, B2, B3 and B4. EVD only performs slightly better than OLR. If we further look at the numbers of falses, we could see that SVR tends to give more false positives, while OLR gives more false negatives. All methods give no false positives and negatives when there is no trend in the data. TSE is consistent and has the best performance on average.

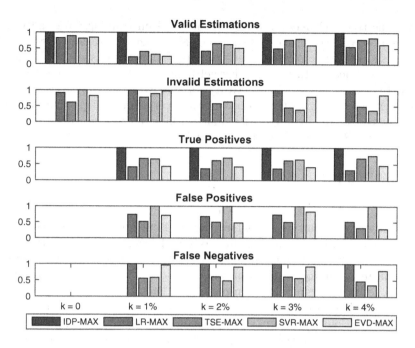

Fig. 5. Experiment result - normalized false negatives/positives

To further compare these methods, we summarize penalties that come from the results of all datasets for each method, which is shown in Table 4. From the table it can be seen that TSE has least mean penalties with all three data selection methods, comparing with the other three methods. This is identical to the conclusion we described earlier. For methods using block maxima, OLR obtained the largest penalty, while for r-largest, it is SVR.

Table 4. Mean penalties over all datasets for each prediction method

	OLR	TSE	SVR	EVD
Raw	62	62	62	62
Maxima	58.28	29.02	42.26	49.68
r-largest	58.2	53.82	77.58	55.76

There are other considerations of a trend prediction method which include its efficiency, sensitivity to data variation, and support of multiple dependent variables. In all four methods, TSE is the most computationally efficient method, and it is least sensitive to the characteristic of a dataset. OLR is median in computation, but it is sensitive to the composition of the dataset, and it will be biased if a large percentage of non-relevant data is involved. SVR is computational intensive has additional parameters that can be tuned: the cost C that controls the trade-off between errors of the SVM on training data and margin maximization, and the epsilon ϵ that controls the size of insensitive region. The ability of supporting non-linear trends is supported by SVR as well. SVR directly supports non-linear data by using Kernel functions, while other methods have to be extended to support non-linearity. In this work, we only considered one inference variable: the system duration. However if more dependent variables need to be considered, a support for multi-variable regression will be necessary, which both OLR and SVR can support while the other two cannot.

5   Conclusions

In this work, we have introduced the motivation of identifying long-term trends in worst-case execution times to achieve timing fault prediction. We have shown four different trend identification methods and compared their performance. The results suggest that data preprocessing should be used as the procedure can significantly improve estimation performance. It also can be seen that the Theil-Sen estimator, which is a non-parametric method, achieved the best performance in this particular experiment. It is robust against noise and outliers, and is computational effective. The other non-parametric method, SVR, is also an outstanding method as it can predict non-linear trends and can be used in multi-variable regression. Extreme value did not perform well because it needs a large amount of data to fit the distribution, i.e., a large data block. However, this will decrease the ability of early detection of failures. Finally for OLR, the performance is not satisfactory as the assumption of normally distributed residuals is violated. This can be improved by assuming a more accurate distribution of data, which requires to further examine the characteristics of WCET. The experiment result suggests a preference for using non-parametric methods with either block-maxima or r-largest.

For future work, we will consider more dependent variables that influence a WCET to improve the precision of prediction. The use of ensemble learning to combine two or three identification methods could also benefit the result of analysis, and multiple successive predictions should be considered to confidently make a control decision. We also aim to obtain real-life data from industrial applications, to examine if a similar result would be obtained. All these issues will form topics for future work.

References

1. Akritas, M.G., Murphy, S.A., LaValley, M.P.: The Theil-sen estimator with doubly censored data and applications to astronomy. J. Am. Stat. Assoc. **90**(429), 170–177 (1995)
2. Fisher, R.A., Tippett, L.H.C.: Limiting forms of the frequency distribution of the largest or smallest member of a sample. In: Mathematical Proceedings of the Cambridge Philosophical Society, vol. 24, pp. 180–190. Cambridge Univerisity Press (1928)

3. Frei, C., Schär, C.: Detection probability of trends in rare events: theory and application to heavy precipitation in the Alpine region. J. Climate **14**(7), 1568–1584 (2001)
4. Hess, A., Iyer, H., Malm, W.: Linear trend analysis: a comparison of methods. Atmos. Environ. **35**(30), 5211–5222 (2001)
5. Hill, T., O'Connor, M., Remus, W.: Neural network models for time series forecasts. Manage. Sci. **42**(7), 1082–1092 (1996)
6. Kunkel, K.E., Andsager, K., Easterling, D.R.: Long-term trends in extreme precipitation events over the conterminous United States and Canada. J. Climate **12**(8), 2515–2527 (1999)
7. Lu, C., Stankovic, J.A., Son, S.H., Tao, G.: Feedback control real-time scheduling: framework, modeling, and algorithms. Real Time Syst. **23**(1–2), 85–126 (2002)
8. McLeod, A.I., Hipel, K.W., Bodo, B.A.: Trend analysis methodology for water quality time series. Environmetrics **2**(2), 169–200 (1991)
9. Qi, M., Zhang, G.P.: Trend time-series modeling and forecasting with neural networks. IEEE Trans. Neural Netw. **19**(5), 808–816 (2008)
10. Reinsel, G.C., Tiao, G.C.: Impact of chlorofluoromethanes on stratospheric ozone: a statistical analysis of ozone data for trends. J. Am. Statist. Assoc. **82**(397), 20–30 (1987)
11. Sen, P.K.: Estimates of the regression coefficient based on Kendall's tau. J. Am. Statist. Assoc. **63**(324), 1379–1389 (1968)
12. Shang, H., Yan, J., Gebremichael, M., Ayalew, S.M.: Trend analysis of extreme precipitation in the Northwestern Highlands of Ethiopia with a case study of Debre Markos. Hydrol. Earth Syst. Sci. **15**(6), 1937–1944 (2011)
13. Smith, R.L.: Extreme value analysis of environmental time series: an application to trend detection in ground-level ozone. Statist. Sci. **4**(4), 367–377 (1989)
14. Smola, A.J., Schölkopf, B.: A tutorial on support vector regression. Statist. Comput. **14**(3), 199–222 (2004)
15. Stankovic, J.A., Lu, C., Son, S.H., Tao, G.: The case for feedback control real-time scheduling. In: Proceedings of the 11th Euromicro Conference on Real-Time Systems, pp. 11–20. IEEE (1999)
16. Tiao, G.: Use of statistical methods in the analysis of environmental data. Am. Statist. **37**(4b), 459–470 (1983)
17. Visser, H., Molenaar, J.: Trend estimation and regression analysis in climatological time series: an application of structural time series models and the Kalman filter. J. Climate **8**(5), 969–979 (1995)
18. Wilhelm, R., Engblom, J., Ermedahl, A., et al.: The worst-case execution-time problem overview of methods and survey of tools. ACM Trans. Embedded Comput. Syst. (TECS) **7**(3), 36 (2008)
19. Zhang, G.P., Qi, M.: Neural network forecasting for seasonal and trend time series. Eur. J. Oper. Res. **160**(2), 501–514 (2005)
20. Zhang, X., Harvey, K.D., Hogg, W., Yuzyk, T.R.: Trends in Canadian streamflow. Water Res. Res. **37**(4), 987–998 (2001)

MC2: Multicore and Cache Analysis via Deterministic and Probabilistic Jitter Bounding

Enrique Díaz[1,2], Mikel Fernández[1], Leonidas Kosmidis[1], Enrico Mezzetti[1], Carles Hernandez[1], Jaume Abella[1], and Francisco J. Cazorla[1,3(✉)]

[1] Barcelona Supercomputing Center (BSC), Barcelona, Spain
{enrique.diaz,mikel.fernandez,leonidas.kosmidis,enrico.mezzetti,
carles.hernandez,jaume.abella,francisco.cazorla}@bsc.es
[2] Universitat Politècnica de Catalunya, Barcelona, Spain
[3] IIIA-CSIC, Bellaterra, Spain

Abstract. In critical domains, reliable software execution is increasingly involving aspects related to the timing dimension. This is due to the advent of high-performance (complex) hardware, used to provide the rising levels of guaranteed performance needed in those domains. Caches and multicores are two of the hardware features that have the potential to significantly reduce WCET estimates, yet they pose new challenges on current-practice measurement-based timing analysis (MBTA) approaches. In this paper we propose *MC2*, a technique for multilevel-cache multicores that combines deterministic and probabilistic jitter-bounding approaches to reliably handle both the variability in execution time generated by caches and the contention in accessing shared hardware resources. We evaluate *MC2* on a COTS quad-core LEON-based board and our initial results show how it effectively captures cache and multicore contention in pWCET estimates with respect to actual observed values.

Keywords: WCET · MBTA · Multicore contention · Probabilistic timing analysis · Jitter bounding

1 Introduction

Computing power needs are steadily increasing in the critical real-time embedded domains, fuelled by the complexity and sheer amount of data a modern on-board software is expected to handle [3,7,33]. At hardware level, while high-performance features, such as caches and multicore processors, provide the demanded performance, they also bring about hard-to-model *jitter* (variability) in execution time, which complicates timing validation and verification. This has resulted in an increased attention on timing in safety standards (e.g., ISO26262 [15] in automotive) and support documents (e.g., CAST32-A [8] in aerospace).

MBTA is the dominant timing analysis approach in most real-time domains [34]. MBTA aims at deriving a worst-case execution time (WCET)

© Springer International Publishing AG 2017
J. Blieberger and M. Bader (Eds.): Ada-Europe 2017, LNCS 10300, pp. 102–118, 2017.
DOI: 10.1007/978-3-319-60588-3_7

estimate that holds for the program during *system operation* from the execution time measurements captured during the tests executed at various stages in the *analysis phase*. The quality of the derived WCET estimates lies on the user's ability to design stressful test scenarios (conditions) that are presumably close to the worst-case conditions that can arise during system operation. The degree of control available to the user, while adequate on simple processor designs, diminishes with the inclusion of complex hardware that challenges: (i) designing worst-case scenarios, e.g., identifying the memory object allocation (code and data) that results in cache set mappings with high impact on execution time, and the worst contention scenarios that the application can suffer in a multicore; and (ii) designing experiments in which bad (pathological) behavior for several resources occurs simultaneously. Overall, despite the user may perform thousands of experiments, there is no guarantee on whether the bad behavior in the sources of jitter (*soj*), like the cache, has been sufficiently captured. This reduces the confidence on the MBTA WCET estimates, which in turn can prevent the use of some high-performance hardware features in critical real-time embedded systems.

Measurement-Based Probabilistic Timing Analysis (MBPTA) [5,32] is a variant of MBTA that aims at increasing the confidence on WCET estimates. MBPTA, which has been successfully evaluated on several case studies (e.g., [31,32]), aims at relieving the user from controlling hardware *soj*. Instead, MBPTA makes that their impact on the measurements emerges naturally, reducing user's burden to only controlling the number of runs to perform [17]. To that end, MBPTA implicitly controls the impact of jittery resources on measurements captured at analysis. In particular, some resources are forced to work on their worst latency during analysis (upperbounding), hence ensuring measurements conservatively capture their impact. The latency of other resources is instead randomized so that their execution times at analysis vary according to a probabilistic execution time distribution that can be used to upperbound the latencies during operation.

In this paper we propose the *MC2* (multicore and cache) MBPTA approach for the analysis of a Commercial-Off-The-Shelf (COTS) multicore processor equipped with multilevel-caches. While hardware designs have been proposed [14,19] for MBPTA compliance, and some of them have hit pre-silicon (RTL) readiness level [14], analyzing MBPTA applicability on COTS multicore processors is fundamental to favor a fast and widespread adoption of MBPTA. MC2 exposes, in a combined MBPTA-compliant manner, the jitter of caches and multicore contention to the execution time measurements taken at analysis. As a result, the WCET estimates MBPTA generates from those measurements upperbound the impact of both resources on program execution time. MC2 combines two techniques that have been classified as MBPTA compliant: software randomization [20] for cache-jitter management, and delay upperbounding for multicore contention management [16]. For the latter, since multicore contention can lead to very pessimistic WCET estimates [13] when contention bounds are provisioned for the worst possible contention, MC2 provides adaptable WCET estimates that depend on contenders' contention. Our results provides evidence that MC2 effectively captures the impact on execution time - and hence on WCET estimates - of both resources, and provides tight WCET estimates.

2   Background

When selecting the timing analysis technique to use, industrial users balance the cost-effectiveness of the technique and the evidence that it can provide to satisfy the level of confidence required by the domain-specific standards [1]. MBTA techniques are less rigorous than static analysis methods but, in general, are more attractive because of their cost-effectiveness and major affinity with the consolidated industrial practice. The quality of MBTA's derived WCET estimates relates to the evidence on their coverage of the worst-case conditions. When evidence obtained is sufficient, MBTA can be used for high-integrity software, e.g., DAL-A functions in avionics [22]. In practice, all techniques require user-provided inputs, e.g., worst-case scenarios for measurements for MBTA and hardware timing models for static timing analysis (with hardware documentation potentially being inaccurate or incomplete [1], thus eventually resorting to measurements to reverse engineering the timing model [26]). This makes complex argue about the quality of a WCET figure. In this paper, we focus on MBTA with the intent to increase the confidence that can be placed on the provided WCET estimates.

MBPTA. MBPTA applies Extreme Value Theory [9] (EVT) on execution time observations from the analysis phase to derive the probabilistic WCET (pWCET) distribution that upperbounds program's execution time during operation. MBPTA requires guaranteeing that the observations obtained at analysis capture those events that can impact execution time at operation, and so pWCET estimates [1]. MBPTA, by deploying EVT (see Fig. 1), is able to derive the probability that bad behavior of several of the *soj* (whose impact has been

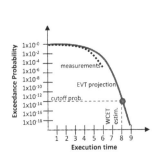

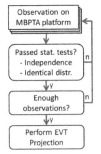

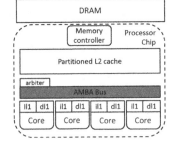

Fig. 1. pWCET example.   **Fig. 2.** MBPTA steps.   **Fig. 3.** Reference architecture.

captured in the analysis-time runs) are triggered in the same run. Hence, EVT has to be seen as a method to predict pathological combinations of observed events in the analysis-time measurements. In general, EVT cannot predict the appearance of unobserved events since their impact on execution time can be arbitrarily large. To cover this gap, MBPTA builds an argument on representativeness by means of (i) either injecting randomization in the timing behavior of certain hardware resources (e.g., caches and buses) so that it is possible to determine the probability of their worst behavior to be captured in the analysis-time measurement runs; or (ii) making resources to work on their worst latency so the analysis time measurements capture their worst timing behavior.

MBPTA application procedure starts by (1) collecting a set of representative observations, see Fig. 2. MBPTA then (2) applies some statistical test such as independence and identical distribution tests [5] required for EVT application. Since in a MBPTA-compliant platform these *probabilistic* properties hold by construction[1], in case *statistical* tests are failed, the user is simply asked for more runs until statistical tests – which are subject to false positives/negatives – are passed. (3) MBPTA checks whether the size of the sample is enough to include all relevant events and ensure certain statistical stability of the results. To that end we use the initial findings in [24] and ask the user for more runs until this condition is satisfied. As final step, (4) MBPTA derives an EVT distribution (pWCET estimate) as shown in Fig. 1.

Software Randomization. MBPTA handles resources with small jitter (usually in the order of few cycles) by means of upperbounding, i.e., by forcing the resource to operate on its worst latency during analysis time [14]. However, cache resources exhibit high jitter between hit and miss events, especially when these events span across multiple levels of cache. For this reason, timing randomization is used. In particular we use software randomization which, by randomly varying the memory layout between distinct program executions, causes cache events (hits/misses) to have a probabilistic behavior that holds during operation. This allows cache jitter to be properly modelled by MBPTA. In this work we use our custom implementation of TASA (Toolchain Agnostic Software rAndomization) [18,21], a static variant of software randomization, applied at source-code level. TASA randomizes the position in memory for any memory object in the software under analysis such as functions, stack frames and global data. Moreover, TASA can randomly affect the internal memory layout of several memory objects such as stack frames and structures.

In general, compilers allocate memory objects in the order they are in the source file. Very few compiler options violate this principle, which can be disabled during compilation with small (if any) impact in the compiler performance [18]. TASA, by randomly rearranging the order of declarations for the corresponding

---

[1] Despite time-randomization, programs might exhibit a degenerate distribution of timing, e.g., having a single or very few different execution times. While extremely rare in practice for real-size programs, the lack of jitter would suggest that the maximum observed execution time could be reasonably used as a precise WCET indicator.

objects in the source file, modifies their relative position in the binary. This, in combination with additional random-sized padding in the form of nop instructions or unused data, increases the potential difference among binary layouts. When the binary is loaded to main memory for the program execution, the random binary memory layout translates into random main memory mapping and hence, a random cache layout, i.e., memory objects are allocated in random cache sets.

3   Reference Platform

We use a 4-core LEON3 [2] platform implemented on an FPGA. Each LEON3 core implements a 7-stage pipeline and comprises first level instruction (ic) and data (dc) caches, with the dc implementing a write-through no write allocate policy, see Fig. 3. An AMBA AHB bus propagates stores, dc misses and ic misses to the partitioned L2 cache deploying a write-back policy. Requests sent to the bus are not split. Hence, the bus is locked all the time a request accesses the L2. If it misses in L2, the bus is locked until the request is solved in main memory and answered back. Requests are arbitrated in the bus using round-robin which provides time analyzability [12]. Hence, our reference architecture comprises two main hardware shared resources, the bus and the memory, with the bus arbiter controlling the contention in both of them. Our platform also comprises performance monitoring counters (PMCs) from which we track ic misses, dc misses, store operations and L2 misses, as detailed in Sect. 4.

In our experiments we consider one task under analysis (tua or τ_a) and several (up to three) contender tasks, referred to as $c(\tau_a)$ or τ_b, τ_c and τ_d. τ_a is always a time-critical task for which a WCET estimate is to be derived.

4   Handling Multicore Contention and Cache Jitter

Goals and Challenges. MC2 aims at reliably capturing the impact that multicore contention (handled by the bus arbiter in our reference architecture) and cache jitter have on pWCET estimates. This requires ensuring that the execution time observations collected at analysis capture the impact of the jitter of both. To ease MC2 adoption, this goal has to be achieved under the following restrictions:

1. MBPTA compliance. The proposed technique must be MBPTA-compliant requiring minimum changes to the single-core MBPTA timing analysis approach, which has already been evaluated with several industrial case studies [32].
2. pWCET estimates should be time composable, so that they are independent of the load contenders put on resources. Time composability enables incremental integration of applications, performing timing analysis of applications mostly in isolation, without the need of regression tests. Time composability also allows updating functionality during system operation without the need of analysing the entire task set, but just those tasks that are updated.

3. The information required by MC2 from the tasks should be obtained via PMCs to facilitate its applicability to real hardware.
4. WCET estimates should be obtained as early as possible in the design process to facilitate incremental software integration [23] (ideally during unit testing) and should hold across integrations for incremental verification purposes.

Overall Process. MC2 process starts by running the software-randomized task under analysis (τ_a) in isolation, see Fig. 4. This exposes the impact of cache jitter to the observed execution time (oet^i) in each run r^i. As a side effect, since the hit/miss pattern of τ_a changes across runs (due to software-randomization), its number of accesses to the bus and the memory also varies. Hence, τ_a has an access distribution to cache/memory rather than a single value (with small variations) as it would be the case if τ_a had not been time randomized.

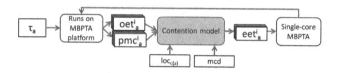

Fig. 4. Schematic view of the proposed pTC contention model.

MC2 also factors in the maximum contention delay (mcd) for each request type and the level of contention generated by τ_a's contenders ($c(\tau_a)$), which is refereed as $loc_{c(a)}$. Δ_{cont} in Eq. (1) captures both mcd and $loc_{c(a)}$. By feeding MBPTA with enlarged execution times (eet), MC2 provides MBPTA with representative information on the impact of cache and multicore contention.

$$eet^i = oet^i + \Delta_{cont} \tag{1}$$

Detailed Explanation. MC2 builds upon the following assumptions and inputs:

1. *τ_a's observed execution times (oet_a^i)* in each run r_a^i of τ_a's in isolation.
2. *τ_a's number of requests (pmc_a^i)* obtained with PMC readings in each run r_a^i of τ_a's in isolation. The particular counters are discussed later.
3. *Worst-case request overlap assumptions*: MC2 assumes that contenders' requests align in the worst possible manner with each τ_a request causing maximum impact on τ_a's execution time. While this assumption is pessimistic, it relieves the end user from modelling the particular cycle when requests occurs, which would be an overly expensive effort, and would only be doable after integration. Instead, assuming mcd delay for each contenders' request brings some pessimism but allows MC2 enable WCET estimates during unit testing to favor incremental integration [23]. This is in contrast to the number of requests that can be derived during unit testing and do not change (for our architecture) at integration, i.e., the number of requests of a task to the bus/memory is not affected by its contenders.

Table 1. Request types and their latency in our reference board.

Type	mcd	Description
sh	$l^{sh} = 1$	L2 st hit
lh	$l^{lh} = 8$	L2 ld hit in L2
lmc	$l^{lmc} = 28$	L2 ld clean miss
smc	$l^{smc} = 28$	L2 st clean miss
lmd	$l^{lmd} = 31$	L2 ld dirty miss
smd	$l^{smd} = 31$	L2 st dirty miss

Table 2. PMCs available in the reference processor.

Name	Description
pmc^{icm}	Bus reads caused by ic misses
pmc^{dcm}	Bus reads caused by dc misses
pmc^{st}	Writes to L2
pmc^{m}	Misses in the L2

4. *User-provided contender's level of contention* ($loc_{c(a)}$): MC2 factors in the contention (i.e., number of requests) of $c(\tau_a)$. To that end, we follow two models. The first one, called fully Time Composable (fTC), assumes each contender task makes as many requests of the longest duration as total number of requests generated by τ_a. The fTC models results in fully time-composable estimates, but at the cost of over-estimation. To reduce the latter, a second model, called partially Time Composable (pTC), is adjustable to the expected level of contention of the contenders (i.e., its number of requests and their type). The pTC model derives the WCET estimate for τ_a in isolation under a given level of contention of its contenders. At integration time, composability can be assessed by simply checking that the contention level of the particular contenders is smaller than the level assumed at analysis. Both models are detailed in Sects. 5 and 6 respectively.

Request Characteristics. MC2 requires information about the types of requests to the bus, with emphasis on those having different usage of the bus, and the maximum time each request holds the bus (mcd).

From processor manuals, we identify six types of request to the bus (see Table 1): load/store requests that hit/miss in L2, and for the case of misses, since the L2 is write-back, request evicting and not evicting dirty data. The former are called dirty misses and the latter clean misses.

The mcd for each request, see the second column of Table 1, is the time interval (measured in cycles) since a request is granted access to the bus until it relinquishes the bus. Hence, mcd is the maximum contention that a request of each type can incur on other requests. We have derived mcd values empirically following the process described in [16]. The general approach consists in generating small benchmarks that generate a single-type of requests (e.g., load hits in L2) and architect experiments so tight bounds to request latencies can be derived.

5 fTC Contention Model

fTC derives a WCET estimate that is an upper bound to the slowdown τ_a can suffer regardless of the load its contender tasks put on the shared resources. This requires the model to pessimistically assume that the number of contenders equals $Nc - 1$ where Nc is the number of cores – four in our platform. Further, the model assumes that for every τ_a request its contenders have one request of the worst type, i.e., causing the longest contention on it that in our architecture corresponds to lmd and smd (indistinctly referred to as xmd). Hence, fTC assumes that each request of τ_a is delayed 31 $cycles = l^{smd} = l^{lmd}$ by each contenders' request. Overall, fTC builds a set of enlarged execution time observations as shown in Eq. (2), where n_a^i is the total number of request that τ_a performs in run r^i.

$$eet_a^i = oet_a^i + \Delta_{cont}^{i,fTC} = oet_a^i + \left[n_a^i \times (Nc - 1) \times l^{xmd} \right] \tag{2}$$

6 pTC Model

The fTC model may result in noticeably pessimistic WCET estimates. The partially Time Composable (pTC) model presented in this section trades time composability to tighten WCET estimates. With pTC [12], the user can yet enjoy benefits of incremental integration with small effort to assess time composability. The pTC model, instead of assuming $Nc - 1$ contenders, takes the actual number of running τ_a contenders. Also, unlike fTC, pTC tracks the number of requests of each type. This offers a powerful solution to tighten WCET estimates with a reasonable low impact on time composability. pTC assumes that an upper bound to the number of contenders' request of each type can be derived.

The pTC model derives the impact that the number of requests for each contender task τ_b can cause on τ_a. Ideally, we would like to have a PMC for the number of requests of each type made by the task. We refer to that ideal counter as n^{xxx} where xxx corresponds to one of the types in Table 1. However, in the target platform there is not a specific set of PMCs measuring those values as shown in Table 2, which lists the relevant PMCs we used.

We performed an analysis of the relation we derive among the events needed by the pTC model and the PMCs in the architecture (pmc^{yyy}) as shown in Fig. 5: the number of loads to L2 (n^l) matches the number of misses to the dc and the ic ($pmc^{dcm} + pmc^{icm}$); the number of stores matches pmc^{st}; and the number of misses pmc^m covers those caused by clean and dirty evictions ($pmc^m = n^{lmc} + n^{smc} + n^{lmd} + n^{smd}$). Further, the number of stores n^{st} matches $pmc^{st} = n^{sh} + n^{smd} + n^{smc}$.

With the existing PMC we approximate the number of requests of each type made by each contender task. In doing so, we take into account the request latency so that the resulting impact that τ_b causes on τ_a derived with PMCs is an upperbound to the actual one we would derive if we had the ideal PMCs. The approach consists in upper bounding high-latency requests first, which in our architecture are dirty misses (lmd and smd).

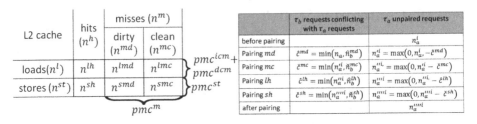

Fig. 5. Events and PMCs   **Fig. 6.** Pairing steps

Bounding Dirty Misses: The number of L2 misses evicting a dirty line is upper bounded by the minimum between the number of stores ($n^{st} = pmc^{st}$) that cause lines to be dirty and the number of L2 misses ($n^m = pmc^m$) that evict cache lines, see left part of Eq. (3).

$$\boxed{\hat{n}^{md} = min(pmc^m, pmc^{st})} \quad \rightarrow \quad \boxed{\check{n}^{mc} = pmc^m - \hat{n}^{md}} \tag{3}$$

Since $n^m = n^{md} + n^{mc}$, the approximation in Eq. (3) may result in assuming that some misses generate dirty evictions while, in reality, they do not, thus introducing some pessimism. In particular, it results in a lower bound to the number of clean misses ($\check{n}^{mc}$), see the right side of Eq. (3).

Bounding Load Hits: The number of loads that hit in cache is upper bounded by the minimum between the number of hits (n^h) and the number of loads (n^l) to the L2, see Eq. (4). They are respectively computed from PMCs as follows:

The number of loads performed to the L2 cache (n^l) equals the number of misses in the dc and ic, i.e., $n^l = pmc^{icm} + pmc^{dcm}$. Note that the number of loads to the L2 includes hits and misses (dirty and clean), i.e., $n^l = n^{lh} + n^{lmc} + n^{lmd}$.

The number of hits in L2, n^h is obtained with existing PMCs as $n^h = (pmc^{icm} + pmc^{dcm} + pmc^{st}) - pmc^m$, that is, the number of read/write accesses to the L2, which include load misses in the ic and the dc plus stores (due to the write-through policy of the dc cache), minus the number of L2 misses. Note that pmc^m does only count the number of direct misses. More specifically, it does not count the number of memory accesses due to write backs.

$$\boxed{\hat{n}^{lh} = min(n^h, n^l)} \quad \rightarrow \quad \boxed{\check{n}^{sh} = n^h - \hat{n}^{lh}} \tag{4}$$

Since $n^h = n^{lh} + n^{sh}$, a lower bound to the number of store hits is derived as shown in the right side of Eq. (4).

Bounding Contention: Once bounds to τ_b accesses have been computed, the pTC model assumes that requests from τ_b delay τ_a requests by their respective mcd. This is implemented by iteratively "pairing" each request from a run r^i of τ_a with one request of τ_b from worst to best latency, see Fig. 6.

1. First, the number of requests from task τ_b of type miss dirty ($\hat{n}^{md}$), i.e. the type with highest mcd, that contend with requests of τ_a, n_a^i, is given

by: $\hat{c}^{md} = min(n_a^i, \hat{n}_b^{md})$. Hence the number of unpaired requests from τ_a is $n_a^{'i} = max(0, n_a^i - \hat{c}_b^{md})$ requests of τ_a unpaired.

2. Those $n_a^{'i}$ requests contend with $\check{n}^{mc}$ (second most impacting type) requests of τ_b: $\check{c}^{mc} = min(n_a^{'i}, \check{n}_b^{mc})$. This results in $n_a^{''} = max(0, n_a^{'i} - \check{c}^{mc})$ τ_a's unpaired requests.

3. Those $n_a^{'''i}$ requests contend with $\hat{n}_b^{lh}$ (third most impacting type) requests of τ_b: $\hat{c}^{lh} = min(n_a^{'''i}, \hat{n}_b^{lh})$ with $n_a^{'''} = max(0, n_a^{'''i} - \hat{c}^{lh})$ requests unpaired.

4. Finally, the $n_a^{''''i}$ remaining τ_a's requests contend with $\check{n}_b^{sh}$ (fourth most impacting type) requests of τ_b: $\check{c}^{sh} = min(n_a^{''''i}, \check{n}_b^{sh})$. With the remaining τ_a's request $n_a^{'''''i} = max(0, n_a^{''''i} - \check{c}^{sh})$ not contending with any request of τ_b.

The obtained pTC contention is the result of assuming that each of these contentions among τ_a and its contender τ_b are aligned in the worst way, causing a contention delay as long as each τ_b request (see Eq. (5)). This process is repeated for the other potential contender tasks τ_c and τ_d. The overall pTC contention bound is given by Eq. (6).

$$\Delta_{\tau_b \to \tau_a}^{i,pTC} = (\hat{c}^{md} \times l^{md}) + (\check{c}^{mc} \times l^{mc}) + (\hat{c}^{lh} \times l^{lh}) + (\check{c}^{sh} \times l^{sh}) \qquad (5)$$

$$\Delta_{cont}^{i,pTC} = \Delta_{\tau_b \to \tau_a}^{i,pTC} + \Delta_{\tau_c \to \tau_a}^{i,pTC} + \Delta_{\tau_d \to \tau_a}^{i,pTC} \qquad (6)$$

Other Considerations. The fTC model has the advantage of breaking the dependence between scheduling and WCET. In an exact model, the WCET figure to be used depends on the schedule of tasks, which creates a circular dependence as WCET is also an input for deriving a feasible schedule. This issue has been initially tackled by an iterative approach to simultaneously attack WCET and scheduling [10]. With fTC the WCET estimate is not affected by the load contender tasks put on the shared resources, and hence it does not depend on task scheduling. However, this comes at the cost of inflated WCET estimates.

It is worth noting that the principles of the presented model does not only apply to the studied processor but also to other multicore processors. In order to adapt the model, it is necessary to understand the type of events using the shared resource and their duration. The quality of the results, however, depends on the PMC support available and the accuracy it guarantees in tracking the desired events, see Fig. 5. As part of our current work we are extending the model to multicore processors in other domains, e.g., automotive.

7   Experimental Results

We first demonstrate our combined approach on a synthetic application and then with benchmarks of the EEMBC Automotive suite [28].

Hardware Setup. We used an FPGA implementation of the LEON3 [2] platform, as introduced in Sect. 3. Each core comprises separate 16KB 4-way setassociative L1 caches for instruction and data, with write-through, no write allocate policy. The cache hierarchy is complemented by a shared 128KB 4-way unified L2 cache, with write-back policy. An AMBA AHB bus provides connections among private caches, the L2 and the DRAM memory controller. In our setting, we configured the L2 to be partitioned among cores (contention is still to be suffered on bus accesses), so each core has a 32 KB direct-mapped L2.

MBPTA Setup. We applied MBPTA to the target program, considering 10^{-12} as the pWCET exceedance probability threshold of interest. We collected 3,000 runs to meet the representativeness requirements, as determined by the ReVS method [24]. The obtained set of observations successfully passed the statistical independence and identical distribution tests, prerequisites to the application of EVT, and allowed MBPTA to converge on a pWCET distribution.

7.1 Synthetic Application

Our synthetic application resembles an "aggressive" program uniformly accessing the shared bus for 30% of its execution time. It consists of several functions that are sequentially accessed within a loop a total of one hundred times. Each function comprises a variable number of instructions, performing a mixture of purely arithmetic and read/write operations.

Our empirical evaluation proceeds through two incremental steps. First, we assess the effectiveness of software randomization in enabling MBPTA to capture intra-core cache jitter. To that end, we execute and analyze our program in isolation (i.e., no contention at all), in a simple single-core setup. Second, we show how the results in isolation can be complemented with the analysis of inter-core contention jitter. We therefore assess our analytical model, combining cache and contention jitter, against representative execution scenarios where all cores in the system are concurrently enabled.

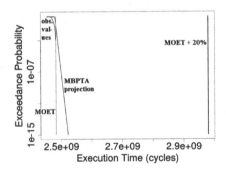

Fig. 7. Results of TASA and MBPTA on a single-core setup.

Capturing Cache Jitter. We exploited TASA to enable MBPTA to capture the execution time variability incurred by caches. To this extent, we analyzed our application in a single-core setup, guaranteeing complete isolation. Figure 7 reports the pWCET distribution computed by MBPTA for the target program.

Observed values are upperbounded by the MBPTA projection and pWCET result is obtained by selecting the value of the projection at the 10^{-12} exceedance threshold. In this case the pWCET distribution is particularly close to the maximum observed execution time (MOET). It is worth noting that, since plain observed values do not provide any worst-case guarantee, it is common (though pretty unscientific) industrial practice to resort to a *fudge factor* to account for unknown factors. This factor is typically in the order of magnitude of 20% of the MOET. Notably, the pWCET computed with MBPTA is not only much tighter than the 20% margin, but also comes with scientific reasoning.

Multicore Contention. The MC2 approach extends single-core pWCET estimates by capturing the effect of inter-core contention through a contention model based on PMCs. In order to assess the precision of our analytical model, we performed a set of experiments on representative execution scenarios where all cores in the system are concurrently enabled and compared against the results of our analytical (fTC and pTC) models. In our setting and platform, the theoretical worst-case inter-core contention suffered by an application corresponds to the fTC scenario where all bus access requests are triggered one cycle after the reserved slot and all other cores already have pending requests, each one incurring the latency of a L2 dirty-miss. While being fully time-composable, this scenario can be extremely pessimistic in practice as it can only occur under extremely bad and rare overlapping of bus requests and cache miss patterns.

fTC. We consider first the fTC contention model as it is used as a reference for the pTC one. Our application, τ_a, is executed under two different scenarios of contention: (1) against three stressing kernels performing loads that miss in L2 (i.e., clean misses) and (2) against three stressing kernels performing stores in L2 overwriting data (i.e., dirty misses). Figure 8 shows the execution time of τ_a under the two scenarios of contention and the bound derived with the fTC model. Values are normalized against the MOET from baseline observations (i.e., no contention). As expected the model is accurate when the execution conditions are matching the fTC assumptions (i.e., worst request latencies and alignment). In practice, contenders will not generate those overly-conflictive scenarios. The pTC model cures the pessimism coming from the worst-case latency assumption.

pTC. To compare the accuracy of the pTC model and how it adapts to contenders' load on the bus, we run our application τ_a against three copies of a benchmark that performs a variable number of bus accesses depending on the configuration, which we express as a percentage of τ_a accesses. Figure 9 compares the observed execution times against the predictions of the pTC model. Results from applying the fTC are included as well for the sake of comparison. As expected, the fTC model yields pessimistic pWCET estimates. Conversely, we observe that the pTC model computes pWCET estimates decrease in parallel with the load put by contenders on the shared bus. Note that the difference among fTC and $pTC - 100\%$ is that the former assumes that all requests contribute the worst-case latency (dirty misses), whereas the latter accounts for the actual type of requests of the contenders. For any value of p, e.g., $pTC - 40\%$,

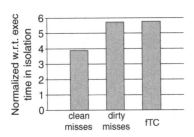

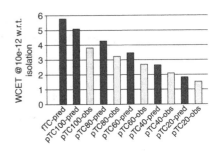

Fig. 8. Execution time when $c(\tau_a)$ create clean/dirty misses and fTC.

Fig. 9. Result of the pTC under different load scenarios generated by the contenders

the derived $pWCET@10^{-12}$ with pTC tightly upperbounds the actual observed value.

All in all this synthetic evaluation confirms that the MC2 method effectively captures both cache and multicore contention into pWCET estimates that are analytically reliable and tightly upperbounding the observed values.

7.2   EEMBC

To further evaluate our approach we applied MC2 on the EEMBC automotive benchmarks [28]. In particular, we analyzed a2time, cacheb, idctrn, iirflt, puwmod, and tblook on the same platform. Figure 10 reports, for each benchmark, MOET in both singlecore and multicore scenarios, and the results of the fTC and pTC models. For the pTC model contention was generated by deploying three copies of the benchmark itself. All results are normalized with respect to the multicore MOET.

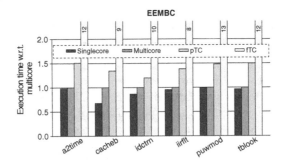

Fig. 10. Results of EEMBCs against 3 copies of themselves

First we observe that fTC WCET estimate are in general extremely high ($\sim$11x). This is explained by the fact that fTC model assumes not only the worst-case alignment scenario but also the worst-case latencies for each contender access, which is generally unrealistic. The pTC model, instead, provides quite good results, with all values below 1.5x the multicore MOET. The only pessimism in the pTC model comes from its conservative assumptions on the alignment of requests. pTC estimates provides a good compromise between tightness and flexibility: a further reduction in pessimism cannot be had without exact knowledge on how bus accesses interleave, which is not flexible and typically too difficult to derive.

8   Related Work

Several approaches have been proposed to account for inter-core contention by computing an upper bound to the delay a task or application may suffer [11]. Some of those approaches require extending classic timing analysis framework to account for the effect of shared resources [4], but they are generally unsustainable owing to the entailed computational complexity. Other approaches suggest a separate (compositional) analysis approach [6,29,30]. They propose a separate analysis for contention and, frequently, rely on splitting tasks into sub-tasks or phases so that worst-case alignment in (typically) TDMA-based arbiters can be reasonably computed. Assuming that tasks can be split into phases allows refining the analysis model and reducing the overall pessimism; however, this assumption is quite application-dependent and cannot be generalized. Moreover, the above approaches typically rely on insightful information on all the applications in the system and a preliminary static analysis step to characterize the pattern of memory accesses. Conversely, the contention analysis approach we rely on limits the pessimism while at the same time making no assumption on how memory accesses are distributed. Our model only requires support for PMCs, which is often available (though at variable extent) in COTS platforms.

Other approaches make use of specific hardware and/or RTOS mechanisms to enforce precomputed bounds to the maximum contention caused/suffered at run time [25,27]. While interesting, those approaches do rely on domain-specific and custom run-time hardware mechanisms that are not typically available, and yield results that are only valid under the specific task set and system configuration. Our approach, instead, derives bounds on the inter-core contention that are at the same time realistic and only partially dependent on the co-runners characteristics, as a first step towards enabling incremental development and qualification.

The use of PMCs to model contention and derive an upper bound to multicore contention delays has been originally introduced in [16], where the analytical model for *fTC* and *pTC* is tailored to the NGMP platform. In this work, we readapt the same concept to the MBPTA framework and combines the contention model in [16] (adapted to the LEON3) with software randomization to provide holistic pWCET bounds, accounting for both cache jitter and contention effects.

9   Conclusions

We have proposed MC2, a technique for COTS multilevel-cache multicores that derives WCET estimates factoring in the jitter generated by caches and multicore contention. To that end, each measurement fed in input to MBPTA systematically accounts for the impact of both resources, effectively enabling MBPTA to factor them in when deriving pWCET estimates. Our results on a COTS platform confirm that MC2 effectively captures the impact of both multi-level cache variability and inter-core contention in realistic WCET estimates, that tightly upperbound observed values.

Acknowledgments. This work has been partially supported by the Spanish Ministry of Economy and Competitiveness (MINECO) under grant TIN2015-65316-P and the HiPEAC Network of Excellence. Jaume Abella has been partially supported by the MINECO under Ramon y Cajal postdoctoral fellowship number RYC-2013-14717. Carles Hernández is jointly funded by the MINECO and FEDER funds through grant TIN2014-60404-JIN. Authors would like to thank Pedro Benedicte for his technical feedback on the camera ready version of this article.

References

1. Abella, J., Hernandez, C., Quinones, E., Cazorla, F.J., Conmy, P.R., Azkarate-askasua, M., Perez, J., Mezzetti, E., Vardanega, T.: WCET analysis methods: pitfalls and challenges on their trustworthiness. In: 2015 10th IEEE International Symposium on Industrial Embedded Systems (SIES), pp. 1–10. IEEE (2015)

2. Gaisler, A.: Leon3 Processor (2016). http://www.gaisler.com/index.php/products/processors/leon3

3. Buttle, D.: Real-time in the prime-time, ETAS GmbH, Germany. In: Keynote talk at 24th Euromicro Conference on Real-Time Systems, Pisa, Italy (2012)

4. Chattopadhyay, S., Chong, L.K., Roychoudhury, A., Kelter, T., Marwedel, P., Falk, H.: A unified WCET analysis framework for multi-core platforms. In: 2012 IEEE 18th Real Time and Embedded Technology and Applications Symposium, pp. 99–108, April 2012

5. Cucu-Grosjean, L., Santinelli, L., Houston, M., Lo, C., Vardanega, T., Kosmidis, L., Abella, J., Mezzetti, E., Quinones, E., Cazorla, F.J.: Measurement-based probabilistic timing analysis for multi-path programs. In: 2012 24th Euromicro Conference on Real-Time Systems (ECRTS), pp. 91–101. IEEE (2012)

6. Dasari, D., Nelis, V., Akesson, B.: A framework for memory contention analysis in multi-core platforms. Real Time Syst. **52**(3), 272–322 (2016). http://dx.doi.org/10.1007/s11241-015-9229-9

7. Edelin, G.: Embedded systems at THALES: the Artemis challenges for an industrial group. In: Lecture at ARTIST Summer School, Autrans, France (2009)

8. Federal Aviation Administration, Certification Authorities Software Team (CAST): CAST-32A Multi-core Processors (2016)

9. Feller, W.: An Introduction to Probability Theory and Its Applications. Wiley, New York (1968)

10. Fernandez, G., Abella, J., Quiones, E., Fossati, L., Zulianello, M., Vardanega, T., Cazorla, F.J.: Seeking time-composable partitions of tasks for cots multicore processors. In: 2015 IEEE 18th International Symposium on Real-Time Distributed Computing, pp. 208–217 (2015)

11. Fernandez, G., Abella, J., Quiñones, E., Rochange, C., Vardanega, T., Cazorla, F.J.: Contention in multicore hardware shared resources: understanding of the state of the art. In: OASIcs-OpenAccess Series in Informatics, vol. 39. Schloss Dagstuhl-Leibniz-Zentrum fuer Informatik (2014)

12. Fernandez, G., Jalle, J., Abella, J., Quiñones, E., Vardanega, T., Cazorla, F.J.: Resource usage templates and signatures for cots multicore processors. In: Proceedings of the 52nd Annual Design Automation Conference (DAC 2015) (2015)

13. Fernández, M., Gioiosa, R., Quiñones, E., Fossati, L., Zulianello, M., Cazorla, F.J.: Assessing the suitability of the NGMP multi-core processor in the space domain. In: Proceedings of the Tenth ACM International Conference on Embedded Software (EMSOFT 2012), NY, USA, pp. 175–184 (2012). http://doi.acm.org/10.1145/2380356.2380389

14. Hernandez, C., Abella, J., Gianarro, A., Andersson, J., Cazorla, F.J.: Random modulo: a new processor cache design for real-time critical systems. In: 2016 53rd ACM/EDAC/IEEE Design Automation Conference (DAC), pp. 1–6, June 2016

15. International Organization for Standardization: ISO/DIS 26262. Road Vehicles - Functional Safety. ISO, Geneva, Switzerland (2009)

16. Jalle, J., Fernandez, M., Abella, J., Andersson, J., Patte, M., Fossati, L., Zulianello, M., Cazorla, F.J.: Bounding resource contention interference in the next-generation microprocessor (NGMP). In: 8th European Congress on Embedded Real Time Software and Systems (ERTS 2016) (2016)

17. Kosmidis, L., Quiones, E., Abella, J., Vardanega, T., Broster, I., Cazorla, F.J.: Measurement-based probabilistic timing analysis and its impact on processor architecture. In: Euromicro Conference on Digital System Design (2014)

18. Kosmidis, L., Vargas, R., Morales, D., Quiones, E., Abella, J., Cazorla, F.J.: TASA: toolchain-agnostic static software randomisation for critical real-time systems. In: International Conference on Computer-Aided Design, pp. 1–8 (2016)

19. Kosmidis, L., Abella, J., Quiñones, E., Cazorla, F.J.: A cache design for probabilistically analysable real-time systems. In: Proceedings of the Conference on Design, Automation and Test in Europe (DATE 2013) (2013)

20. Kosmidis, L., Curtsinger, C., Quiñones, E., Abella, J., Berger, E., Cazorla, F.J.: Probabilistic timing analysis on conventional cache designs. In: Proceedings of the Conference on Design, Automation and Test in Europe (DATE 2013) (2013)

21. Kosmidis, L., Quiñones, E., Abella, J., Farrall, G., Wartel, F., Cazorla, F.J.: Containing timing-related certification cost in automotive systems deploying complex hardware. In: Proceedings of the 51st Annual Design Automation Conference (DAC 2014), pp. 22: 1–22: 6, NY, USA (2014). http://doi.acm.org/10.1145/2593069.2593112

22. Law, S., Bate, I.: Achieving appropriate test coverage for reliable measurement-based timing analysis. In: 2016 28th Euromicro Conference on Real-Time Systems (ECRTS), pp. 189–199, July 2016

23. Mezzetti, E., Vardanega, T.: A rapid cache-aware procedure positioning optimization to favor incremental development. In: Real-Time and Embedded Technology and Applications Symposium (RTAS), pp. 107–116, April 2013

24. Milutinovic, S., Abella, J., Cazorla, F.J.: Modelling probabilistic cache representativeness in the presence of arbitrary access patterns. In: International Symposium on Real-Time Distributed Computing (ISORC), pp. 142–149, May 2016

25. Nowotsch, J., Paulitsch, M., Bhler, D., Theiling, H., Wegener, S., Schmidt, M.: Multi-core interference-sensitive WCET analysis leveraging runtime resource capacity enforcement. In: Euromicro Conference on Real-Time Systems (July 2014)

26. Nowotsch, J., Paulitsch, M., Henrichsen, A., Pongratz, W., Schacht, A.: Monitoring and WCET analysis in COTS multi-core-SoC-based mixed-criticality systems. In: Conference on Design, Automation & Test in Europe (DATE) (2014)

27. Paolieri, M., Quiñones, E., Cazorla, F.J., Bernat, G., Valero, M.: Hardware support for WCET analysis of hard real-time multicore systems. In: 36th Annual International Symposium on Computer Architecture (ISCA) (2009)

28. Poovey, J.A., Conte, T.M., Levy, M., Gal-On, S.: A benchmark characterization of the eembc benchmark suite. IEEE Micro **29**(5), 18–29 (2009). http://dx.doi.org/10.1109/MM.2009.74

29. Schliecker, S., Negrean, M., Nicolescu, G., Paulin, P., Ernst, R.: Reliable performance analysis of a multicore multithreaded system-on-chip. In: 6th International Conference on Hardware/Software Codesign and System Synthesis (CODES 2008) (2008)

30. Schranzhofer, A., Chen, J.J., Thiele, L.: Timing analysis for TDMA arbitration in resource sharing systems. In: 16th IEEE Real-Time and Embedded Technology and Applications Symposium (RTAS) (2010)

31. Wartel, F., Kosmidis, L., Lo, C., Triquet, B., Quiones, E., Abella, J., Gogonel, A., Baldovin, A., Mezzetti, E., Cucu, L., Vardanega, T., Cazorla, F.J.: Measurement-based probabilistic timing analysis: lessons from an integrated-modular avionics case study. In: International Symposium on Industrial Embedded Systems (2013)

32. Wartel, F., Kosmidis, L., Gogonel, A., Baldovin, A., Stephenson, Z., Triquet, B., Quiñones, E., Lo, C., Mezzetti, E., Broster, I., Abella, J., Cucu-Grosjean, L., Vardanega, T., Cazorla, F.J.: Timing analysis of an avionics case study on complex hardware/software platforms. In: Proceedings of the 2015 Design, Automation & Test in Europe Conference & Exhibition, pp. 397–402 (2015). http://dl.acm.org/citation.cfm?id=2755753.2755843

33. West, A.: NASA Study on Flight Software Complexity. Final Report. Technical report, NASA Excellence Program (2009)

34. Wilhelm, R., Engblom, J., Ermedahl, A., Holsti, N., Thesing, S., Whalley, D., Bernat, G., Ferdinand, C., Heckmann, R., Mitra, T., Mueller, F., Puaut, I., Puschner, P., Staschulat, J., Stenström, P.: The worst-case execution-time problem: overview of methods and survey of tools. ACM Trans. Embed. Comput. Syst. **7**(3), 36: 1–36: 53 (2008). http://doi.acm.org/10.1145/1347375.1347389

Programming Models

Lock Elision for Protected Objects Using Intel Transactional Synchronization Extensions

Seongho Jeong, Shinhyung Yang, and Bernd Burgstaller[✉]

Department of Computer Science, Yonsei University, Seoul, Korea
{seongho.jeong,shinhyung.yang,bburg}@yonsei.ac.kr

Abstract. Lock elision is a technique to replace coarse-grained locks by optimistic concurrent execution. In this paper, we introduce lock elision for protected objects (POs) in Ada. We employ Intel Transactional Synchronization Extensions (TSX) as the underlying hardware transactional memory facility. With TSX, a processor can detect dynamically whether tasks need to serialize through critical sections protected by locks. We adapt the GNU Ada run-time library (GNARL) to elide locks transparently from protected functions and procedures. We critically evaluate opportunities and difficulties of lock elision with protected entries. We demonstrate that lock elision can achieve significant performance improvements for a selection of three synthetic and one real-world benchmark. We show the scalability of our approach for up to 44 cores of a two-CPU, 44-core Intel E5-2699 v4 system.

1 Introduction

Since the advent of multicore processors, software developers have been relying on multi-threaded software to achieve performance improvements. Multi-threaded software requires synchronization to protect data shared among multiple threads. Locks allow to transform code into a critical section, which is a block of code that can only be executed by one thread at a time. This property of critical sections is called mutual exclusion. Employing locks to achieve mutual exclusion is well-understood and the most prevalent form of synchronization. However, because threads serialize to gain access to shared data, locks negatively impact performance and hamper scalability.

A coarse-grained lock protects a large amount of shared data and thus is prone to become a highly-contended scalability bottle-neck. Fine-grained locking protects shared data at a finer granularity, which allows a higher degree of parallel access because empirically not all threads require access to the same data-item. To achieve fine-grained locking, a programmer must partition a shared data-structure into parts and introduce a mutual exclusion lock for each part. E.g., instead of protecting an entire linked list with a single, coarse-grained lock, individual list nodes can be protected by a lock. This thought-process is error-prone and complex: obtaining locks without a global order among locks (a locking hierarchy) will result in dead-locks, and the higher degree of parallelism associated with fine-grained locking makes race-conditions harder to avoid.

© Springer International Publishing AG 2017
J. Blieberger and M. Bader (Eds.): Ada-Europe 2017, LNCS 10300, pp. 121–136, 2017.
DOI: 10.1007/978-3-319-60588-3_8

Lock-free programming relies on hardware primitives to provide concurrent operations on data-structures [15, 20]. Although such algorithms provide high scalability, they are mostly complex.

Lock elision [22] is a technique to reduce serialization with lock-based code. The key insight with lock elision is that many dynamic data sharing patterns among threads do not conflict and thus do not require the acquisition of a lock. E.g., a concurrent hash-map [11] contains multiple key-value pairs. Two threads updating different keys will not conflict and hence do not require serialization (locking). Serialization is only required among threads updating the same key's value.

With lock elision, a thread will *speculatively* execute a critical section (called transactional region) without acquiring the associated lock (the lock is said to be elided). In the absence of inter-thread data conflicts, the memory updates (write operations) of the thread are committed to memory. If a data conflict with another thread is detected, speculative execution of the transactional region is aborted and the thread's write operations are not committed to memory. The failed thread must then re-execute the transactional region. With lock elision, programmers are thus granted the convenience of using coarse-grained locks, which will exhibit the scalability of fine-grained locking in the absence of inter-thread data conflicts.

To detect data conflicts and ensure an atomic commit of a thread's memory updates, a read-set and a write-set are maintained for a transactional region. The read-set consists of addresses the thread read from within the transactional region, and the write-set consists of addresses written to within the transactional region. The updates to the write-set will be committed atomically to memory in the absence of data conflicts (see Definition 1), and discarded otherwise.

Definition 1. Data Conflict. *Assume a thread executing a transactional region. A data conflict occurs if another thread either reads a location that is part of the transactional region's write-set or writes a location that is a part of either the read- or write-set of the transactional region (adopted from [17]).*

Lock elision requires hardware support to be efficient. Recent CPU architectures from Intel, IBM and Sun/Oracle provide hardware transactional memory (TM) extensions [13, 17, 27], which allow a processor to dynamically detect data conflicts. (Transactional memory was originally proposed in 1993 by Herlihy and Moss [14].).

In this paper, we focus on lock elision for protected objects (POs) in Ada. As the underlying hardware mechanism we employ Intel TSX [17]. To the best of our knowledge, lock elision for Intel TSX until now has only been attempted with mutual exclusion locks in C and C++ [18, 28]. In contrast, Ada's POs [24] implement the monitor concept [16]. The PO synchronization mechanism goes beyond "plain" mutual exclusion, because POs provide protected functions, procedures and entries. Protected functions do not update shared data and hence multiple protected functions of a PO may execute in parallel. Protected procedures and entries require mutual exclusion. Protected entries provide programmed guards for conditional synchronization.

Introducing lock elision with the Ada PO implementation is a promising concept, because it will make coarse-grained concurrent data-structures susceptible to fine-grained locking, at the cost of no or only minor changes of the application source-code. Our paper makes the following contributions:

1. We adapt the GNU Ada run-time library (GNARL) to elide locks transparently from protected functions and procedures.
2. We investigate opportunities and difficulties for lock elision with protected entries. We outline two possible elision schemes for protected entries.
3. We experimentally evaluate our approach for a selection of three synthetic benchmarks and one real-world benchmark. We show the scalability of our approach for up to 44 cores of a two-CPU, 44-core Intel E5-2699 v4 system.
4. We provide programming- and language-design directions to leverage the parallelism obtainable from lock elision with POs in Ada.

The remainder of this paper is structured as follows. In Sect. 2, we discuss lock elision for Ada POs. Section 3 contains our experimental results. We discuss the related work in Sect. 4 and draw our conclusions in Sect. 5. For an accessible introduction to Intel TSX, we refer the reader to [18, 23].

2   Lock Elision with GNARL

To access the Intel TSX instruction set extensions from Ada code, we created a package with a procedural interface to each TSX instruction. The specification of this package is depicted in Fig. 1.

A transaction is started via instruction xbegin. Upon execution of xbegin, the processor returns the value XBEGIN_STARTED in the EAX-register and "memorizes" the next instruction's address. When the processor detects a data conflict, it will abort the transaction and transfer control to this "memorized" address. The processor commits a transaction when it reaches instruction xend. The memory updates of a transaction become visible to other processors (and cores) when the transaction commits. A commit happens atomically. Instruction xtest allows software to test whether the processor is currently inside a transaction. Instruction xabort allows software to explicitly abort the current transaction.

Whenever a transaction aborts, control is transferred to the address "memorized" by xbegin. In case of an abort, the processor sets a specific bit in the EAX register to signal the type of conflict which caused the abort. Unless the EAX value is 0xffffffff, which denotes XBEGIN_STARTED, software must make a decision whether to retry or fall back to the locking code. Note that there is no guarantee from the processor that a transaction will eventually succeed. Thus, the fall-back path with the conventional lock-based code is required.

We employ inline assembly to emit bytes corresponding to Intel TSX instructions. Figure 2 depicts our implementation for the xbegin instruction. The remaining TSX instructions are implemented in a similar manner.

```
 1  package TSX_inst is
 2  pragma Preelaborate;
 3    type uint32 is mod 2**32;
 4    -- Status codes returned by the CPU in the x86's EAX register:
 5    XBEGIN_STARTED   : constant uint32 := 16#ffffffff#;
 6    XABORT_EXPLICIT  : constant uint32 := 2**0;
 7    XABORT_RETRY     : constant uint32 := 2**1;
 8    XABORT_CONFLICT  : constant uint32 := 2**2;
 9    XABORT_CAPACITY  : constant uint32 := 2**3;
10    XABORT_DEBUG     : constant uint32 := 2**4;
11    XABORT_NESTED    : constant uint32 := 2**5;
12    function XABORT_CODE (state : uint32) return uint32;
13
14    function xbegin return uint32;    -- start transaction
15    procedure xend;                   -- end transaction
16    function xtest return uint32;     -- test for execution inside transaction
17    procedure xabort;                 -- abort transaction
18    procedure pause;                  -- processor hint (not part of Intel TSX)
19  private
20    pragma Inline (XABORT_CODE);
21    pragma Inline_Always (xbegin);
22    pragma Inline_Always (xend);
23    pragma Inline_Always (xtest);
24    pragma Inline_Always (xabort);
25    pragma Inline_Always (pause);
26  end TSX_inst;
```

Fig. 1. Specification of package TSX_inst to use Intel TSX with Ada

```
 1  function xbegin return uint32 is
 2    ret : uint32 := XBEGIN_STARTED;
 3  begin
 4    Asm(".byte 0xc7,0xf8 ; .long 0",
 5    Outputs => uint32'Asm_Output ("+a", ret),
 6    Clobber => "memory", Volatile => True);
 7    return ret;
 8  end xbegin;
```

Fig. 2. Ada implementation for TSX instruction xbegin

2.1   Lock Elision for Protected Functions and Procedures

The Ada 2012 RM [24, Chap. 9.5.1(5)] states that execution of a protected procedure requires exclusive read-write access to the PO. Speculative execution of critical sections with elided locks does not fulfill this requirement. Rather, serialization is achieved by re-executing a critical section in case of a transactional abort [18,23].

GNARL employs one lock per PO for synchronization. We perform lock elision of such locks as follows. (1) Check if the lock is free. If not, wait until it is released by another task. (2) Once the lock is free, the task starts its transaction without actual lock acquisition, and executes the critical section (the body of a protected function or procedure). (3) If the task proceeds through the critical section without a data conflict, it commits the updates in the write-set to memory (where they become visible to other tasks). During this entire process, the lock appears to be free to all tasks.

Because transactions tend to abort frequently, we must keep the existing lock-based code as a fall-back solution (to prevent infinite aborts). If any single task proceeds with the lock-based code, all other tasks competing for access to the PO must wait (serialize) until the lock is released (alike the conventional GNARL implementation).

```
 1 procedure Write_Lock          -- GNARL lock acquisition procedure
 2   result := Try_Elision       -- Added: attempt to elide lock
 3   if result = fail then
 4     acquire PO.lock           -- Lock elision failed -> acquire lock
 5   end if
 6   return                      -- Proceed to critical section, lock is
 7 end Write_Lock                -- either elided or acquired.
 8
 9 -- GNARL extension for lock elision:
10 MAX_RETRY : constant Natural := ...   -- Tuning-knob 1
11 BACKOFF   : constant Natural := ...   -- Tuning-knob 2
12
13 procedure Try_Elision
14   retry = 0
15   while retry < MAX_RETRY loop              -- Attempt elision multiple times
16     state := xbegin        -- Start transaction; resume at abort or conflict
17     if state = XBEGIN_STARTED then
18       -- From here we execute in transactional mode
19       if PO.lock = open then
20         return success   -- Report that elision succeeded
21       else               -- Another task is holding lock:
22         xabort           --   Abort transaction (-> resume at line 16)
23       end if
24     else if state = XABORT_CAPACITY or state = XABORT_RETRY then
25       return fail         -- Report that elision failed
26     else                  -- Transaction failed, but might succeed next time
27       if state = XABORT_CONFLICT then
28         -- Data conflict: defer to competing tasks:
29         Exponential_Backoff ((2**retry)*BACKOFF)
30       end if
31       wait until PO.lock = open -- Data conflict or xabort
32       retry := retry + 1
33     end if
34   end loop
35   return fail              -- Report that elision failed
36 end Try_Elision
```

Fig. 3. Elision of a PO lock in GNARL (in pseudo-code). Try_Elision is called from procedure Write_Lock before entering a critical section. The call returns either inside of a transaction (line 20) or to acquire the PO's lock (lines 25 and 35). Only in the first case will the lock be elided.

Figure 3 depicts the PO lock elision scheme that we implemented within GNARL. Procedure Write_Lock is called from inside GNARL before entering a PO's critical section. In our implementation, Write_Lock calls procedure Try_Elision to attempt lock elision. The transaction retry count is initialized in line 14, before the start of the transaction. Line 16 (xbegin) marks the start of the transaction. If the PO's lock is found open, Try_Elision returns in transactional mode (line 20). Otherwise, a task will abort the transaction (in line 22). The abort will transfer control to line 16 and from there to line 31, where the task will wait until the lock becomes available. If retry exceeds

MAX_RETRY, procedure Try_Elision terminates the retry-loop and returns "fail" (line 35). As a result, procedure Write_Lock will acquire the PO's lock (line 4) and return in non-transactional mode. Note that line 4 can only be reached in non-transactional mode.

The GNARL function for exiting a critical section is conceptually much simpler and has been omitted due to space constraints.

We require read-access to the PO's lock to detect data conflicts. If task A is inside a transaction and task B acquires the lock, task A must abort its transaction. This can be achieved by keeping the PO's lock in the read-set of task A's transaction. However, the lock library underneath GNARL does not allow to read a lock without changing it. As a work-around, we introduced a shadow-lock variable per PO lock (as outlined in [5]). The shadow-lock is of type integer, and we added it to the protected object package inside GNARL. The original PO lock is used with the lock-based code, but not used with transactions. The shadow-lock is the one kept in the read-set of a transaction. We set the shadow-lock if a task acquires the PO's lock. To ensure atomicity, we use GCC's atomic built-in functions to access the shadow-lock.

To improve performance, we applied the following three adjustments. First, we employ the x86 pause instruction inside the busy-waiting loop used by a task to wait for a PO lock to be released. The pause instruction is a hint to the CPU to limit speculative execution, which increases the speed at which the release of the lock is detected [2]. This optimization yielded a considerable performance improvement. Second, a task attempts transactional execution several times before falling back to the lock. As depicted in Fig. 3 (lines 10 and 15), a task tries up to MAX_RETRY times to execute a critical section as a transaction. Lastly, depending on the conflict type, a task may already fall back to the PO lock before reaching the MAX_RETRY limit. On a transaction abort the CPU provides a status code. If the XABORT_RETRY-flag is not set in the status code, the transaction will not succeed in a re-try either (e.g., if the task attempts a system-call inside the critical section). If the XABORT_CAPACITY-flag is set, the transactional memory capacity reached its limit. When we detect one of these flags, we fall back to the conventional lock without further retries. Note that this is a heuristic: depending on control-flow, a task might refrain from executing a system call during the retry, or the transactional memory capacity limit was exceeded because of another task inside of a transaction on the same processor core. (A scenario possible with processors that support hyperthreads.) Note that in line 29 of Fig. 3 a task which encountered a data conflict will wait to allow competing tasks to finish their transactions before re-trying. Procedure Exponential_Backoff contains a busy-waiting loop with the iteration count specified by the procedure's argument. The waiting time increases with every unsuccessful re-try ("exponential backoff"). Thereby situations are avoided where tasks keep mutually aborting each other's transactions without overall progress.

Lock elision may not always improve performance. For example, critical sections which routinely lead to capacity overflow will always fall back to the lock. Different values for the maximum number of attempted lock-elisions and the calibration of the busy-waiting loop (lines 10 and 11 in Fig. 3) will differ across benchmarks and HW platforms. Putting the before-mentioned tuning parameters and the decision whether to elide a PO lock under programmer control (e.g., via a pragma) seems advisable. Alternatively, GNARL itself may be extended with dynamic profiling capabilities to take decisions at run-time. At the present stage, we have hand-tuned these values, as described in Sect. 3.

2.2   Lock Elision for Protected Entries

The Ada 2012 RM [24, Chap. 9.5.3(16)] states that queued entry calls with an open barrier take precedence over all other protected operations of the PO (known as the "eggshell model"). The reason for this requirement is likely to avoid starvation, according to the following definition.

Definition 2 Freedom from Starvation: *every task that attempts to acquire the PO eventually succeeds (adopted from [15]).*

Obviously, RM Clause 9.5.3(16) restricts the degree of parallelism obtainable with lock elision: consider Task A queued at an open entry and Task B calling the same entry (or another entry, or a protected procedure or function of the PO): Task A is required to proceed first, which requires Task B to serialize irrespective of inter-task data conflicts.

It should be noted that for many parallel workloads, freedom from starvation is not a concern (latency and/or throughput is). E.g., both with the "stencil" and the more general "map" programming pattern from [19], the amount of work is usually constant and known *a priory*. The order in which tasks enter a critical region is immaterial, and it is impossible to starve a task because the amount of work is bounded. Even if work is not bounded, e.g., with streaming applications, then individual work items will be bounded, and tasks will synchronize at a barrier before moving from one work-item to the next.

A not entirely unrelated issue has been discussed by the Ada Conformity Assessment Authority (ACAA) in June 2016 to allow parallel processing of Ada standard containers [1].

To elide locks from POs with entries, we have envisioned the following two schemes.

Permissive Lock Elision. One possible elision-scheme for protected entries is to waive Clause (16), at least in response to a programmer-supplied PO type annotation such as a pragma. Protected functions, procedures and entries will then execute in any order in parallel, subject only to serialization due to inter-task data conflicts.

Restrictive Lock Elision. A more restrictive scheme will provide a mode-switch from elided to non-elided, serialized execution as soon as an entry call enqueues at a closed barrier. Such semantics can be achieved by an is_queued-flag, which is added to the read-set of every PO transaction. The task which is about to enqueue will write to the is_queued-flag, which will abort all ongoing transactions. Procedure Try_Elision from Fig. 3 must be adapted such that no transactional execution is attempted if the is_queued-flag is set. The flag will be cleared and the PO switched back to elided mode once all queues are empty.

The core part of the Ada language does not specify the order in which entry queues shall be served. (The real-time systems annex of the Ada RM addresses (implementation-dependent) queuing policies, which we did not consider for this paper.) If a first-come-first-served fairness property is not required, parallelism can be leveraged with the restrictive scheme by allowing the tasks in the front position of each queue to proceed to the critical section in parallel.

One note is due to the controlling variables that occur in barrier expressions. If these variables are frequently written inside of protected operations, the success-rate of transactions will be negatively impacted. A possible remedy can be to encourage programmers to re-queue entry calls from a barrier with a non-trivial condition to a true barrier after the update of control variables has been completed. If the PO selectively performs elision for entries with true barriers, only the barrier evaluation and controlling variable update is serialized, and the remaining work of the protected operation can proceed in transactional mode. One example that will benefit from this approach is a grow-able hash-map which allows insert operations up to a certain load-factor and then temporarily suspends to grow the hash-map. The number of elements inserted will be a controlling variable for the barrier of the insert operation, and this variable will be decremented with every insert operation. Without a re-queue to an entry that performs the actual insertion, the transactional success rate can be expected to be very low.

3   Experimental Results

To evaluate the effect of lock elision with Ada POs, we selected three synthetic benchmarks: a concurrent linked-list, Dijkstra's Dining Philosophers, and a concurrent hash-map. The purpose of the synthetic benchmarks was to study lock elision in isolation, without perturbing effects that a large application (client) might incur. We investigated one real-world application, K-means clustering, from the Stanford Transactional Applications for Multi-Processing (STAMP) benchmark suite [9,21]. STAMP benchmarks are implemented in C, and we ported the K-means clustering benchmark to Ada.

In our evaluation, we used GCC/GNAT version 6.3.0. Lock elision for protected functions and procedures was implemented in GNAT's run-time system as described in Sect. 2. We evaluated our benchmarks on a 2 CPU Intel Xeon E5-2699 v4 system. Each of the E5-2699 CPUs provide 22 cores with 2 hyper-threads per core. Our evaluation platform runs the CentOS Linux distribution (version 7.3, kernel version 4.9.4-1).

We employed likwid-pin from the LIKWID tool-suite [3,26] to pin Ada tasks onto CPU cores. The rationale for task-pinning is to prevent the Linux kernel scheduler from migrating tasks across CPU cores. Such migrations would otherwise perturb the experiments by (1) increasing the cache coherence overhead and (2) increase the transaction failure-rate. The order of our pinning scheme was to assign one task to each core of the first CPU, then one task to each core of the second CPU (tasks 1–44 were assigned this way). Note that we did not use the CPU's hyper-threading facility in our experimental evaluation.

All performance measurements were conducted using hardware performance counters. We created a thick Ada binding to the PAPI C-API. PAPI [7,25] is a library which provides a hardware-independent interface to count micro-architectural events occurring in a CPU during program run-time. In particular, we determined CPU cycle counts and the transactional success rate using PAPI. For the latter, Intel TSX-capable CPUs provide two hardware cycle counters: (1) the total number of transactional cycles and (2) the number of aborted transactional cycles.

We ran each experiment consecutively for three times. Workloads (i.e., the number of times each task would synchronize at a PO), were adjusted such that a benchmark would execute between 2 and 40 s. For each benchmark execution, the execution-time of the longest-running task was obtained. The median of these execution times was reported.

In our lock-elided GNARL implementation, we maintain variable MAX_RETRY to set the number of transactional trials before falling back to lock-based synchronization (see Fig. 3). This variable is a tuning-knob; from our experiments, the value of this variable has to be larger than the number of participating tasks to ensure competitive performance. On our 44-core test platform, we set this value to 200, i.e., a task would try 200x to perform a protected function or procedure in transactional mode before falling back to the lock. Constant BACKOFF was set to 10. This set-up was used with all benchmarks.

Linked Lists—A Counter-Example. We start our evaluation with a data-structure where lock elision is *not* effective. Our linked lists consist of nodes of the following type Node, where each node contains a pointer to the next list element. Because nodes are dynamically allocated, each node ends up in a cache-line of its own, although the size of a node is only 16 B on a 64 bit architecture.

```
1 type Node;
2 type pNode is access Node;
3 type Node is record
4    value : Integer;
5    next : pNode;
6 end record;
```

With coarse-grained locking, a single PO would be employed to synchronize access to a linked list of this type. Each list operation (e.g., insert, lookup, ...) will be implemented as a protected operation. If the PO is elided, each list operation constitutes a transaction. However, traversing a linked list of N nodes will accumulate N cache-lines in the read-set of this transaction, which we found to exceed the CPU resources for all but the smallest linked lists. As a consequence, for linked lists beyond this size constraint, transactions will always fail and fall back to the lock-based code. For this particular example, transactions aborted after traversing 100 nodes. This result will vary with the size of the nodes.

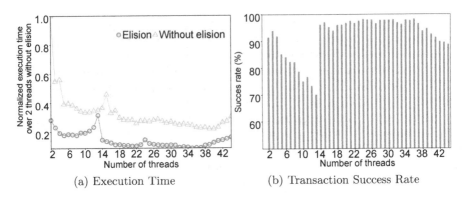

(a) Execution Time   (b) Transaction Success Rate

Fig. 4. Analysis of the Dining Philosophers algorithm at 1 million synchronization steps ("meals") per philosopher

From this example, it becomes clear that lock elision cannot be applied in the general case. Rather, a critical assessment is necessary to decide whether lock elision will be effective for a given use-case. Such an assessment can be done by the programmer (if the programming language provides means to explicitly enable/disable elision), the compiler (through static program analysis), and by the run-time system (through dynamic program analysis).

For the same reason, it seems preferable to conduct lock elision as part of the Ada programming language implementation rather than to divert it to a lower layer such as the glibc library.

Note that for the above example lock elision can be put to work by introducing fine-grained locking of individual list nodes (see, e.g., [15, Chap. 9.5]). We did not pursue this direction, because it would constitute re-factoring of the application source-code rather than lock-elision of course-grained PO locks.

Dining Philosophers. In our implementation of Dijkstra's Dining Philosophers, each philosopher is an instance of an Ada task type and each fork is a PO. Fork acquisition is realized as a protected procedure, which guarantees mutual exclusion. Each fork maintains a state variable that indicates whether a fork is free or taken. When a philosophers acquires a fork, this state variable is set to false. That way, neighboring philosophers aiming at the same fork will find out that the fork is already taken, and re-try calling the acquire procedure until the fork becomes available. After fork acquisition, a philosopher releases the forks immediately by calling the forks' Release procedure (philosophers focus on synchronization only). Scalability of our proposed lock elision is tested by increasing the number of philosophers and forks.

Figure 4a compares the execution time of the Dining Philosophers algorithm with and without lock elision. Execution times are normalized over the execution time for two philosophers without lock elision. The second normalization factor is the workload per task (each philosopher performs 1 million synchronization steps, irrespective of the number of participating philosophers).

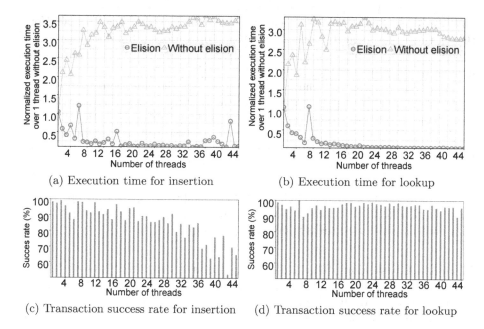

(a) Execution time for insertion

(b) Execution time for lookup

(c) Transaction success rate for insertion

(d) Transaction success rate for lookup

Fig. 5. Concurrent hash-map operations (50 million operations each)

Lock elision shows superior performance from 2 up to 44 tasks. The performance gap is at the largest with the 2-task baseline case. The gap is the smallest for 13 tasks where lock elision suffers from an abnormal increase in execution time.

Concurrent Hash-Map. A concurrent hash-map has high potential to harness the benefits of transactional memory, because data accessed by different tasks tends to be located in different memory locations. The speculative, parallel execution mechanism provided by transactional memory has thus a high chance to succeed.

We implemented a concurrent hash-map using coarse-grained locking via a single PO. Our hash-map provides an insert operation and a lookup function. We employed open addressing for collision resolution. Our hash-map's keys are of type 32 bit unsigned integer, and the value type is `Character`. We purposefully used a value type of small size, to prevent the experiment from being perturbed by costly data movement operations which could arise, e.g., with strings. The purpose of the experiment was to determine the performance improvement possible with lock elision.

We processed insertion and lookup with random keys generated by the random number generator of package `Ada.Numerics.Discrete_Random`. Those operations were performed in a tight loop. One run of the experiment entailed 50 million insert operations on an empty hash-map, and 50 million lookup operations on a pre-filled hash-map. Our hash-map was of size $2 \times X$. Note that in this experiment, the overall number of operations (50 million) was independent of the number of participating tasks. As more tasks are involved, the number of operations per task decrease.

Figure 5a and b depict the execution times for the insertion- and lookup-operations. Clearly the global lock (line-graph "Without Elision") does not scale to multiple tasks. Because of lock contention, tasks serialize at the PO. The result with the elided PO (line-graph "Elision") shows superior scalability and performance. It should be noted that tasks ran these operations in a tight loop, which is an unrealistic scenario for real-world applications.

Figure 5c and d illustrate the success rate of transaction cycles. As more tasks are accessing the PO, the probability of data conflicts during insertion operations increases. Lookup operations do not write shared data in the hash-map hence a data conflict with other tasks is unlikely.

K-means Clustering. The K-means algorithm groups objects located in an N-dimensional space into K clusters. This algorithm is commonly used for data-mining. The STAMP [9, 21] version of the K-means algorithm partitions objects and employs threads such that each thread processes a subset of objects iteratively. With STAMP, a transaction is used to protect the update of the cluster centers, which occurs during each iteration. The algorithm spends most of the time computing cluster centers, and data conflicts resulting from cluster center updates are rare. The algorithm thus benefits from the optimistic concurrency of transactional memory.

To evaluate the effects of lock elision with K-means clustering in Ada, we ported the C-implementation from STAMP to Ada. Instead of using transactional memory, we protected the cluster center updates by a PO. Compared to the previous examples, the percentage of CPU-cycles spent inside of the critical sections is very small (restricted to the cluster center updates), which results in smaller impact from lock elision. Figure 6 depicts the performance difference for elided and non-elided POs for the K-means clustering benchmark. A constant number of points was clustered for varying numbers of clusters. A larger number of clusters reduces the potential for data conflicts during the tasks' joint update of the cluster centers. Higher-dimensional data points incur more parallelizable work and hence diminish the non-parallelizable part (i.e., synchronization) relative to the total amount of work. With ten clusters (Fig. 6a), scalability cannot be maintained past 18 tasks, because of the high probability of data conflicts. On the other hand, with 100 clusters of the same dimension (Fig. 6c), performance does not degrade. This is due to the fact that with 100 cluster centers there is a lower probability of conflicts than with 10 cluster centers. For data points of higher dimension (Fig. 6d), the benefit from lock elision diminishes, because the computation-to-communication ratio increases. Figure 6b clearly shows the benefits of lock elision for a small computation-to-communication ratio. Lock elision can decrease the execution time by more than a factor of 5 in this case.

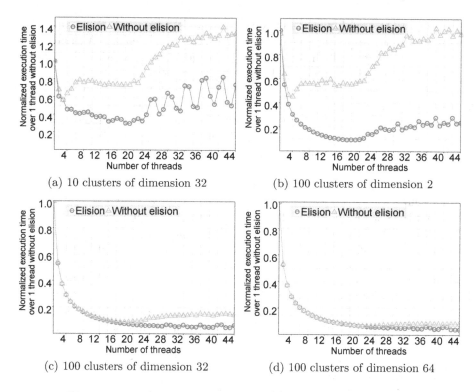

(a) 10 clusters of dimension 32

(b) 100 clusters of dimension 2

(c) 100 clusters of dimension 32

(d) 100 clusters of dimension 64

Fig. 6. Execution time of Ada K-means clustering (65536 points)

4   Related Work

In [18], a comprehensive introduction to lock elision with Intel TSX is provided. The same author implemented lock elision for the glibc library [10]. There, POSIX mutexes are incorporated with Intel TSX. Lock elision is enabled on TSX-capable systems via the "`--enable-lock-elision=yes`" parameter stated at compile time. While lock elision promises to provide the scalability of non-blocking synchronization, its actual performance will vary regarding the frequency and cost of data conflicts. The author proposes an "adaptive elision" policy which is currently used in glibc and subject for improvement. In the author's description of the policy, transactional aborts and unsuccessful transactional execution will adaptively enable elision skips for a given period of time. The author opens possibilities for improving the heuristics in future versions of the library. It will improve C programs which are built against glibc. However, such volatility can introduce an unwanted threat to Ada run-time systems. The Ada programming language strictly specifies the behavior of its protected objects due to the language's provision for reliability and safety. Glibc's lock elision support depends on the capabilities of the underlying hardware and the adaptive heuristic elision algorithm which is not directly accessible to Ada programmers who utilize POs. Our Linked Lists counter example supports the necessity of a means to assess the practicality of lock elision for each use-case. A more effective solution is to provide fine-grained lock elision policies for Ada POs tailored in-line with the design principles of the Ada programming language.

In [28], Yoo et al. apply Intel TSX to a set of benchmarks in the high-performance computing domain (HPC). They survey a broad spectrum of workloads, including a parallel, user-level TCP/IP stack. Their benchmarks are all implemented in C/C++ and do not contain monitor constructs like Ada's POs. Their evaluation is restricted to a 4th generation Intel Core processor with 4 cores (2 hyperthreads per core). In contrast, we investigated lock elision with Ada POs. Our evaluation platform is a state-of-the-art 2 CPU 44 cores Xeon E5-2699 v4 system. Our experiments show scalability up to 44 cores in almost all cases.

In previous work on Ada's protected objects in real-time systems [12], the term *transaction* is employed with single atomic primitives (e.g., read-modify-write operations) in conjunction with lock-free programming. In contrast, our approach allows to combine multiple statements of a protected procedure into a transaction, with TSX as the underlying hardware mechanism. The work in [12] imposes several restrictions to achieve *transactional* behavior, such as disallowing the use of multiple memory locations and loop statements. These restrictions are due to the use of hardware atomic primitives when hardware TM was not available.

Lock-free data-structures provide concurrent access to shared data without relying on locks to achieve mutual exclusion [15,20]. They rely on hardware primitives such as a compare-and-swap (CAS) instruction and it is an agreed-upon fact that the design of lock-free algorithms is complex. Compared to lock elision, lock-free programming shifts the burden of achieving fine-grained parallelism to the programmer. Nevertheless, this approach can achieve good scalability. Both Simple Components [8] and Non-Blocking Ada [6] are collections of lock-free data-structures implemented in Ada. As of June 2016, the Ada Conformity Assessment Authority (ACAA) has been concerned with the provision of concurrent access to Ada's container libraries [1].

5   Conclusions

We have implemented hardware lock elision for protected functions and procedures in Ada 2012. For entries, we presented two possible schemes for lock elision, with varying degrees of parallelism. We demonstrated that lock elision can achieve significant performance improvements. We showed the scalability of our approach for several benchmarks up to 44 cores of a two-CPU, 44-core Intel E5-2699 v4 system. To the best of our knowledge, this is the first approach to lock elision for monitor constructs. Our benchmark source code and the GNARL implementation have been made available on GitHub [4].

Acknowledgements. Research supported by the Next-Generation Information Computing Development Program through the National Research Foundation of Korea (NRF), funded by the Ministry of Science, ICT & Future Planning under grant NRF-2015M3C4A7065522.

References

1. ACAA Web site on "Concurrent access to Ada container libraries". http://www.ada-auth.org/cgi-bin/cvsweb.cgi/ai12s/ai12-0196-1.txt?rev=1.4. Accessed 20 Jan 2017
2. Intel Developer Zone: Pause Intrinsic. https://software.intel.com/en-us/node/524249. Accessed 12 Jan 2017
3. LIKWID GitHub page. https://github.com/RRZE-HPC/likwid/wiki. Accessed 10 Jan 2017
4. Lock-elided protected object resources on GitHub. https://github.com/bbur/pobj-tsx.git. Accessed 28 Mar 2017
5. Lock elision anti-patterns. https://software.intel.com/en-us/articles/tsx-anti-patterns-in-lock-elision-code. Accessed 20 Mar 2017
6. NBAda: non-blocking data structures for Ada Web site. http://www.gidenstam.org/ada/Non-Blocking/. Accessed 20 Jan 2017
7. Performance application programming interface (PAPI) Web site. http://icl.cs.utk.edu/papi/. Accessed 20 Jan 2017
8. Simple Components Web site. http://www.dmitry-kazakov.de/ada/components.htm. Accessed 20 Jan 2017
9. STAMP GitHub page. https://github.com/kozyraki/stamp. Accessed 20 Jan 2017
10. The GNU C Library is now available. https://lists.gnu.org/archive/html/info-gnu/2013-08/msg00003.html. Accessed 22 Jan 2017
11. The world's simplest lock-free hash table, Preshing on programming blog. http://preshing.com/20130605/the-worlds-simplest-lock-free-hash-table/. Accessed 22 Jan 2017
12. Bosch, G.: Lock-free protected types for real-time Ada. Ada Lett. **33**(2), 66–74 (2013)
13. Dice, D., Lev, Y., Moir, M., Nussbaum, D.: Early experience with a commercial hardware transactional memory implementation. In: Proceedings of the 14th International Conference on Architectural Support for Programming Languages and Operating Systems (ASPLOS XIV), pp. 157–168. ACM, New York (2009)
14. Herlihy, M., Moss, J.E.B.: Transactional memory: architectural support for lock-free data structures. In: Proceedings of the 20th Annual International Symposium on Computer Architecture (ISCA 1993), pp. 289–300. ACM, New York (1993)
15. Herlihy, M., Shavit, N.: The Art of Multiprocessor Programming. Morgan Kaufmann Publishers Inc., San Francisco (2008)
16. Hoare, C.A.R.: Monitors: an operating system structuring concept. Commun. ACM **17**(10), 549–557 (1974)
17. Intel Corporation: Intel® 64 and IA-32 Architectures Software Developer's Manual, vol. 1, December 2016
18. Kleen, A.: Scaling existing lock-based applications with lock elision. Queue **12**(1), 20: 20–20: 27 (2014)
19. McCool, M., Reinders, J., Robison, A.: Structured Parallel Programming: Patterns for Efficient Computation. Morgan Kaufmann Publishers Inc., San Francisco (2012)

20. Michael, M.M.: The balancing act of choosing nonblocking features. Commun. ACM **56**(9), 46–53 (2013)
21. Minh, C.C., Chung, J., Kozyrakis, C., Olukotun, K.: STAMP: Stanford transactional applications for multi-processing. In: 4th International Symposium on Workload Characterization (IISWC 2008), Seattle, Washington, USA, 14–16 September, 2008, pp. 35–46 (2008)
22. Rajwar, R., Goodman, J.R.: Speculative lock elision: enabling highly concurrent multithreaded execution. In: Proceedings of the 34th Annual ACM/IEEE International Symposium on Microarchitecture (MICRO 34), pp. 294–305. IEEE Computer Society (2001)
23. Scott, M.L.: Shared-Memory Synchronization. Synthesis Lectures on Computer Architecture. Morgan & Claypool Publishers, San Francisco (2013)
24. Taft, S.T., Duff, R.A., Brukardt, R.L., Ploedereder, E., Leroy, P., Schonberg, E. (eds.): Ada 2012 Reference Manual. Language and Standard Libraries. LNCS, vol. 8339. Springer, Heidelberg (2013)
25. Terpstra, D., Jagode, H., You, H., Dongarra, J.: Collecting performance data with PAPI-C. In: Müller, M.S., Resch, M.M., Schulz, A., Nagel, W.E. (eds.) Tools for High Performance Computing 2009. Springer, Heidelberg (2010)
26. Treibig, J., Hager, G., Wellein, G.: LIKWID: a lightweight performance-oriented tool suite for x86 multicore environments. In: Proceedings of PSTI2010, The First International Workshop on Parallel Software Tools and Tool Infrastructures, San Diego, CA (2010)
27. Wang, A., Gaudet, M., Wu, P., Amaral, J.N., Ohmacht, M., Barton, C., Silvera, R., Michael, M.: Evaluation of Blue Gene/Q hardware support for transactional memories. In: Proceedings of the 21st International Conference on Parallel Architectures and Compilation Techniques (PACT 2012), pp. 127–136. ACM, New York (2012)
28. Yoo, R.M., Hughes, C.J., Lai, K., Rajwar, R.: Performance evaluation of Intel transactional synchronization extensions for high-performance computing. In: Proceedings of the International Conference on High Performance Computing, Networking, Storage and Analysis (SC 2013), pp. 19:1–19:11. ACM, New York (2013)

An Executable Semantics for Synchronous Task Graphs: From SDRT to Ada

Morteza Mohaqeqi$^{(\boxtimes)}$, Jakaria Abdullah, and Wang Yi

Uppsala University, Uppsala, Sweden
{morteza.mohaqeqi,jakaria.abdullah,yi}@it.uu.se

Abstract. We study a graph-based real-time task model in which inter-task synchronization can be specified through a rendezvous mechanism. Previously, efficient methods have been proposed for timing analysis of the corresponding task sets. In this paper, we first formally specify an operational semantics for the model. Next, we describe a method for Ada code generation for a set of such task graphs. We also specify extensions of the approach to cover a notion of broadcasting, as well as global inter-release separation time of real-time jobs. We have implemented the proposed method in a graphical tool which facilitates a model-based design and implementation of real-time software.

Keywords: Automated code generation · Ada programming language · The synchronous digraph real-time task model · Schedulability analysis

1 Introduction

Safe, accurate, and efficient timing analysis of real-time applications is an important requirement in safety-critical embedded systems design. To achieve this goal, having formal models which can specify the structure and behavior of the software in an expressive way is essential. At the same time, the models utilized must be of a suitable level of abstraction, through avoiding unnecessary technical details, such that the analysis can be carried out in a reasonable time.

In the past, several models have been proposed to specify real-time workloads, ranging from the periodic and sporadic task models [7] to more complex graph-based ones [4,9,11]. These models are used to describe the computational workload, and accordingly, to perform timing analysis of the software application. While many studies concern theoretical methods for analyzing the task sets specified by these models, less attention has been paid to implementation issues. However, in practice, a designer needs to have a clear definition of the relation between modeling components and the corresponding implementation building blocks. Having such a knowledge, which helps in (automatically) generating executable programs from a set of formal models, is specially important in the model-based development paradigm [6].

In this work, we consider one of the most expressive real-time task models, i.e., Synchronous Digraph Real-Time (SDRT) [9]. SDRT extends the Digraph

© Springer International Publishing AG 2017
J. Blieberger and M. Bader (Eds.): Ada-Europe 2017, LNCS 10300, pp. 137–152, 2017.
DOI: 10.1007/978-3-319-60588-3_9

Real-Time (DRT) task model [11] by introducing inter-task synchronization through a rendezvous mechanism. Efficient analysis methods for dynamic- and fixed-priority scheduling of DRT tasks, and also for fixed-priority scheduling of SDRT tasks, have been previously proposed [9,12]. In this work, we employ a slightly extended version of SDRT and study automatic Ada code generation for the model. We opt for the Ada programming language [8] since the language primitives, specially the provided notions of task and synchronization, match very well with the SDRT task semantics.

As it will be demonstrated, the SDRT task model allows non-deterministic behavior. We attempt to resolve the non-determinism by confining the possible behaviors of an SDRT task. The goal is then to produce source code implementing the behavior such that the timing analyses (performed on (S)DRT task sets [9,11]) remain valid. In summary, the key contributions include:

- Defining a formal operational semantics for SDRT;
- Proposing a code generation approach to implement the specified semantics;
- Showing how to model global inter-release time constraints using SDRT.

In the rest of the paper, we first review related work. The syntax, as well as operational semantics, of SDRT is formally defined in Sect. 3. We present our approach for implementation of the SDRT behavior using the Ada programming language in Sects. 4 and 5. Some extensions of the method are demonstrated in Sect. 6. Concluding remarks and future work are presented in Sect. 7.

2   Related Work

Implementation of real-time tasks using the Ada programming language has been recently studied by Real et al. [10] with an emphasis on preserving release jitter constraints. For this goal, it is proposed to implement jitter-sensitive tasks in a time-triggered manner, running in the highest level of priority, combined with a number of priority-scheduled jitter-tolerant tasks. A given time-triggered plan is managed/scheduled by a *protected type* with the highest priority, which plays the role of a scheduler. Time triggered tasks synchronize with this scheduler via an entry call. In comparison, our approach can also be used to implement the structure of a time-triggered plan with SDRT. Meanwhile, the SDRT model provides more flexibility in the design of a real-time application, through, for instance, allowing to model branches and inter-task synchronizations.

One of the most relevant models to SDRT is task automaton [5] for which a code generation method is proposed in [2]. Compared to task automata, an important feature of SDRT is that the job release times criteria is separated from the application code logic. In terms of the operational semantics, unlike timed automata, SDRT tasks are not allowed to manipulate the clock variables that determine eligibility of a next job for release. In this way, minimum inter-release times are decoupled from the functionality of the jobs. This is a crucial difference which makes the schedulability analysis problem for the (S)DRT model feasible, in contrast to that of task automata which can be even undecidable in the general case [5]. The code synthesis algorithm provided for task automata in [2] suggests to manage synchronizations and scheduling events by the generated application code. In addition, the implementation of the method (integrated in the TIMES tool [3]) is platform dependent. In contrast, we leverage Ada's primitives, including the synchronization mechanism, which inherently match with the SDRT semantics. This leads to simpler and more intuitive codes. Furthermore, the generated code is hardware independent.

A first attempt to generate Ada code from SDRT models has been carried out by Abdullah et al. [1]. Compared to that work, in this paper we provide a formal operational semantics for the model, and also cover a complete semantics of SDRT including conditional branching. Moreover, we present a technique to model/implement end-to-end inter-release separation times using the SDRT synchronization mechanism.

3   Real-Time Task Graphs with Synchronization

In this work, we focus on the Synchronous Digraph Real-Time (SDRT) [9] task model, which is a graph-based model extended with inter-task synchronizations. Informally, an SDRT task is specified by a directed graph where each path of the graph represents a possible execution path of the task. By means of this model, a task which releases different types of jobs, i.e., with a variable behavior, can be modeled. In what follows, we first present a number of definitions and notations that are used throughout the paper. Then, the syntax and semantics of the SDRT task model are formally defined.

3.1   Notations

We use Σ to denote a set of action labels used to specify inter-task synchronizations. Σ is assumed to contain a *null* action, denoted by $\bot$, which shows the absence of a synchronization. Let Y denote a set of variables. A *valuation* over Y is a function which maps each variable in Y to a value from its domain. Any logical condition over the variables in Y is called a *guard*; the set of all guards is denoted by G. For a given valuation σ and a guard g, both defined over a variable set Y, we write $\sigma \models g$ to denote that σ satisfies g (i.e., the guard is evaluated to True). We also use $\mathbb{N}$ to denote the set of all non-negative integers.

3.2   Syntax

The syntax of an SDRT task is specified using a directed graph. More specifically, considering a set of actions Σ, a set of variables Y, and a set of guards G defined over Y, we define an SDRT task as follows.

Definition 1 (SDRT Task). *An SDRT task is defined as a tuple (V, v_0, E), where*

- V *is a set of vertices,*
- $v_0 \in V$ *is the initial vertex,*
- $E \subseteq V \times \mathbb{N} \times G \times \Sigma \times V$ *is a set of edges.*

Each vertex $v \in V$ represents a *job type* and is associated with a non-negative integer, $d(v)$, as its relative deadline. Each instance of a job type is called a job. A task releases a (possibly infinite) sequence of jobs according to the constraints specified by edges. Intuitively, an edge $(v_i, p, g, a, v_j) \in E$ indicates that if the latest job of the task has been released at time t_0 and is of type v_i, and also the guard g is satisfied after the completion of the job, then the task can synchronize on the action a at any time $t \geq t_0 + p$, releasing a new job of type v_j. Based on this meaning, p is called the *minimum inter-release* time. The precise semantics of an SDRT task is presented in the next subsection.

Here, we assume that exactly two tasks are involved in each synchronization, that is, there is no action $a \in \Sigma$ appearing on the edges of more than two tasks. We later relax this restriction in Sect. 6. In addition, throughout this paper, we assume constrained deadlines. This means that, for any arbitrary vertex $v \in V$, it holds that $d(v) \leq p$ for all p for which $\exists (v, p, g, a, u) \in E$.

It is worth noting that the syntax of an SDRT task has been originally defined, in [9], in a more abstract level. In this work, as we are dealing with code generation, we consider a more concrete definition. Particularly, in the current work, the task syntax is supposed to specify an initial vertex, as well as guards on edges. As this specification only restricts the behavior of a task, the existing timing analysis methods still provide a safe (although maybe a pessimistic) result.

3.3   Operational Semantics

We first make a set of assumptions based on which the SDRT semantics will be defined.

Assumption 1 (Local Access to the Variables). *Each task's variables can be accessed and updated only by the task itself (and by none of the other tasks). As a result, between the finish time of a job and the start of the next one, the value of the guards are not changed.*

We also assume that the functionality of a job of type v is specified by a function $F_v(.)$ which manipulates the task's variables. More specifically, given a current valuation σ of the task variables, $F_v(\sigma)$ denotes the valuation of the variables immediately after the execution of the job. Further, given a set of n tasks, we assume that the first job of the i-th task, for $1 \leq i \leq n$, initializes task's variables to a valuation $\sigma_{0,i}$.

The operational semantics of the SDRT task model is defined using a labeled transition system. Let $\{(V_1, v_{0,1}, E_1), \ldots, (V_n, v_{0,n}, E_n)\}$ denote a set of n SDRT tasks. A semantic state of the system is then defined as a triple $(\bar{v}, \bar{\sigma}, \bar{c})$, where

- $\bar{v} = \langle v_1, \ldots, v_n \rangle$, with $v_i \in V_i$, for $1 \leq i \leq n$, is a vector of vertices (job types), which keeps track of the type of the latest released jobs,

- $\bar{\sigma} = \langle \sigma_1, \ldots, \sigma_n \rangle$ is a vector of valuations, where σ_i denotes a valuation over the variables of the i-th task,
- $\bar{c} = \langle c_1, \ldots, c_n \rangle$ denotes a vector of n non-negative integers, referred to as *clock* variables. The value of c_i shows the time which has passed after the release of the last job of the i-th task.

Before defining the transition rules, we introduce a number of notations. Take an arbitrary vector of job types $\bar{v}$. By $\bar{v}[v_i/v_i']$, we denote the vector of job types obtained by replacing v_i with v_i' in $\bar{v}$, while the other entries of $\bar{v}$ remain unchanged. Additionally, for a vector of clocks $\bar{c}$ and a set of clock variables r, $\bar{c}[r \mapsto 0]$ denotes the vector derived from $\bar{c}$ after resetting those clock variables of $\bar{c}$ that are in r to 0. Also, for a clock vector $\bar{c} = \langle c_1, \ldots, c_n \rangle$, we define $\bar{c} + 1$ as $\bar{c}$ after incrementing each entry by one, that is $\bar{c} + 1 \doteq \langle c_1 + 1, \ldots, c_n + 1 \rangle$. Additionally, for a valuation $\bar{\sigma} = \langle \sigma_1, \ldots, \sigma_n \rangle$ and a job type $v_i \in V_i$, we define $F_{v_i}(\bar{\sigma}) \doteq \langle \sigma_1', \ldots, \sigma_n' \rangle$, where $\sigma_i' = F_{v_i}(\sigma_i)$, and $\sigma_j' = \sigma_j$ for $j \neq i$. Using these definitions, we now present the SDRT semantics.

Definition 2 (SDRT Operational Semantics). *Consider a set of SDRT tasks* $\tau = \{(V_1, v_{0,1}, E_1), \ldots, (V_n, v_{0,n}, E_n)\}$. *Also, define* $\bar{v}_0 = \langle v_{0,1}, \ldots, v_{0,n} \rangle$, $\bar{\sigma}_0 = \langle \sigma_{0,1}, \ldots, \sigma_{0,n} \rangle$, *and* $\bar{c}_0 = \langle 0, \ldots, 0 \rangle$. *The operational semantics of* τ *is defined by a labeled transition system with an initial state of* $(\bar{v}_0, \bar{\sigma}_0, \bar{c}_0)$, *and two types of transitions:*

1. *Delay transitions, denoted by* $(\bar{v}, \bar{\sigma}, \bar{c}) \xrightarrow{\delta} (\bar{v}, \bar{\sigma}, \bar{c} + 1)$, *which represent the progress of time;*
2. *Release transitions, which are associated with the release of new jobs, and include two types:*
   - $(\bar{v}, \bar{\sigma}, \bar{c}) \xrightarrow{\perp} \left(\bar{v}[v_i/v_i'], F_{v_i'}(\bar{\sigma}), \bar{c}[\{c_i\} \mapsto 0] \right)$ *if* $\exists (v_i, p, g, \perp, v_i') \in E_i$ *such that* $p \leq c_i$ *and* $\sigma_i \models g$,[1]
   - $(\bar{v}, \bar{\sigma}, \bar{c}) \xrightarrow{a} \left(\bar{v}[v_i/v_i'][v_j/v_j'], F_{v_j'}(F_{v_i'}(\bar{\sigma})), \bar{c}[\{c_i, c_j\} \mapsto 0] \right)$ *if there exist edges* $(v_i, p_1, g_1, a, v_i') \in E_i$ *and* $(v_j, p_2, g_2, a, v_j') \in E_j$ *with* $a \neq \perp$ *and* $i \neq j$ *such that* $p_1 \leq c_i$, $p_2 \leq c_j$, $\sigma_i \models g_1$, *and* $\sigma_j \models g_2$.

In this definition, the release transition rules are written assuming that a job takes its effect on the task variables immediately after its release (by applying the function $F_v()$ with no delay), while in practice, it would take some duration to execute the job. Nonetheless, this does not compromise the correctness of the semantics. The reason is that, as we consider constrained deadlines, the execution of a job is always finished before the corresponding minimum inter-release times are passed, given that the job meets its deadline. As a result, the guard conditions, which may depend on the task variables, are evaluated only after the job is completed, and its influence on the variables have taken place. Therefore, the variables are not used before the completion of the job, and thus, it does not matter when they are updated (i.e., at the beginning, or at any time

---

[1] Recall that c_i and σ_i denote the i-th entries of $\bar{c}$ and $\bar{\sigma}$, respectively.

during the execution of the job). Based on this, we can also argure that, the defined initial state corresponds to the instant exactly after the first job of each task has been released and also taken its effect.

We point out that our focus is on the job release pattern of an SDRT task set. Hence, in the system state, we do not keep track of the amount of the executed workload of a job. Nevertheless, the defined semantics truly reflects the behavior of the task set, from a release time perspective, as long as no deadline is missed.

Based on the original definition of SDRT [9] (and also DRT [11]), an edge can be taken, and the corresponding job can be released, at any time after the specified minimum inter-release time is passed (given that the other conditions are met). This entails a non-deterministic release-time, while for the implementation, we need to determine release times deterministically. We resolve this issue using the so-called *maximal progress* assumption [2]. According to this, a job is supposed to be released as soon as possible. In terms of the specified transition system, this assumption is expressed as follows.

Assumption 2 (Maximal Progress). *In the specified transition system in Definition 2, whenever there are both delay transition and release transition(s) doable, the system takes the release transition(s) first.*

The presented operational semantics provides a basis for converting an SDRT task set to an executable code. As code generation for the branching structures plays a major role in implementing an SDRT task, we treat it separately in Sect. 4. Next, in Sect. 5, we present our implementation approach for the whole task graph.

4   Code Generation for Branching Structures

A branching structure can be specified in SDRT by a vertex with multiple outgoing edges. To decide which edge must be taken, the program needs to consider the respective minimum inter-release times, guards, and also the synchronization actions. In this section, after reviewing a number of assumptions, we demonstrate our approach to implement the guard, minimum inter-release time, and synchronization criteria of a set of edges comprising a branch. We exploit the *rendezvous* mechanism of Ada for this goal. Then, we present an algorithm for implementing the complete semantics of such structures.

4.1   Assumptions

In order to follow the semantics of the Ada rendezvous, which is used for inter-task synchronization, we assume that the set of synchronization actions Σ contains two types of actions: any action a is either a *sending* action, denoted by $a!$, or a *receiving* action, denoted by $a?$. As will be seen, when generating source code for a task, sending actions are mapped to (implemented by) an **entry call**, while receiving actions are mapped to the **accept** statement of the Ada rendezvous.

While Ada provides a mechanism for a conditional *accept* (within a `select` block), there is no analogous structure for conditional *entry calls*. Hence, we need to slightly change the semantics of SDRT to comply with this restriction. For this purpose, when the guard of an edge with a sending action is satisfied and the associated minimum inter-release time is also passed, we will choose that edge to be taken (although not immediately if the receiving task is not ready at the moment), without checking the other edges any more. To formalize this, consider an arbitrary edge $e = (v, p, g, a, u)$, and an edge $e' = (v, p', g', b!, u')$ with a sending action. Edge e' is said to be *enabled* before e if $p' < p$ and g' is satisfied (irrespective of whether the rendezvous on b can be done at the moment). Given this definition, the release transition rules in Definition 2 are rewritten as:

- $(\bar{v}, \bar{\sigma}, \bar{c}) \xrightarrow{\perp} \left(\bar{v}[v_i/v_i'], F_{v_i'}(\bar{\sigma}), \bar{c}[\{c_i\} \mapsto 0]\right)$ if $\exists e = (v_i, p, g, \perp, v_i') \in E_i$ such that $p \le c_i$ and $\sigma_i \models g$, and there exists no edge outgoing from v_i in E_i with a sending action which is enabled before e;

- $(\bar{v}, \bar{\sigma}, \bar{c}) \xrightarrow{a} \left(\bar{v}[v_i/v_i'][v_j/v_j'], F_{v_j'}(F_{v_i'}(\bar{\sigma})), \bar{c}[\{c_i, c_j\} \mapsto 0]\right)$ if there exist edges $e_i = (v_i, p_1, g_1, a?, v_i') \in E_i$ and $e_j = (v_j, p_2, g_2, a!, v_j') \in E_j$ with $a \ne \perp$ and $i \ne j$ such that $p_1 \le c_i$, $p_2 \le c_j$, $\sigma_i \models g_1$, and $\sigma_j \models g_2$, and there exists no edge with a sending action outgoing from v_i in E_i enabled before e_i and also no such an edge from v_j in E_j enabled before e_j.

4.2   Realizing Basic Blocks

In order to conform with the maximal progress assumption (Assumption 2), the implemented task needs to be notified as soon as a *release* transition becomes eligible. According to the specified semantics, release transitions depend on the corresponding guards, minimum inter-release times, and synchronizations. In the following, we specify that how each of these criteria can be checked at runtime to trigger a release transition.

Guards. In edges with no synchronization, or with a sending action, the guard condition can be checked by an `if-then-else` structure. If evaluated to True, the transition will be chosen to take. However, if an edge is related to a receiving action, we will use the "conditional accept" structure of Ada to restrict the synchronization to be done only if the guard is satisfied and the edge with the corresponding sending action is also ready to be fired. This case is elaborated shortly.

Minimum Inter-release Times. To respect a minimum inter-release time between two jobs, we use the `delay until` statement of Ada, which provides a way to wait until a (absolute) time instant. As an example, consider the branching structure shown in Fig. 1a, where p_1 and p_2 denote the minimum inter-release times assuming $p_1 < p_2$. Further, assume g_1 and g_2 to denote the corresponding

(a) A choice with two edges   (b) A choice with three edges with synchronization

Fig. 1. Sample branching structures in SDRT.

guards. The Ada code generated for this part of the model is seen in Listing 1.[2] In this example, the release time of the current job, which is of type s, has been assumed to be 0.

```
   -- After completion of the last released job
   delay until p1;
   if g1 then
       next_state := u;
       goto loop_start; -- Skipping the rest
   end if;
   delay until p2;
   if g2 then
       next_state := v;
       goto loop_start;
   end if;
```

Listing 1. Implementing the branching structure shown in Fig. 1a

Synchronization. An edge with a receiving action can be fired only if the task sending that action is ready to synchronize. If there are multiple such edges having the required minimum inter-release time passed, the program needs to wait until one of the synchronizations becomes doable. We use the *selective accept* structure to implement this semantics. For example, consider the branch structure shown in Fig. 1b, where p_1, p_2, and p_3 denote the minimum inter-release times, with $p_1 < p_2 < p_3$. Further, let g_1, g_2, and g_3 denote the corresponding guards. The code presented in Listing 2 implements this structure. As seen in Lines 1 to 9, when p_1 expires, the program attempts to evaluate guard g_1, and if satisfied, synchronize on action A. If such a synchronization cannot be accomplished until p_2, then the guard g_2 is checked. If it is satisfied, the program takes the second edge (Lines 10 to 14). Otherwise, synchronization on A is tried again until p_3. If it is not performed by that time, then both the first edge and the third edge are eligible, which are tried using a selective accept block (Lines 20 to 27).

---

[2] We use `goto` to avoid lengthy and redundant codes. The same logic can be easily implemented without this statement.

```
 1    delay until p₁;
 2    select
 3        when g₁ =>
 4        accept A;
 5        next_state := u;
 6        goto loop_start;
 7    or
 8        delay until p₂;
 9    end select;
10    if g2 then
11        Task_2.B;        -- Entry call to Task_2
12        next_state := v;
13        goto loop_start;
14    end if;
15    select
16        -- Repetition of the code appeared in Lines 3 to 6
17    or
18        delay until p₃;
19    end select;
20    select      -- A selective accept
21        -- Repetition of the code appeared in Lines 3 to 6
22    or
23        when g₃ =>
24        accept C;
25        next_state := w;
26        goto loop_start;
27    end select;
```

Listing 2. Ada implementation of the branching structure shown in Fig. 1b.

4.3   Implementation Algorithm for Branching Structures

Our method for generating Ada code for the semantics of a branching structure is shown in Algorithm 1.

In Algorithm 1, the input E is the list of all outgoing edges from a certain vertex, where $E[i]$ denotes the i-th entry of E. Also, $E[i].p$ and $E[i].a$ denote the associated minimum inter-release time and synchronization action, respectively. For simplicity and without loss of generality, in the presented pseudo-code, it is assumed that the latest job has been released at time zero.

The algorithm iterates over the set of edges E. If an edge is not marked with a receiving action, then the decision for taking that edge will be made only based on the guard through the code printed by Lines 7 to 9. Otherwise, the edge is added to the set R. As a result, R contains all edges with a receiving action whose minimum inter-release time has been passed. After examining the edge, if R is empty, then the program needs to just wait until the minimum inter-release time of the next edge (if any) is passed; see Lines 13 to 16. Besides, if R is not empty, i.e., if there are pending receiving actions, the selective accept structure of Ada is used (as shown in Algorithm 2, which is called in Line 18 of Algorithm 1). In this case, the program waits for the first entry call to one of the pending accept statements, until a new edge becomes eligible, if any.

Algorithm 1. Generating Ada code for a branching structure

Input: E: List of edges sorted by inter-release times ascendingly.

```
 1: procedure BRANCHCODE(E)
 2:     n ← |E|                                    ▷ Number of entries in E
 3:     R ← {}                      ▷ Used to keep edges which have a receiving action
 4:     print("delay until " + E[1].p + ";")
 5:     for i ← 1 to n do
 6:         if E[i] is not labeled with a receiving action then
 7:             print("if " + E[i].g + " then ")
 8:             print code for taking edge E[i]
 9:             print("end if;")
10:         else
11:             R ← R ∪ {E[i]}
12:         end if
13:         if R = {} then
14:             if i ≠ n then
15:                 print("delay until " + E[i + 1].p + ";")
16:             end if
17:         else
18:             SELECTIVEACCEPT(E, R, i, n);
19:         end if
20:     end for
21: end procedure
```

Algorithm 2. Generating the selective accept code

```
 1: procedure SELECTIVEACCEPT(E, R, i, n)
 2:     print("select ")
 3:     print("when " + R[1].g + " => ")
 4:     print("accept " + R[1].a + ";")
 5:     for k ← 2 to |R| do
 6:         print("or ")
 7:         print("when " + R[k].g + " => ")
 8:         print("accept " + R[k].a + ";")
 9:     end for
10:     if i < n then
11:         print("or ")
12:         print("delay until " + E[i + 1].p + ";")
13:     end if
14:     print("end select; ")
15: end procedure
```

5   Implementation of a Task Graph

Each SDRT task graph is implemented as a `task` in Ada, running an infinite loop. Inside the loop, the graph structure is implemented by keeping track of the latest released job, and realizing the branching structures. We demonstrate it through a sample task graph shown in Fig. 2. Minimum inter-release times are assumed

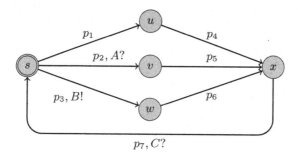

Fig. 2. A sample SDRT task T1.

as $p_1 = 100\,\text{ms}$, $p_2 = 200\,\text{ms}$, $p_3 = 500$ ms, and $p_4 = p_5 = p_6 = p_7 = 100\,\text{ms}$. Further, let g_1, g_2, and g_3 denote the guards on edges from s to u, v, and w, respectively. The guard of the other edges is assumed to be always True.

The Ada code realizing this task model is seen in Listing 3. In the task body, first, a type **State** is defined which includes a distinct value for each vertex (Line 14). The variable **Current_State** is defined of this type to store the latest released job of the task. Also, the variable **Last_Release** is defined to keep the release time of the latest released job. Additionally, minimum inter-release times are declared as constants (Lines 17 to 20). The functionality of each job type is also implemented as a procedure (Lines 22 to 31). As seen, the task priority is dynamically changed before and after execution of the job code. We will talk about priority assignment shortly.

```
1   -- Context clauses and pragmas omitted
2   procedure Taskset_1 is
3       ----   Task declaration ----
4       task T1 is              -- A singleton task
5           pragma Priority(System.Priority'Last);
6           entry A;
7           entry C;
8       end T1;
9
10      ----   task body ----
11      task body T1 is
12          ---------- Variable declaration -------
13          T1_prio : System.Any_Priority := 20;   -- Task priority
14          type State is (s, v, w, u, x);
15          Current_State : State := s;   -- The first job
16          Last_Release  : Ada.Real_Time.Time;
17          p1 : constant Time_Span := Milliseconds(100);
18          p2 : constant Time_Span := Milliseconds(200);
19          p3 : constant Time_Span := Milliseconds(500);
20          -- p4, p5, p6, p7 are defined similarly
21
22          -- Procedures for the job types of T1:
23          procedure s_code is
24          begin
25              Ada.Dynamic_Priorities.Set_Priority(T1_prio);
26              -- The code for job type s goes here
27              Ada.Dynamic_Priorities.Set_Priority(System.Priority'Last);
28          end s_code;
29
30          -- Procedures for v, u, w, and x are specified as well
31          ...
```

```
32
33              --------------- Task logic ---------------
34       begin
35          Last_Release := Clock;
36          loop
37             <<T1_loop>>
38             case Current_State is
39                when s =>
40                   s_code;
41                   delay until Last_Release + p1;
42                   if g1 then
43                      Current_State := u;
44                      Last_Release := Last_Release + p1;
45                      goto T1_loop;
46                   end if;
47                   delay until Last_Release + p2;
48                   select
49                      when g2 =>
50                      accept A;
51                      Last_Release := Clock;
52                      Current_State := v;
53                      goto T1_loop;
54                   or
55                      delay until Last_Release + p3;
56                   end select;
57                   if g3 then
58                      T2.B;              -- Entry call to task T2
59                      Last_Release := Clock;
60                      Current_State := w;
61                      goto T1_loop;
62                   end if;
63                   select
64                      -- Repetition of the code in Lines  49  to  53
65                   end select;
66                when u =>
67                   u_code;
68                   delay until Last_Release + p4;
69                   if True then
70                      Current_State := x;
71                      Last_Release := Last_Release + p4;
72                      goto T1_loop;
73                   end if;
74             -- Similar code is generated for v and w
75                   ...
76                when x =>
77                   x_code;
78                   delay until Last_Release + p7;
79                   select
80                      when True  =>
81                      accept C;
82                      Last_Release := Clock;
83                      Current_State := s;
84                      goto T1_loop;
85                   end select;
86             end case;
87          end loop;
88       end T1;
89       --------------------------------------------------
90    begin
91       null;
92    end Taskset_1;
```

Listing 3. Ada implementation of the task shown in Fig. 2

In the task implementation, the task first initializes Last_Release by the current time (in Line 35), considered as the release time of the first job. Inside the loop, Current_State is examined, through a **case** statement, to find the type of the latest released job. For each job type, Algorithm 1 is employed to implement the respective behavior. For instance, when the job type is s, a branch with three edges must be treated. After the minimum inter-release time p_1 is passed, if g_1 is True, u is selected as the next job. In addition, the current time, which would be equal to Last_Release plus p_1, is assigned as its release time (see Lines 41 to 44). If g_1 is not satisfied, the next edge must be tried. For this, after waiting until p_2 is passed, a select statement is executed. If g_2 is evaluated to True and the rendezvous on entry A can be done before p_3 is passed, the next job will be of type v (Line 52). In this case, the release time of the job is not calculated by adding p_2 to the previous release time. Instead, it is obtained by reading the current clock value (Line 51). The reason is that, in such a case, the job is released when the synchronization is done, which is determined by the other task involving in the rendezvous. The respective code for other situations is similarly generated, as seen in Lines 57 to 85.

Priority Assignment: An important step in realizing each task is determining the respective priority. For this, we note that, in our implementation, a task consists of two different types of code: codes for controlling the release timings of the jobs, and codes implementing the actual functionality of the jobs as defined by the application. An essential requirement is that the release semantics of a task must not be influenced by the execution of the jobs from other tasks. To respect this, we opt to run the logic controlling release instants of the jobs in the highest priority level. For this purpose, the initial priority of all tasks is set to the highest priority level; see Line 5 in of Listing 3. The priority of a task is then adjusted to its actual (user-defined) priority whenever it wants to execute the functionality of a job. One such dynamic priority adjustment is seen in Lines 25 and 27.

6   Extensions

This section extends our approach to cover a broadcast semantics. Additionally, we describe how an end-to-end inter-release separation time can be modeled by SDRT tasks.

6.1   Broadcasting

Up to now, we have assumed that a synchronization involves no more than two tasks. One can extend the model to include a broadcast semantics as well. In a broadcast synchronization, there may be several tasks with the same receiving action, while there is one task with the corresponding sending action. Whenever the task with the sending action wants to take the respective edge, it will try all the relevant tasks, but in a non-blocking way. For instance, consider a broadcasting on an action A, where two tasks Task1 and Task2 contain the respective receiving action. Then, the task associated with the sending action will execute the following code:

```
select
    Task1.A;
else
    null;
end select;
select
    Task2.A;
else
    null;
end select;
```

The `else` part lets the task continue its progress with no blocking if the other task is not accepting the entry at the moment.

6.2 End-to-End Inter-Release Times

Basically, in an SDRT task, the minimum inter-release time constraint can be specified only between two *consecutive* jobs. However, sometimes it is needed to respect a minimum separation time between the release of two jobs which are not necessarily released successively. As an example, in the task shown in Fig. 2, we may need to add a minimum separation time constraint between any job of type u and any subsequent job of type s. Such a constraint is called an *end-to-end* minimum inter-release separation time. In [12], a method has been proposed to transform a DRT graph with such a constraint to an ordinary DRT task. However, the obtained DRT may contain pseudo-polynomially many number of vertices compared to the original one. Instead, one can use the synchronization mechanism of SDRT to allow putting this constraint with less effort (although the computational complexity of the respective analyses may ultimately be the same).

For instance, in the mentioned example, to preserve a minimum separation time of p_8 between the jobs of type u and subsequent jobs of type s, we can

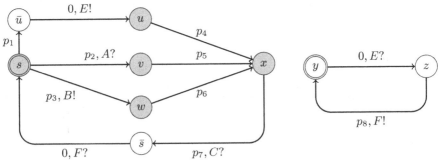

(a) Task in Fig. 2 augmented with two vertices.   (b) The auxiliary task.

Fig. 3. Modifying the task in Fig. 2 to respect an end to end inter-release time separation constraint.

add an auxiliary task with two vertices as seen in Fig. 3b. Also, we augment the DRT task in Fig. 2 with two vertices, namely $\bar{s}$ and $\bar{u}$, seen in Fig. 3a. Whenever a job of type u is released, the task sends a signal, through the action $E!$, to the auxiliary task. On the other side, in order for a job of type s to be released, the task synchronizes on the signal F. According to Fig. 3b, this can be done not earlier than p_8 time units after the release of u's instance. In this way, a job of type s may be released only if the intended delay after the last release of u is observed.

7   Conclusion and Future Work

In this paper we defined an operational semantics for the SDRT task model and provided a method for generating Ada code for this semantics. The method has been implemented in a graphical tool.[3] Also, we discussed extensions of the approach to cover a broadcast synchronization, as well as global and end-to-end inter-release time constraints.

As a future work, we want to formally prove that the provided implementation conforms to the model, i.e., it does not generate a behavior not specified by the SDRT semantics (when neglecting scheduling overheads). Another direction of extending this work is to tackle the model non-determinism. The semantics provided in this work does not specify a deterministic choice in the release of new jobs when more than one are possible at the same time; the actual behavior of the implemented program depends on the Ada run-time system. But, it may be possible to assign a priority to the transitions, and then, utilizing existing mechanisms in Ada, such as `pragma Queuing_Policy`, to preserve orderings enforced by such priorities.

References

1. Abdullah., J., Mohaqeqi, M., Yi, W.: Synthesis of Ada code from graph-based task models. In: 32nd Symposium on Applied Computing, pp. 1466–1471 (2017)
2. Amnell, T., Fersman, E., Pettersson, P., Yi, W., Sun, H.: Code synthesis for timed automata. Nordic J. Comput. **9**(4), 269–300 (2002)
3. Amnell, T., Fersman, E., Mokrushin, P., Pettersson, Yi, W.: TIMES - a tool for modelling and implementation of embedded systems. In: 8th International Conference on Tools and Algorithms for the Construction and Analysis of Systems (TACAS), pp. 460–464 (2002)
4. Sanjoy, K.B.: The non-cyclic recurring real-time task model. In: Real-Time Systems Symposium (RTSS), pp. 173–182 (2010)
5. Fersman, E., Krcal, P., Pettersson, P., Yi, W.: Task automata: schedulability, decidability and undecidability. J. Inf. Comput. **205**(8), 1149–1172 (2007)
6. Kim, B., Feng, L., Sokolsky, O., Lee, I.: Platform-specific code generation from platform-independent timed models. In: Real-Time Systems Symposium (RTSS), pp. 75–86 (2015)

---

[3] The tool is not publicly released at the moment of writing this work. A primary version is available at http://user.it.uu.se/~mormo492/TimesPro.zip.

7. Liu, C.L., Layland, J.W.: Scheduling algorithms for multiprogramming in a hard-real-time environment. J. ACM **20**(1), 46–61 (1973)
8. McCormick, J.W., Singhoff, F., Hugues, J.: Building Parallel, Embedded, and Real-Time Applications with Ada. Cambridge University Press, Cambridge (2011)
9. Mohaqeqi, M., Abdullah, J., Guan, N., Yi, W.: Schedulability analysis of synchronous digraph real-time tasks. In: 28th Euromicro Conference on Real-Time Systems (ECRTS), pp. 176–186 (2016)
10. Real, J., Sáez, S., Crespo, A.: Combining time-triggered plans with priority scheduled task sets. In: 21st Ada-Europe International Conference on Reliable Software Technologies, pp. 195–212 (2016)
11. Stigge, M., Ekberg, P., Guan, N., Yi, W.: The digraph real-time task model. In: 17th IEEE Real-Time and Embedded Technology and Applications Symposium, pp. 71–80 (2011)
12. Stigge, M.: Real-time workload models: expressiveness vs. analysis efficiency. Ph.D. thesis, Uppsala University (2014)

RxAda: An Ada implementation
of the ReactiveX API

Alejandro R. Mosteo[1,2](✉)

[1] Instituto de Investigación en Ingeniería de Aragón (I3A),
Mariano Esquillor s/n, 50018 Zaragoza, Spain
[2] Centro Universitario de la Defensa de Zaragoza (CUD),
Ctra. de Huesca s/n, 50090 Zaragoza, Spain
amosteo@unizar.es

Abstract. The ReactiveX API, also known as the Reactive Extensions in the .NET world, is a recently popularized reactive programming framework for asynchronous, event-based, multi-threaded programming. Presented by its proponents as a solid tool for applications requiring a simple yet powerful approach to event-driven systems, it has seen favorable adoption in many popular languages. Although Ada has been long-favored by powerful tasking capabilities that reduce the need for additional multi-threading support, the reactive approach has properties that are well-suited to the safety and maintainability culture predominant in the Ada world, such as complexity reduction, race-condition and deadlock avoidance, and enhanced maintainability by means of concise and well-defined information flows. This work presents the design for a ReactiveX Ada implementation that aims to balance desirable library properties such as compile-time checks, reasonable user-required generic instantiations, and a shallow learning curve for both library clients and maintainers. The Ada programmer can henceforth benefit from the abundant documentation existing for the language-agnostic ReactiveX approach without stepping out of the Ada tool chain.

Keywords: ReactiveX · Observer pattern · Reactive programming · Ada 2012

1 Introduction

Modern applications are becoming increasingly complex, in many cases driven by external events with unpredictable latencies caused by user interaction, external sources of information, or remote components in distributed systems, for example. Such changes in turn require modifications to local states and generate new internal or remote events. The reactive programming paradigm [9] arises as a response to the challenge of implementing such systems, in which imperative languages have shown shortcomings: the traditional model in which the program imposes the control flow is reversed, becoming a loop that awaits for events to which is necessary to react. This reversal of the logic flow presents challenges [1],

© Springer International Publishing AG 2017
J. Blieberger and M. Bader (Eds.): Ada-Europe 2017, LNCS 10300, pp. 153–166, 2017.
DOI: 10.1007/978-3-319-60588-3_10

like poor understanding by novice programmers, unresponsive systems that fail to exploit parallelism, convoluted state management, among others. A traditional approach has been callbacks, which typically present difficulties to scalability. The interactions between callbacks through shared states can rapidly become too complex, and callbacks themselves can be spread through many locations, complicating maintenance tasks. The term *callback hell* [4] is not unheard of.

The reactive paradigm is not particularly novel; formalization efforts have been shown [13], and proposals using the Ada syntax have been described [12]. It is however relatively recently that reactive programming has become popular, with examples like the .NET standard reactive extensions [10], subsequently ported to many languages, and the publication of the Reactive Manifesto [2]. At least part of the appeal in reactive programming is the ability for the imperative programmer to represent logical sequences much like in typical imperative syntax, while retaining control of the concurrency involved, and without requiring complex state management. By generalizing the observer pattern [6], the ReactiveX approach [10] to reactive programming provides composable abstractions [5] that allow programmers to represent responses to events as complete information flows that dynamically transform data, simultaneously removing concerns about blocking input-output.

This work presents a high-level port of the ReactiveX framework to the Ada 2012 language, named as RxAda [8], focusing on design aspects of the implementation. Ada, lacking functional facilities of other languages like lambda functions and implicit instantiation, presents challenges in the way of a practical ReactiveX implementation which the authors have addressed by means of a combination of object-oriented and generic-based design. The paper is written assuming no prior knowledge of the ReactiveX framework and highlights aspects of the library that are relevant to would-be users, and that could also be interesting to Ada architects and practitioners in general.

The paper is structured as follows: Sect. 2 introduces with examples the basics of the ReactiveX framework. Section 3 discusses RxAda design challenges and the solutions adopted with its advantages and drawbacks. Next, Sect. 4 presents library organization details of relevance to users and maintainers. Lastly, concluding remarks and future directions close the paper in Sect. 5.

2   Reactive Extensions Overview

The definitions of the main concepts that transpire the ReactiveX API are presented before some introductory examples. In-depth documentation is available at the official website [10]. In the following presentation, italized words are Rx-specific jargon with precise meaning, whereas fixed-size font is used for Rx types and subprograms. Since RxAda has followed where possible the RxJava specification [7], its documentation would be the most useful to new RxAda users. Also, some Java examples are provided for comparison.

The foundation of the ReactiveX approach are the `Observable` and `Observer` interfaces, along with the Rx grammar (also termed the reactive contract [11]).

An observer *subscribes* to an observable, after which it may receive at any time a new datum (an *item*) from the observable via the observer On_Next subprogram. The RxAda implementation of these interfaces is shown in Listing 2.1. Per the reactive contract (in POSIX-like regular expression syntax),

$$On\_Next^*(On\_Complete|On\_Error)?,$$

after subscribing, the observer may receive any number of On_Next calls (even none) possibly followed by either On_Complete, to mark the end of the sequence, or On_Error, if something untoward happened upstream, but not both, and never more than once. Also part of the contract is that these three methods will always be called in mutual exclusion in a given observer, thus freeing implementers from local concurrency concerns. Since data propagation is performed by the observable calling On_Next on its subscribers, it is clear that Rx is a push-based framework. Observers cannot know when a new item will arrive, nor can they request items at will.

Listing 2.1. Ada interfaces for the Rx contract in package Rx.Contracts

```
generic
   type T (<>) is private; -- T is the type to be received by the Observer
package Rx.Contracts is

   type Observer is interface; -- Someone interested in receiving data

   procedure On_Next     (This : in out Observer; V : T) is abstract;
   procedure On_Complete (This : in out Observer) is abstract;
   procedure On_Error    (This : in out Observer; Error : Errors.Occurrence) is abstract;
   -- Errors encapsulate an Exception_Occurrence

   type Observable is interface; -- An emitter of data to which an observer can subscribe

   procedure Subscribe (Producer : in out Observable;
                        Consumer : in out Observer'Class) is abstract;

end Rx.Contracts;
```

Although superficially similar to traditional callback programming with an enriched dynamic behavior, the true expressiveness of the Rx approach emanates from its *operators*, which are themselves both observables and observers that can be composed one after another, with each operator implementing a modification to be applied to the items traveling through them. In other words, a chain or sequence of observables can be built, rooted at some source observable. When an observer subscribes to this chain, the root observable will begin emitting data by calling the On_Next in the next operator in the chain. Operators apply their action and push down the item until it reaches the subscriber.

To illustrate these concepts, an example in both Java and Ada is presented in Listing 2.2. It is worth stressing that concatenating operators does not trigger a subscription. Thus, operators are passive elements that by themselves do not cause an observable to start emitting items[1]. Figure 1 details these aspects of Rx operation.

---

[1] A related Rx concept that does create a subscription is a **Subject**, that is out of the scope of this introduction. This is of importance for *cold* observables, which is another Rx concept left out of this introduction.

Listing 2.2. Rx Java/Ada example. For conciseness, appropriate functions used in the Ada example are assumed to exist, and "use" clauses are omitted. The complete compilable example can be found at `https://goo.gl/7bh97d`

```
{
  rx.Observable
    .interval(1, TimeUnit.SECONDS)
      // The interval observable is a counter
         that emits successive values
         separated by the given time period
         in a background Thread
    .observeOn(Schedulers.computation())
      // Switch the data flow to a computation
         thread
    .map(Object::toString)
      // Method reference notation
    .map(s -> s.hashCode())
      // Lambda notation
    .observeOn(Schedulers.io())
      // Switch to an Input/Output thread
    .subscribe(System.out::println);
}
// Java allows ignoring the returned
   subscription, whereas the Ada example has
   to explicitly capture it.
// Java benefits from implicit instantiation and
   in-line lambda expressions, introduced
   with Java 8
```

```
declare
  S : Subscription :=
    Interval (First => 1, Period => 1.0) &
      -- The RxAda Interval observable uses
         Duration as the time unit, and
         uses Ada tasks to implement Rx
         threads
    Observe_On (Schedulers.Computation) &
      -- Switch to a computation task
    Map (Image'Access) &
      -- Image takes an Integer and returns
         its String image
    Map (String_Hash'Access) &
      -- E.g. instance of System.String_Hash,
      -- returns an Integer
    Observe_On (Schedulers.IO) &
      -- Switch to an Input/Output thread
    Subscribe (Put_Line'Access);
begin
  null; -- At this point the previous chain is
         already subscribed and hence active.
end; -- In RxAda, lambda functions are replaced
       by either accesses to functions or
       overridable interfaces from Rx.Actions
```

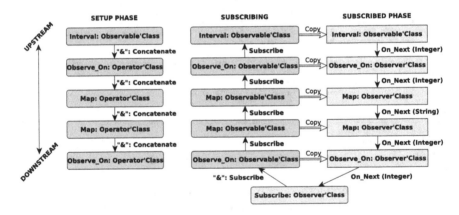

Fig. 1. Anatomy of a data chain in RxAda (based on Listing 2.2). During the setup phase (leftmost), operators are concatenated one after the other with the "&" function, hence the program flow goes from top to bottom. When an observer subscribes (center) using the overloaded "&" function, the subscription progresses from bottom to top via `Subscribe` calls until reaching the source observable, that emits the items. It is at this time that operators are copied, so that each potential subscriber gets fresh operators, as later explained in Listing 2.3. Once the subscribed phase starts, item propagation takes place from source observable to subscribed observer, with each operator in turn applying its operation before pushing down the item. The relevant interfaces for each stage are indicated after the object name. Rounded boxes are used to indicate passive chains, whereas sharp ones indicate a live subscription.

Indeed, the process of chain building and subscription can be separated in two parts as exemplified in Listing 2.3. As a consequence, while chain building is synchronous (that is, it happens as the program execution reaches that point), the data flow may be asynchronous to the program flow, which is sometimes a confusing point for beginners. For example, in Listing 2.2, one item is emitted per second, in some unspecified Rx task, whereas the main program task can be anywhere else. Another important property is that fresh operators are used for each subscription, meaning that both subscribers in Listing 2.3 will see the same final count instead of a cumulative count.

Listing 2.3. Separated chain building and subscription. Each subscription causes the From observable to emit its items, and both subscribers will see the same final count, since a fresh Count operator instance is created for each subscription.

```
declare
    S1, S2 : Rx.Subscriptions.Subscription; -- A subscription is returned when subscribing to allow
                                    -- asynchronous premature cancellation of a flow
    Chain  : Rx.Std.Integers.Observable'Class :=
        Rx.Std.Integers.From (1, 2, 3, 4, 5) &   -- From emits these five integers in sequence
        Rx.Std.Integers.Filter (Is_Even'Access) & -- Filter drops items not passing the test
            -- function Is_Even (I : Integer) return Boolean declared elsewhere
        Rx.Std.Count; -- Emits the count of items received when On_Complete arrives, and completes
begin
    S1 := Chain & Subscribe (On_Next => Rx.Debug.Print'Access); -- Prints 2
    S2 := Chain & Subscribe (On_Next => Rx.Debug.Print'Access); -- Prints 2 too
end;
```

Another observation to be made is that Rx is lazy in regard to task creation [11], and the user should assume that tasks are reused unless explicitly requested by scheduling operators or otherwise necessary for the operator proper working (as in the Interval example in Listing 2.2). That is, in the example in Listing 2.3, all data emission, filtering, counting and output will happen in the task that performs the subscription, because no scheduling operators like Observe_On have been used.

Going back to the basic example in Listing 2.2, the main visual difference is that Java uses dot notation to create Rx chains (also termed flows), whereas in Ada the "&" operator has been chosen. The reasons will become apparent in the next section. To summarize this Rx introduction:

- Anything that can be made observable can serve as the root of a chain.
- There are two distinct *setup* and *subscribed* phases.
- A chain is a pipeline in which items are sent, one at a time, to subscribers.
- Operators are composable and during the subscribed phase they perform data transformations on one item at a time until the final result is delivered to the subscribed observer.
- Each subscription is isolated from others that use the same chain.
- Once a flow completes or errs, no further data will reach the observer.

The takeaway from this Rx introduction is that operator chains allow the representation of item transformations in a naturally ordered flow with cohesive temporal logic that includes task switching. Hence, operators may take as much time as needed without blocking concerns and spaghetti callback jumps, letting the user focus on the application logic.

3   RxAda Design

In this section some all-pervasive design decisions are discussed. More precisely, the genericity model of the library is first introduced. This model in turn affects the library implementation facilities and the way clients can use the library. The general dependency architecture is summarized last.

3.1   Typed Operators

As evidenced by Listing 2.1, observers receive items of a single type in On_Next calls. Observables, in turn, must be aware of this type to be able to call On_Next on subscribers. Seemingly not a big deal, (e.g. any collection library has the stored type as a generic formal), the inconvenience arises from operators that transform the type being emitted. Operators exhibit both observable and observer interfaces, but not necessarily of the same type. For example, the Map operator allows the conversion or processing of a type into another by means of a function parameter that, given the upstream incoming type, returns a possibly different type that is passed downstream. Listing 3.1 shows the Java specification:

Listing 3.1. Map operator definition in RxJava

```
public class Observable<T> { // T is the type emitted by this observable

    public final <R> Observable<R> map(Func1<? super T,? extends R> func);
    // R is the result of func, and the type emitted by the observable returned by Map

    // Other operators omitted
}
```

This is par for the course with implicit instances in Java or C++. In Ada, however, this requires instances with two formal parameter types, or two instances with the second one nested inside the first one. An alternative design was considered which would have eliminated the need for these instantiations. A root interface type could be declared, like demonstrated in Listing 3.2:

Listing 3.2. Possible definition not requiring generic user types

```
package Rx.Contracts is -- No longer generic

    type Rx_Item is interface;

    type Observer is interface; -- Someone interested in receiving data
    procedure On_Next (This : in out Observer; V : Rx_Item'Class) is abstract;
```

This approach is tempting from a developer point of view since it removes numerous instantiations when using the library. Furthermore, the whole library can become non-generic. The price is, however, the lack of type consistency checks between chained operators at compile time, since all of them would deal with the same Rx_Item'Class classwide data. Furthermore, user types would have to be made descendants of the root Rx_Item interface, which is a distributed pollution imposed outside of the library and may discomfort some users. In addition, user functions should either perform casts that could fail at runtime or generic marshallers should be instantiated for convenience (that could not be compile-time checked anyway).

For these reasons this approach was not adopted. The consequence, imposed by Ada's explicit nature, is that one instantiation is needed per user type involved in a chain. To mitigate the issue for beginners, and since some operators emit known data types (e.g., Count emits integers), String, Integer and Float types come preinstantiated and ready for use in the package Rx.Std in RxAda.

The materialization of a user type, from an RxAda implementer point of view, is in package Rx.Impl.Typed. This package is used as a generic formal through the rest of the implementation, and contains information related to a user type in relation with the Rx contract that other parts of the RxAda implementation require. A traits-based approach [3] is used for user types, enabling storage control. See Listing 3.3 for details.

Listing 3.3. RxAda helper implementation package for a user type

```
generic
    with package Type_Traits is new Rx.Traits.Types (<>);
    -- Traits are used to efficiently work with both definite and indefinite user types
package Rx.Impl.Typed is

    subtype T is Type_Traits.T; -- Remember that T (<>) is the user supplied type

    package Contracts is new Rx.Contracts     (T);
    package Actions   is new Rx.Actions.Typed (T);

    subtype Observable is Contracts.Observable;
    subtype Observer   is Contracts.Observer;

    -- And more...
```

3.2   Type Transformations

Once it is accepted that observers are statically typed, the issue of chaining operators arises. In Java, as seen in the Map example, the Map operator is a primitive operation of the Observable type. In Ada, primitive operations must be declared in the same package as the type. Hence, to use the same dot notation for operator chaining, all operators should be declared within the same Observable package. Unfortunately, when two types are involved a new instantiation would be required, which would no longer be primitive. Alternatively, a single instantiation with two types could be adopted, but then operators that preserve the type (e.g. the Filter operator) would be repeated if several packages with the same input type existed. Another problem in this case would be that for circular conversions (from Integer to String and back to Integer), an obvious circular dependence for the instantiations would appear.

These reasons preclude a natural Ada solution that uses dot notation. The adopted solution in RxAda is the use, as in the C++ implementation, of a binary operator function. Whereas C++ uses the pipe "|" operator, in Ada the "&" operator was chosen, which furthermore already conveys the sense of concatenation to Ada programmers. This is realized as seen in Listing 3.4 where the root Operator class of RxAda is defined.

Listing 3.4. RxAda root package for operators

```
generic
   with package From is new Rx.Impl.Typed (<>);
   with package Into is new Rx.Impl.Typed (<>);
package Rx.Impl.Transformers is

   -- The package receives its name from the fact that the input and output types can be different

   type Operator is new          -- Base operator implementation type
      From.Contracts.Observer and -- Observes data of From.T type
      Into.Contracts.Observable  -- Emits data of Into.T type
      with private;

   overriding procedure On_Next (This : in out Operator; V : From.T) is abstract;
   -- Observes pushed data of From.T type

   overriding procedure Subscribe (This : in out Operator; Observer : in out Into.Observer'Class);
   -- Can be subscribed to by observers of Into.T type

   function "&" (Producer : From.Contracts.Observable'Class;
                 Consumer : Operator'Class)
                 return Into.Contracts.Observable'Class;
   -- By making "&" asymmetric, all kinds of properly type-checked chains can be set up
   -- This operator is also renamed as Concatenate
```

As evidenced by the parameters accepted by "&", users have to perform an additional instantiation for every conversion between types, in the proper From→Into direction of transformation. And, since "&" is defined for two precise types, the proper consistency checks for operators forming a chain are performed at compile time. The second parameter of "&" is returned under its Observable'Class view, to be used as first parameter of a subsequent "&" call. Listing 3.5 shows again the initial example of Listing 2.2, this time detailing the different types involved. Other packages shown therein are explained in the following subsections.

Listing 3.5. Detail of "&"-related types with explicit package names

```
-- A fictitious syntax is used in the right-side comments to indicate both the base interface of the
      types and the user type (between parentheses) with which the packages are instantiated (through
      instances of package Typed)

-- package Rx.Std contains instances ready for use for Integer and String types

package Integers renames Rx.Std.Integers;
package Strings  renames Rx.Std.Strings;
package Int_To_Str renames Rx.Std.Integer_To_String;
package Str_To_Int renames Rx.Std.String_To_Integer;

S : Rx.Subscriptions.Subscription :=     -- Allows termination and liveness checking
    Integers.Interval (First => 1, Period => 1.0)  -- Contracts (Integer).Observable'Class
    &                                    -- Concatenation using Preservers (Integer)."&"
    Integers.Observe_On (Rx.Schedulers.Computation) -- Preservers (Integer).Operator'Class
    &                                    -- Concatenation using Transformers (Integer, String)."&"
    Int_To_Str.Map (Image'Access)        -- Transformers (Integer, String).Operator'Class
    &                                    -- Concatenation using Preservers (String)."&"
    Str_To_Int.Map (String_Hash'Access)  -- Transformers (String, Integer).Operator'Class
    &                                    -- Concatenation using Preservers (Integer)."&"
    Integers.Observe_On (Schedulers.IO)  -- Preservers (Integer).Operator'Class
    &                                    -- Subscription using Contracts (Integer)."&"
    Integers.Subscribe (Put_Line'Access); -- Contracts (Integer).Sink'Class
```

3.3   Type-Preserving Operators

With the design explained up to this point, the basic pieces are in place for
the actual implementation of Rx operators. For the issue of type-preserving
operators, the Rx.Transformers package can be directly specialized and reused,
as shown in Listing 3.6.

Listing 3.6. Specialization for type-preserving operators

```
generic
   with package Typed is new Rx.Impl.Typed (<>);
package Rx.Impl.Preservers is

   package Transform is new Rx.Transformers (Typed, Typed);
   -- The same type is received and emitted

   subtype Operator is Transform.Operator; -- Just a shortcut

   function "&" (Producer : Typed.Contracts.Observable'Class;
                 Consumer : Operator'Class)
                 return Typed.Contracts.Observable'Class renames Transform. "&";
   -- Where in Transformer From and Into had to be specified, here Typed suffices,
   -- since both received and emitted types are one and the same
```

3.4   Observers of Several Types and Mutual Exclusion Enforcing

To close the topic of types and operators, a last case has to be considered.
A number of complex operators are able to observe observables of different types
at the same time. For example, a variant of the Sample operator emits the last
seen item from upstream whenever another observable, the sampler, emits an
item whose type is not significant, discarding the rest of upstream items. This
is prototyped in Java as:

```
public final <U> Observable<T> sample(Observable<U> sampler)
// U is the unimportant sampler item type. This operator subscribes to sampler, emitting the last
     observed item from upstream whenever sampler emits one item too
```

Other operators, like Merge or Flatmap, also can receive items from several
observables at the same time. Upstream observables have no way to synchronize
their emissions, which requires enforcing of the mutual exclusion contract at the
point where these observables converge in a single operator. To support that
kind of complex operators, RxAda defines a Multiobserver specific type, which
simplifies maintenance by centralizing the mutual exclusion support and shallow
copy low-level memory management needed for observers subscribed to several
observables.

Mutual exclusion, in Ada, would typically be done with a protected type.
However, there are at least two reasons to avoid this choice in the Rx case. For
once, user supplied functions can last an unknown time, and should hence not
be performed inside a protected call. Furthermore, if items were emitted from
within a protected subprogram, any call further down the chain to a blocking
operation (for example in user-supplied code) would result in a bounded error. To
avoid these pitfalls, semaphores are used internally and transparently to operator
implementers and users. Relevant parts of the multiobserver specification are
shown in Listing 3.7.

Listing 3.7. Multiobserver specification

```
generic
   with package Transformer is new Rx.Impl.Transformers (<>); -- Items being transformed
   with package Observable is new Rx.Impl.Typed (<>);        -- Secondary observed items
package Rx.Impl.Multiobservers is

   type Operator (<>) is new Transformer.Operator with private;
   -- The in-chain operator; specialization is prevented with unknown discriminant

   type Observer (<>) is new Observable.Contracts.Observer with private;
   -- Observer type for the out-of-chain observables

   type Multiobserver is abstract tagged limited private;
   -- This is the support type that operator implementations must override.
   -- This type takes care of mutual exclusion and shallow references

   not overriding procedure On_Next (Multi    : in out Multiobserver;
                                     Op        : in out Operator'Class;
                                     V         :        Transformer.From.T) is abstract;
   -- In-chain values arrive here, thanks to the Operator parameter

   not overriding procedure On_Next (Multi    : in out Multiobserver;
                                     Obs       : in out Observer'Class;
                                     V         :        Observable.T) is abstract;
   -- Out-of-chain values arrive here, thanks to the Observer parameter

   type Multiobserver_Access is access Multiobserver'Class;

   function Create_Operator (Multi : Multiobserver_access) return Operator;
   -- The operator implementer must supply a multiobserver instance to be shared

   function Create_Observer (From : in out Operator) return Observer'Class;
   -- Creation of aditional observers that can watch out-of-chain observables
```

3.5   Executing the Subscription

Previous examples ended the chain with a function named `Subscribe` (e.g. List-ing 3.5). In RxAda, to distinguish between a regular operator concatenation and an actual subscription, and for uniformity, the "&" symbol is used too, but with a different parameter profile. As shown in Listing 3.8, a specific `Sink` inter-face is used that disambiguates for the compiler the precise "&" being called. The returned `Subscription` is in practice a hidden reference-counted pointer to a shared atomic boolean that can be used to externally and asynchronously terminate a subscription, or check its liveness.

Listing 3.8. Subscription-related declarations

```
   type Sink is abstract new Observer with private;
   -- Specialized type to recognize subscription intent and store a shared Subscription.
   -- The shared subscription is returned by the following "&" function

   function "&" (Producer : Observable'Class; Consumer : Sink'Class) return Subscription;
   -- The actual function that calls to Producer.Subscribe (Consumer)

   function Subscribe (Using : Observer'Class) return Sink'Class;
   -- Function that wraps a regular Observer into a Sink.
   -- A version taking procedure accesses for On_Next, On_Complete and On_Error is also available.
   -- See Rx.Subscribe for details
```

3.6   Dependencies and User Instantiations

To conclude this section, dependencies between the already seen parts of the library are graphically depicted in Fig. 2. At this point the reader might rightfully wonder how many and of which package instances should be created to be able to use RxAda. To ease initial learning curve and for simple use cases, RxAda provides two packages that take care of the finer details with sensible defaults, so the new user needs basically to choose between `Rx.Definites` or `Rx.Indefinites` as the entry point into RxAda. These packages take as formal only the user type (see Listing 3.9) and create instances of all single-type observables, ready for use. Finer storage control is available through `Rx.Types`. To obtain operators that transform between types, there is the `Rx.Operators` package for that purpose. For even finer control, the user can dive into the individual operator packages, whose organization is described in the next section.

Listing 3.9. Simplest packages for user instantiations

```
generic
   with package Type_Traits is new Rx.Traits.Types (<>);
package Rx.Types is
   -- Default operator instantiations with user-specified storage
end Rx.Types;
```

```
generic
   type T is private;
package Rx.Definites is
   -- Default operator instantiations optimized
            for definite types
end Rx.Definites;
```

```
generic
   type T (<>) is private;
package Rx.Indefinites is
   -- Default operator instantiations using
            standard Holders whenever necessary
end Rx.Indefinites;
```

4   Library Organization

The RxAda library has been structured in several package families to simplify its maintenance and understanding. For example, the already seen `Rx.Impl.*` hierarchy contains packages that would rarely be of interest for final users, and that contain most of the logic implementing the Rx framework. Other similar branches are presented next, concluding with the multithreading support facilities, which is particularly interesting given that it is the part of Rx that enables such flexible tasking.

4.1   User-Facing Packages

An effort has been made to isolate as much as possible packages that users of the library may want to eventually know about from other implementation packages. This separation is visible in two ways: in the on-disk file organization and in the package names. Source files (available at [8]) are classified in three folders. A first, root folder named `src` contains user-facing packages, like the ones discussed at the end of the previous section. Within this folder, another one named `priv` contains the specifications of implementation packages. Finally, a sibling folder `body` contains all bodies of the library. In summary, basic users

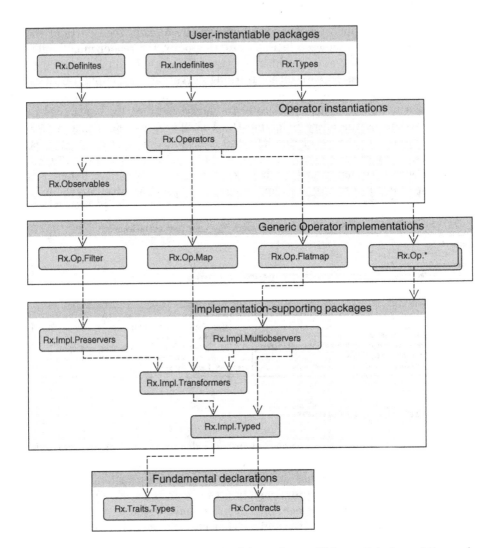

Fig. 2. Dependencies between some RxAda packages. This partial view of the package hierarchy represents the basic interactions described in Sect. 3. From bottom to top: `Rx.Contracts` declares the interfaces for the Reactive Contract, whereas `Rx.Traits.Types` is a generic package where the user specifies a definite representation for an indefinite type, and the proper conversions. The `Rx.Impl.Typed` package takes a user type and combines it with the Rx contract via implementation packages, not shown here. The rest of `Rx.Impl.*` packages depicted are successive specializations of the Operator implementation infrastructure. The `Rx.Op.*` packages are the actual Rx operator implementations, which in turn can be instantiated directly by an advanced user, or through the convenience packages seen in the top layer.

should concern themselves with the `src` folder whereas advanced users might have interest at some point in the `priv` folder too. Packages in the `src` folder are directly named as `Rx.<Name>`, while implementation packages in `priv` follow a `Rx.<Specialization>.<Name>` convention, as detailed next.

4.2   General Implementation Packages

As seen, implementation packages without a more specific classification belong in the `Rx.Impl.*` hierarchy. These packages deal with Rx concepts, contrarily to non-Rx-specific supporting packages (that might as well be provided by third-party libraries, although there no external dependencies at present) that are in `Rx.Tools.*`. The supporting packages include, for example, reentrant semaphores and thread-safe reference-counting pointers used in the few operators that must be shallow-shared with unknown numbers of Observables (that is, those implementing the Multiobserver interface). The rest of the operators mostly rely on copy semantics during chain formation, and reference accesses during data flow, simplifying the library memory management.

4.3   Operator Implementations

To distinguish between observables that create items (sources) and operators that transform data, these packages are classified respectively under the `Rx.Src.*` and `Rx.Op.*` hierarchies, although Rx documentation refers to them indistinctly as operators.

4.4   Scheduling Packages

As seen in the example Listing 2.2, Rx allows simple yet powerful task management. As in other Rx implementations, users need only to use the `Rx.Schedulers` package facilities for task control. The actual implementation of tasking events and pools that are used in `Rx.Schedulers` and the `Subscribe_On`, `Observe_On` operators is filed under the `Rx.Dispatchers.*` branch. An abstract `Dispatcher` interface is defined that allows scheduling events in a particular scheduler at a particular time; this is used to implement the different specialized task pools recommended in the Rx documentation (e.g., I/O and background computation).

5   Conclusions

This work presented an Ada 2012 implementation of the ReactiveX approach to reactive programming. The focus was placed on design and implementation decisions adopted to address the challenges arising from the imperative nature of Ada, tagged types syntax, lack of implicit instantiations of generics and lambda functions, and explicit memory management. The implementation aims at balancing user comfort, maintenance simplicity, and correctness and performance issues such as compile-time type checking. To that end the library is structured in two main layers: the upper layer exposes the operators to users with purely client needs in a type-centric manner, with a single generic instantiation per type and per transformation between types. The lower layer contains features needed for library expansion and advanced client use like the definition of new operators or selective instantiation of parts of the library.

Future work is needed to assess the performance of the library against implementations in other languages. Support for more operator variants and the `Subject` interface is also in the implementation pipeline.

RxAda is available under an Open Source license to interested parties.

Aknowledgements. This work has been supported by projects RoboChallenge (DPI2016-76676-R-AEI/FEDER-UE) and Alerta (CUD2016-17). The author thanks the regulars at `comp.lang.ada` for insightful discussions and the AdaCore support team for their prompt response to bugs uncovered during RxAda development.

References

1. Bainomugisha, E., Carreton, A.L., Cutsem, T.V., Mostinckx, S., Meuter, W.D.: A survey on reactive programming. ACM Comput. Surv. **45**(4), 52:1–52:34 (2013)
2. Bonér, J., Farley, D., Kuhn, R., Thompson, M.: The Reactive Manifesto (2014). http://www.reactivemanifesto.org/
3. Briot, E.: Traits-based containers (2015). http://blog.adacore.com/traits-based-containers
4. Edwards, J.: Coherent reaction. In: Proceedings of the 24th ACM SIGPLAN Conference Companion on Object Oriented Programming Systems Languages and Applications, OOPSLA 2009, pp. 925–932. ACM, New York (2009)
5. Elliott, C.M.: Push-pull functional reactive programming. In: Proceedings of the 2nd ACM SIGPLAN Symposium on Haskell, Haskell 2009, pp. 25–36. ACM (2009)
6. Gamma, E., Helm, R., Johnson, R., Vlissides, J.: Design Patterns: Elements of Reusable Object-Oriented Software. Addison-Wesley Longman, Inc., Boston (1995)
7. Maglie, A.: ReactiveX and RxJava. In: Reactive Java Programming, pp. 1–9. Springer, New York (2016)
8. Mosteo, A.R.: RxAda (2017). https://bitbucket.org/amosteo/rxada
9. Salvaneschi, G., Margara, A., Tamburrelli, G.: Reactive programming: a walkthrough. In: 2015 IEEE/ACM 37th IEEE International Conference on Software Engineering, vol. 2, pp. 953–954, May 2015
10. ReactiveX: An API for asynchronous programming with observable streams. http://reactivex.io/
11. Rx design guidelines. https://blogs.msdn.microsoft.com/rxteam/2010/10/28/rx-design-guidelines/
12. Thornley, J.: Parallel programming with declarative Ada. Technical report, Caltech (1993)
13. Wan, Z., Hudak, P.: Functional reactive programming from first principles. In: Proceedings of the ACM SIGPLAN 2000 Conference on Programming Language Design and Implementation, PLDI 2000, pp. 242–252. ACM, New York (2000)

Panel: The Future of Safety-Minded Languages

A New Ravenscar-Based Profile

Patrick Rogers[1]([✉]), Jose Ruiz[2], Tristan Gingold[2],
and Patrick Bernardi[1]

[1] AdaCore, New York, USA
{rogers,bernardi}@adacore.com
[2] AdaCore, Paris, France
{ruiz,gingold}@adacore.com

Abstract. We describe a new Ada language profile based directly upon the Ravenscar profile, intended to add expressive power for certain applications in the real-time and embedded systems domains. The new profile enhancements result primarily from the removal of selected Ravenscar restrictions but new capabilities are added. We provide the motivation and requirements for such a profile, the corresponding profile changes, and analyses of the results.

Keywords: Ada · The Ravenscar profile · Real-time systems · Run-time library

1 Introduction

The Ravenscar profile is a subset of the Ada concurrency facilities that supports determinism, schedulability analysis, constrained memory utilization, and certification to the highest integrity levels. Four distinct application domains are specifically intended:

- hard real-time applications requiring predictability,
- safety-critical systems requiring formal, stringent certification,
- high-integrity applications requiring formal static analysis and verification,
- embedded applications requiring both a small memory footprint and low execution overhead.

The profile is a subset of full Ada tasking because of the wide range and demanding nature of the analyses involved with these domains, in addition to efficiency and code size concerns. Those tasking constructs that preclude analysis at the source level or analysis of the tasking portion of the underlying run-time library are necessarily disallowed. Complexity is the primary concern.

The profile has proven to be very successful, allowing the use of concurrency in domains that would have otherwise been unlikely at best. It is a major strength of the Ada language. Indeed it is unique among languages with built-in concurrency constructs. Although a reduced subset based on Ravenscar was explored for Java [1] it did not become more than a research topic.

However, a loss of expressive power inevitably results from elimination or restriction of language features. For some applications this loss results in additional complexity at the application level as developers "work around" the restrictions. We argue that the loss can be mitigated if the focus of the profile is narrowed to the hard real-time and embedded systems domains because those domains do not entail the

© Springer International Publishing AG 2017
J. Blieberger and M. Bader (Eds.): Ada-Europe 2017, LNCS 10300, pp. 169–183, 2017.
DOI: 10.1007/978-3-319-60588-3_11

extremely stringent analyses required by the others. In particular, expressive power can be significantly improved without precluding schedulability analysis and without increasing the time and space costs unacceptably.

Therefore, a new language profile specifically for a subset of hard real-time and embedded applications is both desirable and possible. The reader should understand that this new profile is not a replacement for the Ravenscar profile. It is an additional profile based on Ravenscar. When the other domains are involved, or when the smallest and simplest implementation is otherwise required, the Ravenscar profile is most appropriate.

In the remaining sections of this paper we expand on the motivations and issues, introduce a set of requirements and new content, and analyze the implementation.

2 Motivation

Most of the Ravenscar profile restrictions exist to remove complexity, both at the application level and in the run-time library (because that is where tasking is largely implemented). A simpler application is less costly to analyze for certification and safety, as is a simpler run-time library. Indeed, a subset of the language is essential to make these analyses economically feasible. A simplified run-time library can also be far more efficient in both space and speed [2, 3]. For example, abort statements complicate analysis of both the application and the run-time library implementation, as well as impose size and performance penalties even when not used in the application. Asynchronous select statements are another source of considerable complexity, both in the application and the run-time library implementation.

Some restrictions exist for the sake of preventing inappropriate usage. For example, relative delay statements should not be used to (attempt to) express periodic behavior in tasks. Implicit heap allocations are inappropriate for certified systems because they do not appear in the source code directly. Other restrictions exist to define a static synchronization and communication model, such as the prohibition of task entries and selective accept statements. Maintaining determinism is a recurring theme.

However, some of these removed features are so powerful that application developers may "re-implement" the missing capabilities at the application level, using constructs allowed by the profile. The lack of multiple protected entries per protected object is a prime example, as is the lack of multiple callers queued simultaneously on an individual protected entry [4, 5]. For instance, developers may use two protected objects, each with a single entry and some barrier replacement code, to mimic a single entry with multiple queued entry callers [5, Sect. 5.9]. Similarly, they may have an explicit array of Suspension_Object values to implement the behavior that multiple protected entries in a single protected object would provide [5, Sect. 5.10].

Indeed, the prohibition of multiple protected entries per object and multiple queued callers per entry precludes the full power of protected objects. In Ada, the execution of a protected subprogram call or entry call starts a "protected action." When the called body completes execution, the barriers for all the protected entries in the protected object (if any) are evaluated as part of the protected action. If there are callers waiting on entries with entry barriers that are true, one of those entries is selected and that entry body executes. In Ravenscar, that is the end of the protected action because there can be only one caller on the entry "queue" and there is only one entry per protected object. A number of language operations are deferred during a protected action and these are now allowed to happen if any are pending. For example, new calls to the protected object's subprograms and entries are allowed.

Absent the Ravenscar entry restrictions, however, the protected action may continue. During that same protected action, after each subsequent entry body execution, all the protected object's entry barriers are re-evaluated again, so that queued callers on entries with open barriers, if any, can be detected and their calls executed. The completion of that selected entry body execution triggers yet another evaluation and this evaluation/execution continues until there are no callers queued on entries with open barriers in the protected object. Only then does the protected action complete. This iterative, full form of protected action is fundamental to the power of protected objects.

While the protected action is ongoing, any tasks that will eventually call the operations of that protected object, but have not yet done so, cannot interfere. Execution preference is given to the callers already in the protected entry queues while the protected action executes. As a result, the Boolean condition on which a caller is waiting is guaranteed to be true when the body actually executes, unlike the common condition-variable/mutex case.

"Implementation" of these restricted facilities by application developers can add considerable complexity to the application level. Obviously any reintroduced complexity must be acceptable for the domain in question, otherwise the code will be rejected, e.g., in those domains requiring certification. But for some hard real-time applications, predictability is the primary requirement and thus a higher degree of complexity, including within the run-time library, is acceptable.

Without question, there are applications that should use the Ravenscar profile and can be expressed reasonably in that profile's subset. However, there are some real-time/embedded applications that do not require the most stringent analyses supported by Ravenscar and cannot reasonably be expressed in the profile's subset. Such applications are not "Ravenscar applications." This new profile means to address those applications.

3 Goal and Profile Requirements

The goal of the new profile is to maximize the expressive power available to the developers of a certain class of real-time and embedded applications. Specifically, these are applications that can accept additional complexity, both at the application level and within the underlying run-time library.

These applications require the operational benefits that the Ravenscar profile provides to applications in those two domains, such as predictability. These benefits– for these specific applications – can be expressed as requirements for the profile and its underlying run-time library implementation:

1. The new profile must not introduce unpredictable timing behavior. The ability to perform schedulability analysis for applications in the real-time systems domain is key.
2. The new profile must not introduce unpredictable storage utilization.
3. The new profile must minimize additional implementation complexity, to the extent possible.

4. The new profile implementation must maintain both low execution time overhead and a small code memory footprint, to the extent possible.

Requirements #3 and #4 involve compromises, as new functionality will typically require additional run-time library code. We believe the new profile content described in Sect. 4 represents the best compromise of additional complexity for additional functionality that also retains the benefits of Ravenscar expressed in the four requirements above. In Sect. 5 we analyze each new profile feature in terms of these requirements.

4   New Profile Content

The Ravenscar profile (i.e., not this new profile) is described in the language standard by a set of pragmas specifying both behavior and language restrictions [6]:

```
pragma Task_Dispatching_Policy (FIFO_Within_Priorities);
pragma Locking_Policy (Ceiling_Locking);
pragma Detect_Blocking;
pragma Restrictions (
           No_Abort_Statements,
           No_Dynamic_Attachment,
           No_Dynamic_CPU_Assignment,
           No_Dynamic_Priorities,
           No_Implicit_Heap_Allocations,
           No_Local_Protected_Objects,
           No_Local_Timing_Events,
           No_Protected_Type_Allocators,
           No_Relative_Delay,
           No_Requeue_Statements,
           No_Select_Statements,
           No_Specific_Termination_Handlers,
           No_Task_Allocators,
           No_Task_Hierarchy,
           No_Task_Termination,
           Simple_Barriers,
           Max_Entry_Queue_Length => 1,
           Max_Protected_Entries => 1,
           Max_Task_Entries => 0,
           No_Dependence => Ada.Asynchronous_Task_Control,
           No_Dependence => Ada.Calendar,
           No_Dependence =>
             Ada.Execution_Time.Group_Budgets,
           No_Dependence => Ada.Execution_Time.Timers,
           No_Dependence => Ada.Synchronous_Barriers,
           No_Dependence => Ada.Task_Attributes,
           No_Dependence =>
             System.Multiprocessors.Dispatching_Domains);
```

The new profile relaxes, replaces, or removes some of these restrictions. The following sections describe the changes, referring as necessary to the restrictions specified above. *Anything not indicated as removed or altered from the Ravenscar profile remains unchanged in the new profile.*

4.1   Number of Queued Callers

The extended profile does not specify the global restrictionMax_Entry_Queue_Length. As a result, multiple callers can be queued on any given protected entry, rather than only one caller at a time. Note that task entries remain disallowed.

In addition, for any individual protected entry declaration, the developer can specify the maximum number of callers allowed for that entry using a new aspect (or pragma) Max_Queue_Length. (This new aspect should not be confused with the existing Max_Entry_Queue_Length restriction.)The specified maximum number of callers is checked at runtime. Use of the new aspect is optional, but if specified the value must be a static positive integer.

4.2   Number of Entries per Protected Object

The extended profile does not specify a value for Max_Protected_Entries. As a result, multiple entries per protected object are allowed. Note that this change also allows entry families to have more than one member.

Whenever multiple entries are open within a protected object and have callers queued, an entry will be chosen per the text of RM D.4 paragraph 12 (i.e., by priority of the callers or, if necessary, by the textual order of the entry declarations).

4.3   Relaxed Entry Barriers

The extended profile does not specify Simple_Barriers. Instead, a new restriction Pure_Barriers is applied. In addition to simple Boolean local variables, the new restriction also allows more complex Boolean expressions.

Specifically, Pure_Barriers allows the following:

- Variables local to the protected object (thus defined in the private part)
- Discriminants for the protected object
- Numeric literals
- Enumeration (and thus character) literals
- Named numbers
- Predefined relational operators
- Logical operators (**and, or, xor**)
- Short-circuit control forms (**and then, or else**)
- The logical negation operator (**not**)
- The Count attribute

No other language entities are allowed in the barrier expressions. Note that, in Ravenscar, the Count attribute is only allowed within protected entry bodies, whereas this new profile also allows it in the entry barriers.

Although more expressive, these expressions are still limited in content so that side effects, exceptions, and recursion are impossible. Removing the possibility of side effects is particularly important because the language does not specify the number of times a given barrier is evaluated. Allowing exceptions would complicate the implementation, whereas the goal is an efficient and predictable run-time library implementation that minimizes barrier evaluation cost.

4.4   Relative Delay Statements

The extended profile does not specify No_Relative_Delay. As a result, "relative" delay statements are now allowed, in addition to "absolute" (delay-until) delay statements.

Although relative delay statements are not appropriate for expressing periodic behavior, there are cases in which a relative delay has precisely the required semantics. For example, an electro-mechanical relay may have a requirement that it not be actuated more than N times per second in order to prevent burn-out. A relative delay after each actuation directly implements that requirement.

4.5   No_Implicit_Heap_Allocations

The extended profile does not specify No_Implicit_Heap_Allocations. This restriction is in the Ravenscar profile for the sake of the other high-integrity domains addressed by Ravenscar and is not *necessarily* applicable to real-time and embedded systems. Of course, the restriction may be considered appropriate and, if so, developers can specify this restriction in their application code. The new profile does not prohibit the restriction, it simply does not require it.

4.6   Ada.Calendar

The extended profile removes the restriction prohibiting use of the Ada.Calendar package. This restriction is present in Ravenscar because the Ada.Real_Time package has more appropriate semantics for real-time/embedded applications. However, not all usage of Ada.Calendar is unreasonable, for example time-stamping log messages.

5   Analysis

In this section we use the four requirements listed in Sect. 3 to evaluate the changes introduced by the new profile described in Sect. 4. Each new profile feature is examined to show compliance with the four requirements.

5.1   Protected Entry Queueing and Multiple Entry Queues Per Protected Object

The implementation of these two enhancements occurs indivisibly and indeed their semantics are inextricably intertwined, so we examine them as one.

Requirement 1: Maintain timing predictability

The new profile allows multiple protected entries per protected object and multiple queued callers per entry. These changes enable full, iterative protected actions and thus allow many of the design idioms for protected objects. However, support for full protected actions increases the execution times for those tasks that call protected procedures and entries. That increase can reduce the overall schedulability of the set of tasks in the system. Whether or not schedulability is actually precluded will depend upon the application design.

The potential for increased task execution time (beyond that of Ravenscar) for protected procedure and entry calls exists because of the implementation of the iterative protected actions. Specifically, we use the common "last task in" implementation approach, in which the caller that triggers the protected action performs all of the subsequent entry calls on behalf of all of the selected caller tasks. This approach is the most efficient because it avoids a task switch to each queued caller. However, a given caller may therefore execute more than the one procedure or entry body explicitly called in its source code. The result is that a protected procedure or entry call may involve a computation time greater than that of the individual entry/procedure explicitly called.

To precisely show where the increases occur we will use equations for Response Time Analysis, the standard way of analyzing fixed-priority real-time systems such as those using Ravenscar [4]. (The bulk of the following is based directly on [4, 7].) In the most abstract form, the response time R for any single task in the system is the sum of the task's computation time C, blocking time B, and interference time I, as shown in Eq. (1):

$$R_i = C_i + B_i + I_i \tag{1}$$

Specifically, for any single task i in a given interval, C_i is the worst-case execution time (WCET) required for the task to do the work it performs to meet its functional requirements, B_i is the worst-case time the task is waiting for lower priority tasks, and I_i is the worst-case time the task is preempted by the execution of higher priority tasks. The entire task set is schedulable if every task i has a worst-case response time R_i less than or equal to that task's individual dead line D_i. There are other terms that would be included in the equation as well, such as the system overhead (e.g., clock handling) and jitter, but these can be ignored for our purposes.

By definition, for a given task the total interference per interval is the amount of time required for the execution of all the higher priority tasks in that interval. Each higher priority task is released some number of times in the interval because each has a shorter period. When released each executes for their computation time C. For any single higher priority task j, then, the total interference contributed per interval is the product of the number of releases for j and computation time C_j. The total interference experienced by the lower priority task is then the sum of those products from all the higher priority tasks, shown in Eq. (2):

$$I_i = \sum_{j \in hp(i)} \left\lceil \frac{R_i}{T_j} \right\rceil C_j \tag{2}$$

In Eq. (2), hp is the set of tasks with priorities higher than that of task i, referenced elsewhere as P_i. C_j is the computation time for a task j in that set and T_j is the period for that task. To understand the number of releases in the equation, consider that over the time of R_i, the higher priority task j will be released at least once because it has a shorter period. If we divide R_i by the period of the higher priority task, T_j, we get a fractional value representing the number of releases in R_i for task j. The number of releases must be a whole number so the ceiling function is applied to that fractional value (The ceiling function returns the smallest integer greater than the fractional value it operates upon.).

The reader will have observed that R_i appears on both sides of the equation. The easiest way to solve such an equation is with a recurrence relationship [4] but showing that is outside the scope of this paper.

For the blocking term B_i, recall that this is the amount of time spent waiting for lower priority tasks to finish their execution, per interval. Waiting necessarily occurs when a lower priority task has a mutual exclusion lock on one or more shared resources, which in Ada are protected objects. By "shared" we mean that tasks of different priorities, higher and lower relative to a given task, call protected procedures or a protected entry in the same protected object. One or more protected objects can be shared in this way.

The blocking term must be both bounded and quantifiable to support schedulability analyses. Under the Ceiling Priority protocol applied by Ravenscar (and the new profile) the bound is ideal: higher-priority processes can only be blocked once per release by lower-priority tasks locking a shared protected object. There are no iterative protected actions in Ravenscar so a task can only execute one entry per invocation. Therefore, the blocking time in Ravenscar is the maximum execution time required for any single protected entry in a protected object shared among the tasks in question. We can quantify this value precisely using Eq. (3):

$$B_i = \max_{k=1}^{K} usage(k, i) \, C(k) \tag{3}$$

In Eq. (3), K is the number of protected objects *potentially* shared among tasks with higher and lower priorities than P_i. The term $C(k)$ is the execution time required for a protected procedure body or entry body in protected object k. (Note that in [4, 7] $C(k)$ is the sole value provided for protected object k, but it is not necessarily the greatest value experienced when invoking the protected entries in k. In our usage we do assume that it is the largest single value.) A protected object may or may not be shared among a given group of tasks so the equation must be able to ignore some protected objects' $C(k)$ values. Therefore, the function *usage* (k, i) returns either 0 or 1, indicating whether or not protected object k is accessed by at least one task with priority lower than P_i, and at least one task with priority greater than or equal to P_i. If the protected object k is not shared in that manner the product will be zero and those values of $C(k)$ will be ignored. Thus the worst case blocking for task i, B_i, is the maximum of the protected entry execution times $C(k)$ from among all the shared protected objects' operations invoked by lower priority tasks.

In the new profile, a higher priority task is still blocked only once per release by a lower priority task. However, the value of $C(k)$ may now be greater than the time for the invocation of a *single* entry because iterative protected actions are now allowed. In these protected actions, multiple entry bodies may be executed, assuming the application design is such that iterative protected actions will actually occur.

The number of entries executed in the protected actions will be no greater than the number of callers queued on the entries in the protected object. As a result, to compute the worst case value for $C(k)$ we now need to know the worst case number of callers accessing k. Without any additional information, that worst case is the total number of tasks N in the application because it is possible for all tasks to call the same protected object's entries. Moreover, it may be the case that every task in the application has called the entry in k with the highest computation time. If the barrier remains open, that entry will execute once for every caller.

There are two mitigating factors that can limit the number of callers.

First, the new profile allows the developer to specify the maximum number of callers per individual entry, via the new aspect Max_Queue_Length (see Sect. 4.1). Therefore, the worst case value for $C(k)$ is the sum, for all entries in the protected object k, of the product of each individual entry WCET and the maximum number of callers for that entry. That could still be a significant value, depending on the application design, but it is likely much less than N and is under the direct control of the developer. We express this value in Eq. (4):

$$C(k) = \sum_{e \in E(k)} Max\_Queue\_Length(e)\ C(e) \qquad (4)$$

In Eq. (4), k is again a protected object and $E(k)$ is the set of entries declared in k. Max_Queue_Length is the value specified by the aspect for entry e. $C(e)$ is the worst case computation time for the protected entry e. Thus, for each entry e in k, $C(k)$ is the sum of the product of the number of callers for e and the computation time for e. $C(k)$ is therefore the WCET for executing all the entries in k for the possible number of callers.

The second factor reducing the number of callers has to do with the definition of blocking with regard to shared protected objects. Some of the callers queued on the protected entries of protected object k may have higher priority than P_i (the priority of task i), and some may have lower priority. By definition, only the lower priority callers contribute to the blocking term B_i. The execution of entry bodies on behalf of queued higher priority callers is simply part of the interference term I_i, as if task i was preempted by each such caller. The *usage* function in Eq. (3) already ensures that only appropriately shared protected objects are included in the calculation. We repeat the blocking computation from Eq. (3), now as Eq. (5), both for convenience and because the meaning of $C(k)$ has changed:

$$B_i = \max_{k=1}^{K} usage(k, i) \, C(k) \tag{5}$$

The change is that $C(k)$ is now the worst case computation time for executing a protected action in protected object k, rather a single entry in k (see Eq. (4)).

In addition, calls to some entry-specific attributes are somewhat slower and there is a minimum implementation-dependent increase in the run-time library implementation for entry handling, in both cases due to the potential for protected actions. These increases will also appear in the blocking term via $C(k)$. All the increases are examined and explained in the subsection for requirement #4.

The reader should understand that these execution time increases do not introduce non-determinism and so they do not preclude schedulability analysis. The increases may potentially reduce the chances for overall schedulability but the analysis can still be performed.

Note that the new profile does not impose a requirement to have multiple entries in any given protected object, nor is there a requirement to have multiple callers queued per entry. The application designer can choose to have only one entry per protected object and can set the value of Max_Queue_Length to one for each entry. In that case, though, the designer should simply apply the Ravenscar profile. That usage clearly involves a different application design than the one intended for use with the new profile. In other words, an application either has a Ravenscar compliant design or it does not. If not, it requires a different profile. In either case the application will be analyzable for schedulability.

Requirement 2: Maintain storage utilization predictability

Support for multiple entries and multiple callers (entry queues) uses logical linked lists that are physically part of the existing task descriptors in the run-time library. The lists are represented using pointers to task descriptors that are already present in the descriptors. The queue elements are the task descriptors themselves. There is no need to allocate any additional memory.

Requirement 3: Minimize additional complexity

The implementation for multiple entries and multiple callers added fewer than 300 logical SLOCs (declarations and statements) to the existing Ravenscar run-time library implementation.

Requirement 4: Maintain space and speed efficiency

In the early 2000s, the European Space Agency (ESA) funded the development of a vendor-independent Ravenscar benchmarking test suite: the ESA Ravenscar Benchmarks, or ERB [8]. The work was done by AdaCore along with the Technical University of Madrid and the University of Padua. The test suite is available for download via the AdaCore Libre site (http://libre.adacore.com/tools/erb/) using subversion. We used the ERB to measure the efficiency of the new profile's run-time implementation.

The ERB is targeted to the ERC32 and Leon processors and is designed to use the GNAT compiler, among others. We used the GNAT Leon compiler with execution on the "tsim" simulator. We used the original tests for our analysis. To run the tests we followed the instructions in the "GETTING_STARTED" file.

The ERB tests examine a number of characteristics of an implementation, including timing for tasking related features, accuracy of arithmetic operators, subprogram call overhead, dynamic memory allocation and deallocation times, and the amount of memory used. The useful tests for our purposes measure the performance of various tasking constructs so we did not run all the tests defined by the test suite. Instead, we ran all the tasking timing tests, specifically the tests named "tp_t_a_*xxx*" where "*xxx*" is a number and a letter.

We ran the tests using the run-time libraries for the Ravenscar profile and the new profile and got repeatable results. Since the ERB itself and the tsim simulator are designed with exactly that expectation we have confidence in the results and corresponding conclusions.

The tests were not changed from the originals so the source code is consistent with the Ravenscar restrictions. For example, any entry in a protected object is the only entry present and has at most one caller. This approach allows us to discuss performance differences relative to the Ravenscar profile. Therefore, in the results that follow, we provide the percentage difference between the results of the tests when run on our standard Ravenscar run-time library and when run on a run-time library implementing the new profile.

In nearly all cases the resulting percentage differences were either literally zero or were so close to zero as to be insignificant. We do not present those results. In some cases we took one representative result from a set of directly related tests. This was done because those tests showed no differences among the results. For example, some tests measure calls from a task versus calls from a main procedure. Only one result is used for such a group of tests. As a result, only five tests provided informative non-zero results. In addition, one set of tests provided a useful result even though the difference was zero, i.e., there was no change.

Specifically, in those tests in which a protected entry is not declared within a protected object, the timing is unchanged: there is no performance increase for calls to protected procedures declared within such objects. The reason it is unchanged is that an optimized run-time library routine dedicated to that scenario is used in both profiles. This is an important idiom (mutual exclusion alone, without condition synchronization) so the lack of any additional overhead is ideal. This was test tp_t_a_07a.

However, when a protected object does contain an entry declaration, calls to both protected procedures as well as protected entries do encounter a change in performance, due to the potential for an iterative protected action triggered by the completion of the body. In this scenario, we cannot use a dedicated run-time routine to handle a single entry with a single caller, but must use the "standard" run-time routine for the sake of the additional semantics. The performance is therefore not the same as with the Ravenscar profile. Specifically:

- A call to a protected entry with the barrier open is approximately 54% slower, due to the check for other potential entries to execute (although none would ensue since there was only one entry and one caller in Ravenscar). This was test tp_t_a_09a.

- A call to a protected entry with the barrier closed is approximately 25% slower. In this case no entry body is executed so, in combination with the Simple_Barriers restriction, no further protected action execution is possible. The caller is simply queued. (Simple_Barriersentails that 'Count is not used in a barrier.) This was test tp_t_a_10a.
- A call to a protected procedure, when the protected object contains an entry declaration that is closed, is approximately 13% slower. This is the minimal case, in which the potential for another entry body execution must be checked but no resulting processing is required (there is no caller queuing, in particular). This was test tp_t_a_12a.

Other functionality related to protected entries also exhibit performance changes:

- A call to 'Count for an entry, made from a protected procedure within that same protected object, is approximately 21% slower. This was test tp_t_a_13a.
- A call to 'Caller in a protected entry is approximately 58% slower. This was test tp_t_a_14a.

We have presented the differences in terms of percentages relative to the bespoke Ravenscar run-time routines that take advantage of the reduced semantics. However, the numbers themselves are still low and well within the realm of usability.

5.2 Pure_Barriers

See Sect. 4.3 for the definition of the new restriction Pure_Barriers. Recall from that section that, although this new restriction allows more language entities in the barrier expressions, the expressions are by no means fully general.

Requirement 1: Maintain timing predictability
The barrier expression is compiled like any expression. However, although the expression can be more complex than those of Simple_Barriers, it is restricted to simple language-defined operators that have no side-effects and no exceptions. As a direct result, execution time remains predictable.

Requirement 2: Maintain storage utilization predictability
The amount of stack needed to evaluate the barrier is predictable because of the restrictions imposed. In particular, arbitrary Boolean functions and non-local variables are not allowed.

Requirement 3: Minimize additional complexity
Although Pure_Barriers is less restrictive than Simple_Barriers, the complexity is still low and is directly controlled by the user.

Requirement 4: Maintain space and speed efficiency
Likewise, space and speed efficiency depend on the expression complexity and are, therefore, under user control. The restrictions are such that efficiency should remain high.

5.3   Relative Delay Statements

A relative delay statement in the application code is implemented in the run-time library as a procedure with a body that simply contains an absolute delay statement. The value of type Time for this absolute delay is computed as the sum of the result of the Clock function plus the Duration value converted to a Time_Span value. In other words, the implementation contains precisely the work-around used by application programmers under the Ravenscar profile when a relative delay is desired.

Requirement 1: Maintain timing predictability
The implementations of functions Clock, To_Time_Span, and the function "+" prior to the absolute delay statement have consistent, predictable times, as in the Ravenscar profile.

Requirement 2: Maintain storage utilization predictability
There is no additional memory allocation for this feature.

Requirement 3: Minimize additional complexity
This feature does not increase complexity, it is almost transparent.

Requirement 4: Maintain space and speed efficiency
This feature is efficient in terms of both space and speed. The additional time required consists of the execution of the bodies of the functions Clock, To_Time_Span, and the addition function, all of which are minimal and the same as under the Ravenscar profile.

5.4   Non-tasking Restrictions

The removal of the restrictions preventing implicit heap allocation and use of Ada. Calendar does not require run-time library support. There are no performance impacts and no other effects other than to allow the otherwise prohibited functionality in the code. Application developers can specify both restrictions, if desired, and the compiler will detect violations as in the Ravenscar profile.

5.5   Analysis Summary

We have examined each new profile addition in terms of the four general requirements, restated here along with their specific results summary:

1. The new profile must not introduce unpredictable timing behavior. The ability to perform schedulability analysis for applications in the real-time systems domain is key.

   The new profile features maintain the ability to perform schedulability analysis. Full protected actions, if used, increase the blocking time for individual tasks, but that does not preclude schedulability analysis. The new features do not introduce non-determinism.

2. The new profile must not introduce unpredictable storage utilization.

The new profile features do not introduce any unpredictable storage utilization into the run-time library. It does remove the unilateral application of the restriction No_Implicit_Heap_Allocations, but the run-time library does no such allocations. If the application designer wants to ensure no such storage allocation occurs they can reapply the configuration pragma, but removal of the pragma does not introduce unpredictability.

3. The new profile must minimize additional implementation complexity, to the extent possible.

Some of the new profile features introduce complexity into the run-time library, others introduce none whatsoever. In particular, the allowance for multiple entries per protected object and multiple simultaneously queued callers introduces complexity but not beyond an acceptable amount.

4. The new profile implementation must maintain both low execution time overhead and a small code memory footprint, to the extent possible.

The new profile features do affect performance but do not do so to an unacceptable degree. The additional memory footprint in the implementation is quite small and appears in the form of additional object code.

Overall, the new features provide significantly enhanced expressive power while meeting the required constraints.

6   Conclusions

The Ravenscar profile presents an appropriate subset of Ada tasking for the several application domains it addresses when the absolute minimum application and implementation complexity is required. However, the resulting profile is necessarily strict and the resulting loss of expressive power is considerable.

The loss can be mitigated when additional complexity is allowable, i.e., when only schedulability analysis or a small memory footprint is required. That is the case for a class of applications in the real-time and embedded systems domains.

Considerable expressive power can be restored, especially for protected types, without sacrificing predictability and without imposing unacceptable performance degradations. Moreover, the complexity of the added run-time library code is small: much of the additional code consists of declarations, with simple control flow consisting of a few if-statements and a few loops. These changes make possible the expression of a larger set of applications in the two domains without prompting the work-arounds that introduce complexity at the application level.

The reader will have noticed that we have not mentioned the name of the new profile, other than the fact that it is directly based on Ravenscar. AdaCore is currently shipping the new profile in selected products, with the profile named "GNAT Extended Ravenscar Profile," but we hope to have this new profile included in the language standard and as such it would have a vendor-independent name.

The authors would like to thank the reviewers of the 17th International Real-Time Ada Workshop for their comments on our position paper [9] proposing an initial version of the new profile, as well as the meeting members for their very helpful suggestions and feedback.

References

1. Kwon, J., Wellings, A.J., King, S.: Ravenscar-Java: a high-integrity profile for real-time Java. Concurrency Comput. Pract. Experience **17**(5–6), 681–713 (2005)
2. Shen, H., Baker, T.P.: A Linux kernel module implementation of restricted Ada tasking. ACM SIGAda Ada Lett. **19**(2), 96–103 (1999)
3. Dobbing, B.: The Ravenscar tasking profile – experience report. ACM SIGAda Ada Lett. **19** (2), 28–32 (1999)
4. Burns, A., Wellings, A.: Analysable Real-Time Systems Programmed in Ada. CreateSpace Independent Publishing Platform (2016)
5. Burns, A., Dobbing, B., Vardanega, T.: Guide for the use of the Ada Ravenscar profile in high integrity systems. Ada Lett. **XXIV**(2), 1–74 (2004)
6. ISO: ISO/IEC JTC 1/SC 22/WG9 Ada Reference Manual-Language and Standard Libraries-ISO/IEC 8652:2012/Cor 1:2016 (2016)
7. Burns, A., Wellings, A.J.: Real-Time Systems and Programming Languages, 4th edn. Addison-Wesley, Reading (2009)
8. Berrendonner, R., Guitton, J.: The ESA Ravenscar benchmark. In: Reliable Software Technologies – Ada-Europe 2005. Springer, New York (2005)
9. Rogers, P., Ruiz, J., Gingold, T.: Toward extensions to the Ravenscar profile. ACM SIGAda Ada Lett. **35**(1), 32–37 (2015)

OpenMP Tasking Model for Ada: Safety and Correctness

Sara Royuela[1(✉)], Xavier Martorell[1(✉)], Eduardo Quiñones[1(✉)], and Luis Miguel Pinho[2(✉)]

[1] Barcelona Supercomputing Center, Barcelona, Spain
{sara.royuela,xavier.martorell,eduardo.quinones}@bsc.es
[2] CISTER/INESC-TEC, ISEP, Polytechnic Institute of Porto, Porto, Portugal
lmp@isep.ipp.pt

Abstract. The safety-critical real-time embedded domain increasingly demands the use of parallel architectures to fulfill performance requirements. Such architectures require the use of parallel programming models to exploit the underlying parallelism. This paper evaluates the applicability of using OpenMP, a widespread parallel programming model, with Ada, a language widely used in the safety-critical domain.

Concretely, this paper shows that applying the OpenMP tasking model to exploit fine-grained parallelism within Ada tasks does not impact on programs safeness and correctness, which is vital in the environments where Ada is mostly used. Moreover, we compare the OpenMP tasking model with the proposal of Ada extensions to define parallel blocks, parallel loops and reductions. Overall, we conclude that the OpenMP tasking model can be safely used in such environments, being a promising approach to exploit fine-grain parallelism in Ada tasks, and we identify the issues which still need to be further researched.

1 Introduction

There is a clear trend towards the use of parallel computation to fulfill the performance requirements of real-time embedded systems in general, and safety-critical embedded systems in particular (e.g. autonomous driving). In that regard, the use of advanced parallel architectures, like many-core heterogeneous processors, is increasingly seen as the solution. These architectures rely on parallel programming models to exploit their massively parallel capabilities. Thus, there is a need to integrate these models in the development of safety-critical systems [21].

Safety-critical systems are commonly developed with programming languages where concepts as safety and reliability are crucial. In that respect, Ada is widely used in safety-critical and high-security domains such as avionics and railroad systems. The whole language is designed to keep safeness: it enforces strong typing, checks ranges in loops and so eliminating buffer overflows, provides actual contracts in the form of pre- and post-conditions, prevents access to deallocated memory, etc. A long list of language decisions allows compilers to implement correctness techniques to certify algorithms regarding their specification.

© Springer International Publishing AG 2017
J. Blieberger and M. Bader (Eds.): Ada-Europe 2017, LNCS 10300, pp. 184–200, 2017.
DOI: 10.1007/978-3-319-60588-3_12

Ada supports a concurrency model (by means of Ada tasks and protected objects) that is mainly suitable for coarse-grained parallelism. Hence, there has been a significant effort to add support for fine-grained parallelism to Ada, to benefit from parallel architectures. The existent proposal [26] enriches the Ada core with extensions that support parallel blocks and parallel loops (including reductions). This technique is based on the notion of *tasklets* [23]: concurrent logical units within an Ada task. Since adding parallelism also means adding a source of errors (due to concurrent accesses to global data and synchronizations) the proposal addresses safety using new annotations. With that, the compiler is able to detect data race conditions[1] and blocking operations[2].

This paper evaluates the use of the OpenMP [1] tasking model to express fine-grained parallelism in Ada. OpenMP was born in the 90's out of the need for standardizing the different vendor specific directives related to parallelism. The language has successfully emerged as the de facto standard for shared-memory systems. This is the result of being successfully used for decades in the high-performance computing (HPC) domain. Furthermore, OpenMP has recently gained much attention in the embedded field owing to the augmentations of the latest specifications, which address the key issues in heterogeneous embedded systems: (a) the coupling of a main host processor to one or more many-core accelerators, where highly-parallel code kernels can be offloaded for improved performance/watt; and (b) the capability of expressing fine-grained, both structured and unstructured, and highly-dynamic task parallelism.

This paper shows how OpenMP can be integrated with Ada, and how correctness and thus safety are preserved when using the OpenMP tasking model [9] by virtue of compiler analyses. These analyses allow both compile-time detection of errors that may cause runtimes to break or hang, and automatic amendment of errors introduced due to a wrong usage of the user-driven parallelism. The OpenMP tasking model implements an execution pattern similar to the *tasklet* model, for an OpenMP task[3] resembles a *tasklet*. Interestingly, both models map to state-of-the-art scheduling methods, enabling to provide timing guarantees to OpenMP applications [24]. Such points make OpenMP particularly relevant for embedded heterogeneous systems, which typically run applications that can be very well modeled as periodic task graphs.

There are however a few caveats. First, the interplay between OpenMP and Ada runtimes, each with its own model. Second, although the tasking model of OpenMP has been demonstrated to be analyzable for real-time systems using the limited preemptive scheduling model [30], it is still ongoing effort to make it

---

[1] A *race condition* occurs when two or more accesses to the same variable are concurrent and at least one is a write.

[2] *Blocking operations* are defined in Ada to be one of the following: entry calls; select, accept, delay and abort statements; task creation or activation; external calls on a protected subprogram with the same target object as that of the protected action; and calls to a subprogram containing blocking operations.

[3] An *OpenMP task* is a specific instance of executable code and its data environment, generated when a thread encounters a given construct (i.e. `task`, `taskloop`, `parallel`, `target`, or `teams`).

a standard offering. Finally, it remains as a future work to evaluate the complete OpenMP language, including its thread-based model (see Sect. 4.1).

2   Motivation: Why OpenMP?

Programming multi-cores is difficult due to the multiple constraints it involves. Hence, the success of a multi-core platform relies on its productivity, which combines performance, programmability and portability. With such a goal, multitude of programming models coexist. The different approaches are grouped as follows:

Hardware-centric models aim to replace the native platform programming with higher-level, user-friendly solutions, e.g. Intel® TBB [27] and NVIDIA® CUDA [5]. These models focus on tuning an application to match a chosen platform, which makes their use a neither scalable nor portable solution.

Application-centric models deal with the application parallelization from design to implementation, e.g. OpenCL [34] and OmpSs [13]. Although portable, these models may require a full rewriting process to accomplish productivity.

Parallelism-centric models allow users to express typical parallelism constructs in a simple and effective way, and at various levels of abstraction, e.g. POSIX threads (Pthreads) [11], MPI [33] and OpenMP [12]. This approach allows flexibility and expressiveness, while decoupling design from implementation.

Given the vast amount of options available, there is a noticeable need to unify programming models for many-cores [36]. In that sense, OpenMP has proved many advantages over its competitors. On the one hand, different evaluations demonstrate that OpenMP delivers tantamount performance and efficiency compared to highly tunable models such as TBB [16], CUDA [19], OpenCL [31], and MPI [17]. On the other hand, OpenMP has different advantages over low level libraries such as Pthreads: (a) it offers robustness without sacrificing performance [18], and (b) OpenMP does not lock the software to a specific number of threads. Another advantage is that the code can be compiled as a single-threaded application just disabling support for OpenMP, thus easing debugging.

The use of OpenMP presents three main advantages. First, an expert community has constantly reviewed and augmented the language for the past 20 years. Thus, less effort is needed to introduce fine-grained parallelism in Ada. Second, OpenMP is widely implemented by several chip and compiler vendors (e.g. GNU [2], Intel® [4], and IBM [3]), meaning that less effort is needed to manage parallelism as the OpenMP runtime will manage it. Third, OpenMP provides greater expressiveness due to years of experience in its development. The language offers several directives for parallelization and synchronization, along with a large number of clauses that allow to contextualize concurrency, providing a finer control of the parallelism. Overall, OpenMP is a good candidate to introduce fine-grained parallelism to Ada by virtue of its benefits.

Despite its benefits, there is still work to do to fulfill the safety-critical domain requirements. Firstly, OpenMP is not reliable because it does not define any recovery mechanism. In that regard, different approaches have been proposed and some of them have been already adopted, which we discuss in Sect. 5.3. Secondly, both programmers and compilers must satisfy some requirements to make possible whole program analysis (such as programmers adding information in headers libraries, and compilers implementing techniques like IPO [7]).

3   Ada Language Extensions for Fine-Grain Parallelism

Ada includes tasking features as part of the standard by means of tasks, which are entities that denote concurrent actions, and inter-task communication mechanisms such as protected objects or *rendezvous*. However, this model is mainly suitable for coarse-grained parallelism due to its higher overhead [32].

Efforts exist to extend Ada with a fine-grained parallel model based on the notion of *tasklets* [23], where parallelism is not fully controlled by the programmer: the programmer specifies the parallel nature of the algorithm, and the compiler and the runtime have the freedom to organize parallel computations.

Based on this model, specific language extensions have been proposed [35] to cover two cases where parallelization is suitable: parallel blocks and parallel loops, including reductions. The following subsections present the syntax and semantics proposed (which are being considered for future versions of the Ada language [8]), as well as how safety is kept in this model.

3.1   Parallel Blocks

A parallel block (Listing 1.1) denotes two or more parts of an algorithm that can be executed in parallel. A transfer of control[4] or exception[5] within one parallel sequence aborts the execution of parallel sequences that have not started, and potentially initiates the abortion of those sequences not yet completed[6]. Once all parallel sequences complete, then the transfer of control or exception occurs.

Listing 1.1. Parallel block syntax with proposed Ada extensions

```
1   parallel
2       sequence_of_statements
3   and
4       sequence_of_statements
5   {and
6       sequence_of_statements}
7   end parallel;
```

Listing 1.2. Parallel loop syntax with proposed Ada extensions

```
1   for i in parallel lb..ub loop
2       sequence_of_statements
3   end loop;
```

---

[4] A *transfer of control* causes the execution of a program to continue from a different address instead of the next instruction (e.g. a return instruction).

[5] *Exceptions* are anomalous conditions requiring special processing. Ada has predefined exceptions (language-defined run-time errors) and user-defined exceptions.

[6] The rules for abortion of parallel computations are still under discussion [25].

3.2 Parallel Loop

In a parallel loop (Listing 1.2), iterations may execute in parallel. Each iteration can be treated as a separate unit of work. However, this may introduce too much overhead from: (a) the creation of the work item, (b) the communication of results, and (c) the synchronization of shared data (protected objects). To palliate this, both the compiler and the runtime are given the freedom to chunk iterations. Although not mandatory, programmers may gain control by defining sized chunks. The proposal reveals the necessity of providing support for per-thread copies of relevant data to deal with data dependencies and shared data.

The authors also introduce the concept of a parallel array; that is data being updated within a parallel loop. The syntax is shown in Listing 1.3, where the use of <> indicates an array of unspecified bounds. In that case, the compiler may choose the size based on the number of chunks chosen for the parallelized loops where the array is used. Alternatively, the programmer may provide a bound, thus forcing a specific partitioning. The rule regarding transfer of control and exceptions presented for parallel blocks also applies here. For this purpose, each chunk is treated as equivalent to separate sequences of a parallel block.

Listing 1.3. Not chuncked parallel array with proposed Ada extensions

```
1   Arr : array (parallel <>) of a_type
2        := (others => initial_value);
```

3.3 Parallel Reduction

The authors of the proposed Ada extensions define a reduction as a common operation for values in a parallel array that consists in combining the different values of the array at the end of the processing with the appropriate reduction operation. Syntax for parallel reductions is still under discussion [25] and the current proposal is to define this reduction in the type as in Listing 1.4.

Listing 1.4. Parallel reduction with proposed Ada extensions

```
1    ...
2      type Partial_Array_Type is new array (parallel <>) of Float;
3      with Reducer =>"+", Identity => 0.0;
4      Partial_Sum : Partial_Array_Type := (others => 0.0);
5      Sum : Float := 0.0;
6    begin
7      for I in parallel Arr'Range loop
8          Partial_Sum(<>) := Partial_Sum(<>) + Arr(I);
9      end loop;
10     Sum := Partial_Sum(<>)'Reduced; -- reduce value either here or
11                                     -- during the parallel loop
12   ...
```

3.4   Safety

Despite the clear benefits of parallel computation in terms of performance, parallel programming is complex and error prone, and that may compromise correctness and so safety. Hence, it is paramount to incorporate compiler and run-time techniques that detect errors in parallel programming.

There are two main sources of errors when dealing with parallel code: (a) the concurrent access to shared resources in a situation of *race condition*, and (b) an error in the synchronization between parallel operations leading to a *deadlock*. To guarantee safety, Ada parallel code must use atomic variables and protected objects to access shared data. Moreover, the compiler shall be able to complain if different parallel regions might have conflicting side-effects.

In that respect, due to the hardship of accessing the complete source code to perform a full analysis, the proposed Ada extensions suggests a two-fold solution [35]: (a) eliminate race conditions by adding an extended version of the SPARK `Global` aspect to the language (this will help the compiler to identify those memory locations that are read and written without requiring access to the complete code); and (b) address deadlocks by the defined execution model, together with a new aspect called `Potentially_Blocking` that indicates whether a subprogram contains statements that are potentially blocking.

4   OpenMP for Fine-Grained Parallelism in Ada

In this paper, we propose a complementary approach for exploiting fine-grain parallelism in Ada: OpenMP. Our approach is motivated by the threefold advantage of (a) being a well-known parallel programming model supported by many chip and compiler vendors, (b) offering a simple yet exhaustive interface, and (c) providing greater expressiveness as a result of years of experienced development.

4.1   OpenMP Execution Model

OpenMP provides two different models of parallelism:

Thread-parallelism, which defines a conceptual abstraction of user-level threads that work as proxies for physical processors. This model enforces a rather structured parallelism. Representative constructs are `for` and `sections`.
Task-parallelism, tasking model hereafter, which is oblivious of the physical layout. Programmers focus on exposing parallelism rather than mapping parallelism onto threads. Representative constructs are `task` and `taskloop`.

An OpenMP program begins as a single thread of execution, called the *initial thread*. Parallelism is achieved through the `parallel` construct. When such a construct is found, a *team* of threads is spawned. These are joined at the *implicit barrier* encountered at the end of the parallel region. Within that region, the threads of the team execute work. This is the so-called *fork-join model*.

Then, within the parallel region, parallelism is achieved by means of different constructs: for, sections and task, among others.

Mutual exclusion is accomplished via the critical and atomic constructs, and synchronization by means of the barrier construct. Additionally, the tasking model offers the taskwait construct to impose a less restrictive synchronization (while a barrier synchronizes all threads in the current team, a taskwait only synchronizes descendant tasks of the binding task).

Figure 2 shows the execution model of a parallel block with a loop implemented using the parallel for directive, where all spawned threads work in parallel from the beginning of the parallel region as long as there is work to do. Figure 1 shows the model of a parallel block with tasks. In this case, the single construct restricts the execution of the parallel region to only one thread until a task construct is found. Then, another thread (or the same, depending on the scheduling policy), concurrently executes the code of the task.

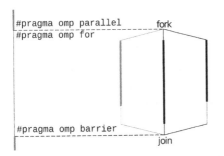

Fig. 1. Fork-join model with unstructured parallelism

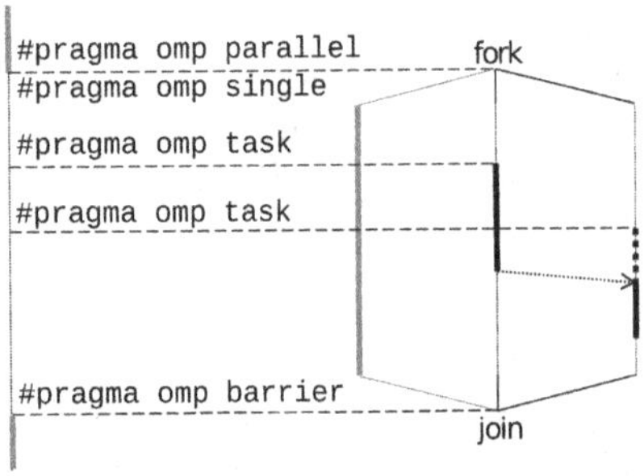

Fig. 2. Fork-join model with structured parallelism

The tasking model adapts better to the parallelism model proposed for Ada, which is oblivious of the threads as well. Thus, even if a thread-parallel version is possible, we focus on the tasking model, remaining the other as future work.

4.2   Data Scoping

One of the most interesting characteristics of OpenMP is that it allows a rich definition of the scoping of variables involved in the parallel computation by means of data-sharing clauses. This scoping can be one of the following:

- *private*: a new fresh variable is created within the scope.
- *firstprivate*: a new variable is created in the scope and initialized with the value of the original variable.
- *lastprivate*: a new variable is created within the scope and the original variable is updated at the end of the execution of the region (only for tasks).
- *shared*: the original variable is used in the scope, thus opening the possibility of data race conditions.

The use of data-sharing clauses is particularly powerful to avoid unnecessary synchronizations as well as race conditions. All variables appearing within a construct have a default data-sharing defined by the OpenMP specifications (Sect. 2.15.1 [1]). Data-scoping rules are not based on the use of the variables, but on their storage. Thus, users are required to explicitly scope many variables, changing the default data-sharing values, in order to fulfill correctness (i.e., avoiding data races) and enhance performance (i.e., privatizing variables).

Listing 1.5 shows a simple C code with two tasks concurrently performing two multiplications. These tasks are synchronized in the taskwait directive previous to adding the two computed values. The code shows the default data-sharing of the variables derived following the data-scoping rules: a, b and res are defined as shared because they have dynamic storage duration, whereas x and y are defined as firstprivate. This code however is not correct because the updated values of x and y are not visible outside the tasks. Hence, programmers must manually introduce the data-sharing clauses as shown in Listing 1.6.

Listing 1.5. OpenMP specification defined data-sharing clauses

```
1  int a, b, res;
2  int foo() {
3      #pragma omp parallel
4      // shared(a, b, res)
5      #pragma omp single nowait
6      {
7          int x, y;
8          #pragma omp task
9          // firstprivate(x) shared(a)
10         x = a*a;
11         #pragma omp task
12         // firstprivate(y) shared(b)
13         y = b*b;
14         #pragma omp taskwait
15         res = x + y;
16     }
17 }
```

Listing 1.6. OpenMP manually defined data-sharing clauses

```
1  int a, b, res;
2  int foo() {
3      #pragma omp parallel shared(res) \
4                              firstprivate(a, b)
5      #pragma omp single nowait
6      {
7          int x, y;
8          #pragma omp task shared(x) \
9                              firstprivate(a)
10         x = a*a;
11         #pragma omp task shared(y) \
12                              firstprivate(b)
13         y = b*b;
14         #pragma omp taskwait
15         res = x + y;
16     }
17 }
```

Manually defining data-sharing clauses is a cumbersome and error-prone process because programmers have to be aware of the memory model and analyze the usage of the variables. Fortunately, compiler analysis techniques have already proved that it is possible to automatically define data-sharing clauses [28] and statically catch incoherences in the user-defined attributes that may lead to non-deterministic results, runtime failures and loss of performance [29]. We further explain these in Sect. 5.

The possibility of defining data-sharing attributes makes an important difference with the proposed Ada extensions, where this task is allotted to the compiler. In that regard, OpenMP adds flexibility to the model without losing simplicity, as the attributes can still be discovered at compile time.

4.3   Supporting OpenMP in Ada

The current OpenMP specification is defined for C, C++ and Fortran. In the examples showed in Sect. 4.2 we use the syntax defined for C/C++. However,

Ada does not group a sequence of statements by bracketing the group (as in C), but uses a more structured approach with a closing statement to match the beginning of the group. Since Ada already defines pragmas of the form `pragma Name (Parameter_List);`, we propose introducing a new kind of pragma, the `pragma OMP`, together with the directive name (e.g. `task`, `barrier`, etc.).

Listing 1.7 shows an example of the proposed syntax when the OpenMP construct applies to one statement, and Listing 1.8 shows an example where the construct applies to more than one statement.

Listing 1.7. OpenMP proposed syntax pragmas applying to one statement

Listing 1.8. OpenMP proposed syntax for pragmas applying to several statements

```
1 pragma OMP (taskloop, num_tasks=>N);
2 for i in range 0..I loop
3   ...      -- statements here
4 end loop;
```

```
1 pragma OMP (task, shared=>var);
2 begin
3   ...      -- statements here
4 end;
```

OpenMP defines the argument of a data-sharing clause as a list of items. This does not match directly with the syntax allowed in Ada for pragmas, which is shown in Listing 1.9. In order to simplify the syntax needed to define data-sharing clauses, we propose to extend the definition of `pragma_argument_identifier` with a list of expressions. We will use this proposed syntax for the rest of the document.

Listing 1.9. Ada syntax for pragmas

```
pragma ::=
      pragma identifier [( pragma_argument_association { , pragma_argument_association })];
pragma_argument_association ::=
      [ pragma_argument_identifier =>] name
    | [ pragma_argument_identifier =>] expression
```

4.4 Parallel Blocks

As previously introduced, a parallel block denotes two or more concurrent sections. In OpenMP a parallel block can be written so that each parallel region is wrapped in a task, and all tasks are wrapped in a parallel region. We use the parallel computation of the Fibonacci sequence to illustrate this scenario. Listing 1.10 shows the implementation using Ada extensions, and Listing 1.11 shows the OpenMP implementation.

In the Ada version, the compiler can detect that no unsafe access is made to N, X or Y in the parallel block, thus concluding no synchronization is required (except the one at the end of the parallel block). Furthermore, it can privatize X and Y, copying out their value after the parallel computation completes. This however, may harm performance due to the extra copies (it remains as a compiler decision). The logic behind the choice to make data-sharing transparent to the user is based on simplicity and readability, whilst safe.

In the OpenMP version, although programmers are not forced to define the data-scoping manually (since the compiler can detect the proper data-sharing attributes as it does in the Ada version), they can specify the intended model for

Listing 1.10. Parallel Fibonacci sequence with Ada extensions

```
1  if N < 2 then
2      return N;
3  parallel
4      X:= Fibonacci(N - 2);
5  and
6      Y:= Fibonacci(N - 2);
7  end parallel;
8  return X + Y;
```

Listing 1.11. Parallel Fibonacci sequence with OpenMP tasks

```
1   if N < 2 then
2       return N;
3   pragma OMP (parallel, shared=>X,Y,
4                         firstprivate=>N);
5   pragma OMP (single, nowait);
6   begin
7       pragma OMP (task, shared=>X,
8                         firstprivate=>N);
9       X:= Fibonacci(N - 2);
10      pragma OMP (task, shared=>Y,
11                        firstprivate=>N)
12      Y:= Fibonacci(N - 2);
13  end
14  return X + Y;
```

data access. Hence, accesses to X and Y are marked as shared because there is no concurrency in the usage of these variables and they are both updated within the corresponding tasks and visible after the tasks. Additionally, the access to N is marked as firstprivate because the value is just read within the task. Since there is an implicit barrier at the end of the parallel construct, the return statement will always access the correct values of X and Y. This model is not as naive as the proposed Ada extensions, being a trade-off between simplicity and flexibility.

4.5 Parallel Loop

As previously explained, a parallel loop defines a loop where iterations may be executed in parallel. The OpenMP tasking model offers the taskloop construct, which specifies that the iterations of the associated loops will be distributed across the tasks created by the construct, and executed concurrently. Users can control the number of tasks and their size with the following clauses:

- num_tasks defines the number of tasks created.
- grain_size defines the number of loop iterations assigned to each task.

We illustrate this scenario with the well-known matrix multiplication benchmark. Consider two matrices M1 and M2, and the matrix RES, where their multiplication is stored. Listing 1.12 shows the code implemented with the syntax proposed for the Ada extensions, and Listing 1.13 shows the implementation using the OpenMP taskloop construct.

Again, OpenMP allows more expressiveness by virtue of the data-sharing clauses. In the Ada version the compiler may not be able to determine that parallel access to RES are not data races. Moreover, the OpenMP version also allows controlling the granularity of the parallelization whereas the Ada extensions are limited to defining the number of elements of a parallel array.

4.6 Parallel Reduction

For the Ada extensions, a reduction is an operation defined over the elements of a parallel array. OpenMP relaxes this constraint and defines a reduction as a

Listing 1.12. Parallel matrix multiplication with Ada extensions

```
1 for i in parallel 0..MAX_I loop
2   for j in range 0..MAX_J loop
3     for k in range 0..MAX_K loop
4       RES(i,j):= RES(i,j)
5                 + M1(i,k) * M2(k,j);
6     end loop;
7   end loop;
8 end loop;
```

Listing 1.13. Parallel matrix multiplication with OpenMP taskloop

```
1 pragma OMP (parallel);
2 pragma OMP (taskloop,
3   private=>i, j, k,
4   firstprivate=>MAX_I, MAX_J, MAX_K,
5   shared=>RES, M1, M2,
6   grainsize=>size);
7 begin
8   for i in range 0..MAX_I loop
9     for j in range 0..MAX_J loop
10      for k in range 0..MAX_K loop
11        RES(i,j):= RES(i,j)
12                  + M1(i,k) * M2(k,j);
13      end loop;
14    end loop;
15  end loop;
16 end
```

parallel operation which result is stored in a variable. Different implicitly declared reduction identifiers are defined in OpenMP (e.g. +, -, *, etc.). Additionally, the specification allows user defined reductions with the syntax specified in Listing 1.14. There, `reduction_identifier` is either a base language identifier or an implicitly declared identifier, `typename_list` is a list of type names, `combiner` is the reduction expression, and `initializer_clause` indicates the value to be used to initialize the private copies of the reduction.

Listing 1.14. OpenMP syntax for user-declared reductions

```
1 #pragma omp declare reduction \
2   (reduction_identifier : typename_list : combiner) \
3   [initializer_clause]
```

The reduction itself is implemented in OpenMP by means of a clause that can be added to multiple constructs like `parallel` and `for` among others. The possibilities with OpenMP reductions underscore their versatility in the face of the proposed Ada extensions. Until OpenMP 4.5, the reduction is limited to the thread-parallelism model. Nonetheless, the planned OpenMP 5.0 [6] defines reductions for taskloops as well. Listing 1.15 shows the syntax adapted to our proposal for Ada. Clauses `num_tasks` and `grain_size` can still be used.

Listing 1.15. OpenMP parallel taskloops reduction example

```
1   pragma OMP parallel (taskloop reduction=>+,TOTAL);
2   begin
3     for i in range 0..MAX_I loop
4       TOTAL := Arr(i);
5     end loop;
6   end
```

OpenMP specifies that the number of times the combiner is executed, and the order of these executions is unspecified. This means that different executions may deliver different results. To avoid this unspecified behavior some restrictions can be added to the use of OpenMP reductions in safety-critical embedded domains, such as: limiting the operations to those that are associative and commutative, and forbidding the use of floating point types.

4.7 Mutual Exclusion

In OpenMP, mutual exclusion is achieved by means of two constructs: `critical` and `atomic`. While the `critical` construct restricts the execution of its associated structured block to a single thread at a time, the `atomic` construct ensures that a specific storage location is accessed atomically.

The `atomic` construct is very restrictive in the sense that it accepts a limited number of associated statements of the form defined in the specifications (Sect. 2.13.6 [1]). Consequently, atomics do not represent a threat concerning safety because no deadlock may be caused by their use. Differently, the `critical` construct accepts any kind of statement and, as a consequence, deadlocks may appear. Although OpenMP forbids nesting `critical` constructs with the same name, this is not sufficient to avoid deadlocks. A `critical` construct containing a task scheduling point[7] may cause a deadlock if the thread executing the critical region jumps to a region containing a `critical` construct with the same name. Section 5 discusses solutions and the work that needs to be done to integrate OpenMP and Ada mutual exclusion mechanisms.

5   Safety in OpenMP

Compilers are key tools to anticipate bugs that may appear at run-time, becoming fundamental when developing safety-critical systems. Although most OpenMP compilers do not diagnose common mistakes that cause execution errors, previous works are encouraging. The following subsections tackle the situations that jeopardize safety when using OpenMP, showing the existent solutions and also explaining additional proposals. The argumentation is orthogonal to the underlying language. The techniques used have been implemented in compilers for C/C++, hence it is possible provide them in Ada compilers as well.

5.1 Correctness: Data Races and Synchronization

Detecting exact data races at compile time is an open challenge, and static tools still struggle to obtain no false negatives and minimal false positives. Current mechanisms have been proved to work properly on specific subsets of OpenMP such as having a fixed number of threads [22] or avoiding the use of non-affine constructs[8] [10]. A more general approach can be used to determine the regions

---

[7] A *task scheduling point (TSP)* is a point during the execution of the a task region at which it can be suspended to be resumed later, and where the executing thread may switch to a different task region. OpenMP defines the list of TSP to be: the point immediately following the generation of an explicit task, after the point of completion of a task region, and in a taskwait region among others.

[8] *Non-affine* constructs are non-affine subscript expressions, indirect array subscripts, use of structs, non-affine loop bounds, and non-affine `if` conditions, among others.

of code that are definitely non-concurrent [20]. Although it is not an accurate solution, it will never deliver false negatives. The previously mentioned techniques can be combined to deliver conservative and fairly accurate results.

It is unattainable that compilers are able to interpret the semantics of an algorithm, thus correctness techniques are limited. However, it is feasible for compilers to observe situations that are incoherent or may lead to runtime errors. In that regard, static analysis techniques have proved to be able to catch tasks and variables that are not properly synchronized, causing both non-deterministic results (due to data races) and runtime failures (due to wrong synchronization -e.g. a task using as shared an automatic storage variable after its lifetime has ended-) [29]. Such techniques adopt a conservative approach, in the sense that performance is secondary when correctness is on the line (e.g. privatize a variable in order to avoid a race-condition). The compiler can provide a report, so users may act in accordance with the decisions taken.

Additionally, it has been demonstrated that the compiler can determine the data-sharing attributes of a task provided that all code concurrent with the task is accessible at compile time [28]. When a variable cannot be automatically determined, the user is warned to manually scope it. Since limitations concern full access to the code, whole program analysis techniques can resolve the problem. Furthermore, the Potentially_Blocking aspect proposed by the authors of the Ada extensions could be used to enable the detection of such problems at compile time, avoiding the necessity of program analysis in some cases.

Listing 1.16 shows a potential OpenMP Ada code computing the number pi as an example of the application of the correctness techniques implemented in an OpenMP-compliant compiler (Mercurium [15]). The constructs added by the user to express parallelism are emphasized, while the parts discovered by the compiler in order for the code to be correct are underlined. Both synchronization (with the taskwait construct) and mutual exclusion (with the atomic construct) can be decided by the compiler. Also the data-sharing clauses needed to avoid race-condition (on variable x) and for the code to make sense (variable sum) are automatically determined. Given the code with none of the underlined clauses and constructs, the compiler detects:

- For tasks 1 and 2: variable x is in a race condition due to concurrency between tasks 1 and 2. Additionally, the value of this variable is defined and used (in that order) within the tasks only, thus the variable can be privatized.
- In all tasks, variable step is a read-only scalar. Thus, it can be firstprivate.
- Variable sum is updated and read among the tasks, so it has to be shared. However, it is in a race condition, so accesses must be synchronized. On the one hand, tasks 1 and 2 read-write the variable, thus the compiler adds an atomic construct. On the other hand, task 3 only reads the variable, so the compiler adds a taskwait before the task.
- For task 3, variable res must be used before exiting the function. Otherwise, if the task is deferred until the function returns, the variable will no longer exist. Thus, a taskwait must be inserted after the task.

Listing 1.16. Example of data sharing

```
1    function Pi (n_steps: in Integer) return Float is
2        x : Float;
3        sum, res: Float := 0.0;
4        step : Float := 1.0/Float(n_steps);
5    begin
6        pragma OMP(task); -- private=>x, firstprivate=>step, shared=>sum
7        begin   -- OpenMP Task 1
8            x := 0;
9            for I in 1 .. n_steps/2-1 loop
10               x := (Float(I)+0.5)*step;
11               pragma OMP(atomic);
12               sum := sum + 4.0/(1.0+x*x);
13           end loop;
14       end;
15       pragma OMP(task); -- private=>x, firstprivate=>step, shared=>sum
16       begin  -- OpenMP Task 2
17           x := 0;
18           for I in n_steps/2 .. n_steps  loop
19               x := (Float(I)+0.5)*step;
20               pragma OMP(atomic);
21               sum := sum + 4.0/(1.0+x*x);
22           end loop;
23       end;
24       pragma OMP(taskwait);
25       pragma OMP(task); -- firstprivate=>step,sum, shared=>res
26       begin  -- OpenMP Task 3
27           res := step * sum;
28       end;
29       pragma OMP(taskwait);
30       return res;
31   end Pi;
```

5.2   Deadlocks

OpenMP offers two ways to synchronize threads: via directives, such as
critical and barrier, and via runtime routines, such as omp_set_lock.
In both cases, a deadlock may occur only if a thread that holds a lock tries to
obtain the same lock. This is a consequence of being a model focused in languages which do not provide higher-level concurrency mechanisms. Ada code
will use protected objects, so work still needs to be performed to integrate both
Ada and OpenMP runtime systems.

5.3   Error Handling

In the critical domain it is important to understand and specify behaviour upon
failures. The technique to enable such property is error handling. There are three
main mechanisms for handling errors: exceptions, error codes and call-backs.
Each method has advantages and disadvantages. The first fits perfectly in the
structure of exception-aware languages such as Ada. The second is suitable for
exception-unaware languages such as C. Finally, the third has the advantage of
isolating the code that is to be executed when an exception occurs. Although
only some minor mechanisms have been included in the specifications (i.e. can-
cellation constructs), there are different proposals to improve OpenMP reliability

by adopting error handling mechanisms in OpenMP [14,37]. The integration of these with Ada exceptions is also in need for future work.

6   Conclusions and Future Work

There is an oportunity for extending Ada with fine-grained parallelism. Extensions to the language with such purpose have already been presented and are still under discussion. Nevertheless, the increasing variety of platforms and their specific programming models force programmers to master multiple complex languages. Comparisons among multiple parallel programming models show the need to provide a common programming model for many-cores. In that regard, OpenMP is the perfect candidate, for it has successfully emerged as the de facto standard for shared-memory parallel programming, and starts to be used for distributed memory systems. In this paper, we show how the OpenMP tasking model can successfully be applied to Ada to define fine-grained parallelism in the form of parallel blocks, parallel loops and parallel reductions. The use of OpenMP is not a threat regarding safeness, for we have shown that both compilers and runtimes can be used to check correctness and recover from failures.

There is nevertheless work to be done to understand the actual impact of mixing OpenMP and Ada tasks, because both will be mapped to the underlying threads of the operating system. Another area for future work is a potential combination of the OpenMP tasking model and the proposed syntax for Ada parallel extensions. The underlying parallel models are sufficiently close to enable this to be considered further.

References

1. OpenMP 4.5 (2015). http://www.openmp.org/wp-content/uploads/openmp-4.5. pdf
2. GOMP (2016). https://gcc.gnu.org/projects/gomp/
3. IBM Parallel Environment (2016). http://www-03.ibm.com/systems/power/ software/parallel/
4. Intel® OpenMP* Runtime Library (2016). https://www.openmprtl.org
5. NVIDIA® CUDA C Programming Guide (2016). https://docs.nvidia.com/cuda/ cuda-c-programming-guide/index.html
6. OpenMP Technical Report 4: version 5.0 Preview 1 (2016). http://www.openmp. org/wp-content/uploads/openmp-tr4.pdf
7. Intel Interprocedural Optimization (2017). https://software.intel.com/en-us/ node/522666
8. Ada Rapporteur Group: AI12-0119-1 (2016). http://www.ada-auth.org/cgi-bin/ cvsweb.cgi/ai12s/ai12-0119-1.txt
9. Ayguadé, E., Copty, N., Duran, A., Hoeflinger, J., Lin, Y., Massaioli, F., Teruel, X., Unnikrishnan, P., Zhang, G.: The design of OpenMP tasks. TPDS **20**(3), 404–418 (2009)
10. Basupalli, V., Yuki, T., Rajopadhye, S., Morvan, A., Derrien, S., Quinton, P., Wonnacott, D.: ompVerify: polyhedral analysis for the OpenMP programmer. In: Chapman, B.M., Gropp, W.D., Kumaran, K., Müller, M.S. (eds.) IWOMP 2011. LNCS, vol. 6665, pp. 37–53. Springer, Heidelberg (2011). doi:10.1007/978-3-642-21487-5_4

11. Butenhof, D.R.: Programming with POSIX Threads. Addison-Wesley, Reading (1997)
12. Chapman, B., Jost, G., Van Der Pas, R.: Using OpenMP: Portable Shared Memory Parallel Programming, vol. 10. MIT press, Cambridge (2008)
13. Duran, A., Ayguadé, E., Badia, R.M., Labarta, J., Martinell, L., Martorell, X., Planas, J.: Ompss: a proposal for programming heterogeneous multi-core architectures. Parallel Process. Lett. **21**(02), 173–193 (2011)
14. Duran, A., Ferrer, R., Costa, J.J., Gonzàlez, M., Martorell, X., Ayguadé, E., Labarta, J.: A proposal for error handling in OpenMP. IJPP **35**(4), 393–416 (2007)
15. Ferrer, R., Royuela, S., Caballero, D., Duran, A., Martorell, X., Ayguadé, E.: Mercurium: Design decisions for a s2s compiler. In: Cetus Users and Compiler Infastructure Workshop in conjunction with PACT (2011)
16. Kegel, P., Schellmann, M., Gorlatch, S.: Using OpenMP vs. threading building blocks for medical imaging on multi-cores. In: Sips, H., Epema, D., Lin, H.-X. (eds.) Euro-Par 2009. LNCS, vol. 5704, pp. 654–665. Springer, Heidelberg (2009). doi:10.1007/978-3-642-03869-3_62
17. Krawezik, G., Cappello, F.: Performance comparison of MPI and three OpenMP programming styles on shared memory multiprocessors. In: SPAA. ACM (2003)
18. Kuhn, B., Petersen, P., O'Toole, E.: OpenMP versus threading in C/C++. Concurrency Pract. Experience **12**(12), 1165–1176 (2000)
19. Lee, S., Min, S.J., Eigenmann, R.: OpenMP to GPGPU: a compiler framework for automatic translation and optimization. SIGPLAN Not. **44**(4), 101–110 (2009)
20. Lin, Y.: Static nonconcurrency analysis of OpenMP programs. In: Mueller, M.S., Chapman, B.M., Supinski, B.R., Malony, A.D., Voss, M. (eds.) IWOMP -2005. LNCS, vol. 4315, pp. 36–50. Springer, Heidelberg (2008). doi:10.1007/978-3-540-68555-5_4
21. Lisper, B.: Towards parallel programming models for predictability. In: OASIcs, vol. 23. Schloss Dagstuhl LZI (2012)
22. Ma, H., Diersen, S.R., Wang, L., Liao, C., Quinlan, D., Yang, Z.: Symbolic analysis of concurrency errors in openmp programs. In: ICPP, pp. 510–516. IEEE (2013)
23. Michell, S., Moore, B., Pinho, L.M.: Tasklettes – a fine grained parallelism for ada on multicores. In: Keller, H.B., Plödereder, E., Dencker, P., Klenk, H. (eds.) Ada-Europe 2013. LNCS, vol. 7896, pp. 17–34. Springer, Heidelberg (2013). doi:10.1007/978-3-642-38601-5_2
24. Pinho, L., Nelis, V., Yomsi, P., Quinones, E., Bertogna, M., Burgio, P., Marongiu, A., Scordino, C., Gai, P., Ramponi, M., Mardiak, M.: P-SOCRATES: a parallel software framework for time-critical many-core systems. MICPRO **39**(8), 1190–1203 (2015)
25. Pinho, L.M., Michell, S.: Session summary: parallel and multicore systems. Ada Lett. **36**(1), 83–90 (2016)
26. Pinho, L.M., Moore, B., Michell, S., Taft, S.T.: Real-time fine-grained parallelism in ada. ACM SIGAda Ada Lett. **35**(1), 46–58 (2015)
27. Reinders, J.: Intel Threading Building Blocks. O'Reilly & Associates Inc, Sebastopol (2007)
28. Royuela, S., Duran, A., Liao, C., Quinlan, D.J.: Auto-scoping for OpenMP tasks. In: Chapman, B.M., Massaioli, F., Müller, M.S., Rorro, M. (eds.) IWOMP 2012. LNCS, vol. 7312, pp. 29–43. Springer, Heidelberg (2012). doi:10.1007/978-3-642-30961-8_3
29. Royuela, S., Ferrer, R., Caballero, D., Martorell, X.: Compiler analysis for OpenMP tasks correctness. In: Computing Frontiers, p. 7. ACM (2015)

30. Serrano, M.A., Melani, A., Bertogna, M., Quinones, E.: Response-time analysis of DAG tasks under fixed priority scheduling with limited preemptions. In: DATE, pp. 1066–1071. IEEE (2016)
31. Shen, J., Fang, J., Sips, H., Varbanescu, A.L.: Performance gaps between OpenMP and OpenCL for multi-core CPUs. In: ICPPW, pp. 116–125. IEEE (2012)
32. Sielski, K.L.: Implementing Ada 83 and Ada 9X using solaris threads. Ada: Towards Maturity **6**, 5 (1993)
33. Snir, M.: MPI-the Complete Reference: The MPI Core, vol. 1. MIT press, Cambridge (1998)
34. Stone, J.E., Gohara, D., Shi, G.: OpenCL: a parallel programming standard for heterogeneous computing systems. CSE **12**(3), 66–73 (2010)
35. Taft, S.T., Moore, B., Pinho, L.M., Michell, S.: Safe parallel programming in Ada with language extensions. ACM SIGAda Ada Lett. **34**(3), 87–96 (2014)
36. Varbanescu, A.L., Hijma, P., Van Nieuwpoort, R., Bal, H.: Towards an effective unified programming model for many-cores. In: IPDPS, pp. 681–692. IEEE (2011)
37. Wong, M., Klemm, M., Duran, A., Mattson, T., Haab, G., Supinski, B.R., Churbanov, A.: Towards an error model for OpenMP. In: Sato, M., Hanawa, T., Müller, M.S., Chapman, B.M., Supinski, B.R. (eds.) IWOMP 2010. LNCS, vol. 6132, pp. 70–82. Springer, Heidelberg (2010). doi:10.1007/978-3-642-13217-9_6

Mixed Criticality

Migrating Mixed Criticality Tasks Within a Cyclic Executive Framework

Alan Burns[1]([⊠]) and Sanjoy Baruah[2]

[1] University of York, York, UK
burns@cs.york.ac.uk
[2] University of North Carolina, Chapel Hill, USA

Abstract. In a cyclic executive, a series of frames are executed in sequence; once the series is complete the sequence is repeated. Within each frame, units of computation are executed, again in sequence. In implementing cyclic executives upon multi-core platforms, there is advantage in coordinating the execution of the cores so that frames are released at the same time across all cores. For mixed criticality systems, the requirement for separation would additionally require that, at any time, code of the same criticality should be executing on all cores. In this paper we derive algorithms for constructing such multiprocessor cyclic executives for systems of periodic tasks, when inter-processor migration is permitted.

1 Introduction

Recent trends in embedded computing towards the widespread use of multi-core platforms, and the increasing tendency for applications to contain components of different criticality, have thrown up major challenges to the developers of reliable software-based systems. In this paper we consider these two challenges in the context of highly safety-critical application domains where cyclic executives remain the scheduling mechanism of choice.

Cyclic executives. A cyclic executive is a simple deterministic scheme that consists, for a single processor, of the continuous executing of a series of *frames* (or *minor cycles* as they are often called). Each frame consists of a sequence of *jobs* that execute in the specified sequence and are required to complete by the end of the frame. The set of frames is called the *major cycle*.

Multicore CPUs. On a multi-core, or multiprocessor, platform each core should have the same frame size and the same major cycle time. The time source from which the run-time support software will execute the jobs contained within each frame, is synchronised so that all cores switch between minor cycles concurrently. Within each frame there are a series of jobs to be executed. If jobs are constrained to execute always within the same minor cycle and always on the same core then the run-time schedule is defined to be *partitioned*. Alternatively, if jobs can migrate from one active frame to another active frame on a different core then the schedule is defined to be *global*. In this paper we allow a

J. Blieberger and M. Bader (Eds.): Ada-Europe 2017, LNCS 10300, pp. 203–216, 2017.
DOI: 10.1007/978-3-319-60588-3_13

small number of constrained job migrations. In a previous workshop paper [5] we focused on independent jobs, in this paper we address the more practical problem of jobs that are derived from periodic tasks. In other work [6,7] we have shown how fully partitioned systems can be constructed.

Mixed criticality. In mixed-criticality scheduling (MCS) theory, tasks are characterized by several different WCET parameters denoting different estimates of the true WCET value, these different estimates being made at different levels of assurance. The scheduling objective is then to validate the correct execution of each task at a level of assurance that is consistent with the criticality level assigned to that task: tasks assigned greater criticality must be shown to execute correctly when more conservative WCET estimates are assumed, while less critical tasks need to have their correctness demonstrated only when less conservative WCET estimates are assumed.

Related work. A cyclic executive is a particularly restricted form of static schedule. The issue of mapping mixed criticality code to static schedules has been addressed by Tamas-Selicean and Pop [13,14]. An alternative approach to implementing the move between criticality levels in a static schedule is by switching between previously computed schedules; one per criticality level - this approach is explored in [3,12]. However, these schemes are only applicable to single processor systems. The notion of separation used in this paper comes from [9].

2   System Model

In a typical implementation, a cyclic executive (CE) is defined by two durations, the length of the minor cycle (or frame) T_F and the duration of the major cycle T_M. These values are related by ($T_M = k.T_F$) where k is a positive integer (usually a power of 2), denoting the number of frames in the repeating major cycle of the CE.

The issue of how to choose T_F and T_M to best support a set of tasks with given periods is beyond the scope of this paper. Rather we follow industrial practice [4] and assume these parameters are fixed by the system definition and that application tasks' periods are constrained to be multiples of T_F (up to the value of T_M).

The mapping of tasks to frames implies that there is a set of jobs allocated to each frame. All jobs within a frame must complete by the end of the frame. However, what it means to complete will depend on the behaviour of the system in terms of its criticality levels – as will be explained shortly.

We assume that the hardware platform consists of m identical (unit speed) processors (or cores). Each job can execute on any core and has identical temporal behaviour on all cores.

In general V criticality levels, L_1 to L_V, may be defined for a system with L_1 being the highest criticality; in this paper we primarily restrict ourselves to just two criticality levels ($V = 2$), and use the notation $L_1 = $ HI and $L_2 = $ LO.

Run-time support

Mixed-criticality scheduling (MCS) theory has primarily concerned itself with the sharing of CPU computing capacity in order to satisfy the computational demand, as characterized by the worst-case execution times (WCET), of pieces of code. However, there are typically many additional resources that are also accessed in a shared manner upon a computing platform, and it is imperative that these resources also be considered.

An interesting approach towards such a consideration was advocated by Giannopoulou et al. [9] in the context of multicore platforms: during any given instant in time, all the cores are only allowed to execute code of the same criticality level. This approach has the advantage of ensuring that accesses to all shared resources (memory buses, cache, etc.) during any time-instant are only from code of the same criticality level. We refer to such a scheme of switching between workloads of different criticality levels as *synchronised switching*.

We focus our attention in this paper on synchronized switching. That is, we seek to construct cyclic executives in which each minor cycle may be considered partitioned into V criticality levels. Initially the highest criticality jobs are executed, when they have finished the next highest criticality jobs are executed, and so on. This continues until finally the lowest criticality jobs are executed. In a simple system with just two criticality levels, HI and LO, there is a switchover time S defined within each minor frame. Before S each core is executing HI-criticality work, after S each core is executing LO-criticality work. To give resilient fault tolerant behaviour, if the HI-criticality work has not completed by time-instant S on any core then the LO-criticality work is postponed (on every core), thereby giving extra time for the HI-criticality work to execute (up to the end of the minor cycle). In this paper we will explore how to find acceptable (safe and efficient) values for the switching times.

Implementing the criticality switches. Giannopoulou et al. [9] advocated, if supported by the hardware platform, the use of synchronisation barriers. In the case of dual-criticality workloads (the generalization to >2 criticality levels is straight-forward), each core calls the barrier upon completing its assigned HI-criticality work. When the final core completes and calls the barrier, all the calls are released from the barrier and each core continues with executing LO-criticality work.

The benefit of this barrier-based scheme is that it can take advantage of time gained by jobs executing for less than their estimated WCETs. So at the end of the HI-criticality executions if the signal occurs before the pre-computed barrier S, then all cores can move to LO-criticality executions early. Additionally, there may be situations arising at run-time when a late switch to one criticality level is compensated by time gained from under-execution within jobs of the next criticality level. For example, the switch occurs at some time $> S$, but the LO-criticality jobs end up executing for less than their LO-criticality WCET values and hence all complete by the end of the frame.

3   Dual Criticality Jobs

In this section, we consider the scheduling of a collection of jobs within a single frame of an m-processor platform, when there are only two criticality levels ($V = 2$). All the jobs are assumed to become available at the start of the frame (without loss of generality, denoted as being at time 0), and they all have a deadline at the end of the frame (denoted D). In keeping with prior work on the scheduling of such dual-criticality systems, we use the notation HI and LO to denote the greater and lesser criticality levels (i.e., $L_1 =$ HI and $L_V = L_2 =$ LO). The criticality of job j_i is denoted by $\chi_i \in \{$LO, HI$\}$; each HI-criticality job is characterized by two WCET parameters $C_i($LO$)$ and $C_i($HI$)$ (with $C_i($LO$) \leq C_i($HI$)$), while each LO-criticality job j_i is characterized by a single WCET parameter $C_i($LO$)$ (for convenience such jobs are also assigned a $C_i($HI$)$ value with $C_i($LO$) = C_i($HI$)$).

Given a collection of such dual-criticality jobs to be scheduled within a frame of duration D upon an m-processor platform, our objective is to determine the switching point S such that only HI-criticality jobs are executed over the interval $[0, S)$. If all HI-criticality jobs complete by time-instant S, then LO-criticality jobs are executed over $[S, D)$; else, the LO-criticality jobs are abandoned and execution of HI-criticality jobs continues over $[S, D)$ as well. It follows that there are three conditions that need to be satisfied:

1. If each HI-criticality job j_i executes for no more than $C_i($LO$)$, then all the HI-criticality jobs must fit into the interval $[0, S)$.
2. All the LO-criticality jobs must fit into the interval $[S, D)$
3. If each HI-criticality job j_i executes for no more than $C_i($HI$)$, then all the HI-criticality jobs must fit into the interval $[0, D)$.

In Sect. 3.1 below, we derive a simple and efficient algorithm for determining S (and the corresponding schedules) such that these conditions are satisfied; in Sect. 3.2, we describe an optimization to this simple method. These algorithms assume minimal run-time support.

3.1   A Simple Scheme for Constructing CEs

We first define two (potential) candidates for the switching point S:

S^{min} The earliest instant at which all HI-criticality jobs have completed if they execute for no more than $C($LO$)$.
S^{max} The latest instant at which a switch must occur for the LO-criticality work to complete by time D.

It is evident that any candidate S must satisfy the two inequalities $S^{\mathrm{min}} \leq S \leq S^{\mathrm{max}}$.

Let us additionally define two interval durations, which constrain the possible values of S^{min} and S^{max}.

Δ^{LO} The duration (makespan) of the interval needed for all the LO-criticality jobs to (begin and) complete execution.

Δ^{HI} The duration of the interval needed for all the HI-criticality jobs to execute the extra work they must do in HI-criticality mode—i.e., the amount $(C_i(\text{HI}) - C_i(\text{LO}))$, for each j_i with $\chi_i = \text{HI}$.

To determine these durations, we employ the optimal scheme of McNaughton [10, p. 6]. Given a collection of n jobs with execution requirements $c_1, c_2, \ldots, c_n$, McNaughton showed that the minimum makespan of a preemptive schedule for these jobs on m unit-speed processors is given by

$$\max\left(\frac{\sum_{i=1}^{n} c_i}{m}, \max_{i=1}^{n}\{c_i\}\right) \tag{1}$$

The actual schedule is obtained by taking the jobs (in any order) and allocating them to m intervals of the size of the makespan, each representing one of the m processors. As one interval is filled, perhaps with part of a job, the next interval starts with the rest of this job. At most $(m-1)$ jobs are split across intervals in this manner. During run-time a job that was split across two intervals will run at the beginning of the time-interval upon one processor, and towards the end of the time-interval on the other processor.

A direct application of McNaughton's result yields the conclusion that the minimum makespan for a global preemptive schedule for the jobs in LO-criticality mode is given by

$$\Delta^{\text{LO}} \stackrel{\text{def}}{=} \max\left(\frac{\sum_{\chi_i=\text{LO}} C_i(\text{LO})}{m}, \max_{\chi_i=\text{LO}}\{C_i(\text{LO})\}\right) \tag{2}$$

We therefore set

$$S^{\max} \stackrel{\text{def}}{=} D - \Delta^{\text{LO}} \tag{3}$$

Similarly, a direct application of the makespan result allows the minimum interval for the HI-criticality work (in LO-criticality mode) to be computed:

$$S^{\min} \stackrel{\text{def}}{=} \max\left(\frac{\sum_{\chi_i=\text{HI}} C_i(\text{LO})}{m}, \max_{\chi_i=\text{HI}}\{C_i(\text{LO})\}\right) \tag{4}$$

Clearly for the whole system to be schedulable, it is necessary that $S^{\min} \leq S^{\max}$ which is equivalent to requiring that

$$S^{\min} \leq D - \Delta^{\text{LO}}$$
$$\Leftrightarrow S^{\min} + \Delta^{\text{LO}} \leq D \tag{5}$$

We now consider the final constraint—the scheduling of HI-criticality jobs executing in HI-criticality mode. It has been shown [2, Example 1] that this is not necessarily ensured by simply computing the makespan (using McNaughton's method, as above) with the $C_i(\text{HI})$ values, and validating that the resulting makespan is $\leq D$. We instead determine the minimal makespan for all the HI-criticality jobs, subject to each such job having received an amount of execution equal to its LO-criticality WCET by time-instant $S^{\min}$. To determine this makespan, we apply McNaughton's scheme to the work that is left to do after time-instant $S^{\min}$ (i.e. $C_i(\text{HI}) - C_i(\text{LO})$ for each job j_i with $\chi_i = \text{HI}$). Letting $C_i(\text{EX})$ denote the "excess" computational requirement of job j_i in HI-criticality mode over LO-criticality mode:

$$C_i(\text{EX}) \stackrel{\text{def}}{=} \left(C_i(\text{HI}) - C_i(\text{LO})\right),$$

we have

$$\Delta^{\text{HI}} \stackrel{\text{def}}{=} \max\left(\frac{\sum_{\chi_i=\text{HI}} C_i(\text{EX})}{m}, \max_{\chi_i=\text{HI}}\left\{C_i(\text{EX})\right\}\right) \tag{6}$$

It is evident that $S^{\min} + \Delta^{\text{HI}} \leq D$ is sufficient for schedulability; earlier (Expression 5) we had shown that $S^{\min} + \Delta^{\text{LO}}$ should also be $\leq D$. Putting these pieces together, we may summarize this method as follows. We compute $S^{\min}, \Delta^{\text{LO}}$, and Δ^{HI} according to Expressions (4), (2), and (6) respectively, and require that

$$S^{\min} + \max\left(\Delta^{\text{LO}}, \Delta^{\text{HI}}\right) \leq D \tag{7}$$

as a sufficient schedulability condition. If this condition is satisfied, $S \leftarrow S^{\min}$ (i.e., we declare $S^{\min}$ to be the switch-point we had set out to compute).

3.2   An Improvement

Let us now suppose that Condition 7 is violated, and $S^{\min} + \max\left(\Delta^{\text{LO}}, \Delta^{\text{HI}}\right) > D$. Since $\left(S^{\min} + \Delta^{\text{LO}} \leq D\right)$ is a necessary condition for schedulability (see Inequality 5), it must be the case that

$$S^{\min} + \Delta^{\text{HI}} > D.$$

Now if $\left(\sum_{\chi_i=\text{HI}} C_i(\text{HI}) \geq mD\right)$, there is nothing to be done. Otherwise, there must be some unused processor capacity in the McNaughton schedule constructed according to Expression 4 for the interval $[0, S)$, and/or in the McNaughton schedule constructed according to Expression 6 for the interval after time-instant S. Let us consider the situation where the schedule has some unused processor capacity over the interval $[0, S)$ (recall that $S \leftarrow S^{\min}$ in the method of Sect. 3.1). An inspection of Expression (4) reveals that this happens if

$$\frac{\sum_{\chi_i=\text{HI}} C_i(\text{LO})}{m} < \max_{\chi_i=\text{HI}}\left\{C_i(\text{LO})\right\}$$

Our idea, intuitively speaking, is that any such unused capacity prior to time-instant S may as well be allocated to some HI-criticality task, for use in the event of the system undergoing a mode-change into HI-criticality mode. (If the system does not undergo such a mode-change, this allocated capacity may end up remaining unused.) Doing so leaves less execution remaining to be completed after the switch instant S in HI-criticality mode, and may thus result in a smaller makespan in HI-criticality modes (i.e., a smaller value for Δ^{HI}).

Such a scheme is particularly effective if the duration of the HI-criticality schedule after S—the one of duration Δ^{HI}—is also dominated by longer jobs, i.e., if in Expression 6

$$\frac{\sum_{\chi_i=\text{HI}} C_i(\text{EX})}{m} < \max_{\chi_i=\text{HI}}\{C_i(\text{EX})\}$$

If this be the case, then the unused capacity prior to time-instant S can be filled so as to minimise the maximum $C_i(\text{EX})$ by bringing forward work to before S— this is accomplished by increasing $C_i(\text{LO})$ for such a job, thereby decreasing its $C_i(\text{EX})$ by the same amount. However, jobs that have $(C_i(\text{LO}) = S)$ cannot have work brought forward in this manner since this would result in S increasing as well.

It is evident that this scheme is effective since:

- Any work brought forward will not change S,
- The first term in Expression (6) is not increased by bringing work forward, and
- The second term in Expression (6) is reduced by always choosing the largest value and decreasing it.

We note that if more than one job has the same $C_i(\text{EX})$ value then an arbitrary choice is made (and has no impact on optimality).

And what if there is no unused processor capacity in the schedule over $[0, S)$? In that case, the switch-point S may be increased to any value $\leq S^{\max}$ (where $S^{\max}$ is as defined by Expression (3)). An obvious choice for S is $S \leftarrow S^{\max}$; an iterative algorithm for achieving the smallest value of S (i.e., the earliest possible switch-time) is as follows. Setting the switch point S to be $S^{\min} + 1$ will generate m free slots. So $C_i(\text{LO})$ values of HI-criticality jobs can be increased by this amount (and the corresponding $C(\text{EX})$ values decreased). If this will reduce the size of Δ^{HI} by more than one then an overall decrease in $S + \Delta^{\text{HI}}$ will have been achieved. This cycle is repeated (i.e. adding 1 to S) until either no further gain is made or S takes the value of $S^{\max}$. At each step of the cycle no $C(\text{LO})$ value should increase beyond the current value of S.

Example 1. We apply this improved scheme to the scheduling of the mixed-criticality instance of Table 1 upon 3 unit-speed processors with a frame length of 8 ($D = 8$).

We can immediately use the equations above to compute: $\Delta^{\text{LO}} = 3$ (and hence $S^{\max} = 5$) and $S^{\min} = 4$. So the first step to schedulability is satisfied (i.e. $S^{\min} \leq S^{\max}$). if we ignore mixed criticality issues then the minimum makespan for the HI-criticality jobs (ignoring LO-criticality work) is 7. So a completely separated scheme would require a frame size of 10 ($7 + 3$).

If we initially focus on $S^{\min}$ then we note that there are no free slots, so Eq. (6) gives a makespan in HI-criticality mode (Δ^{HI}) of 5. So the use of this value for S (i.e. 4) gives a required frame size of 9 ($4 + 5$); since the frame-size is 8, the instance would be deemed unschedulable with $S \leftarrow 4$.

Table 1. An example dual-criticality job instance

	χ_i	$C_i(\text{LO})$	$C_i(\text{HI})$	$C_i(\text{HI}) - C_i(\text{LO})$
j_1	LO	3	-	-
j_2	LO	2	-	-
j_3	LO	2	-	-
j_4	HI	2	7	5
j_5	HI	3	7	4
j_6	HI	3	3	0
j_7	HI	4	4	0

However, if we set $S \leftarrow (S^{\min} + 1)$ which equals $S^{\max} = 5$ then the total work available on three processors by time 5 is 15. The work required using $C(\text{LO})$ values for HI-criticality work is 12. Hence 3 units of work can be added to these $C(\text{LO})$ values. If we make $C_4(\text{LO}) = 4$ and $C_5(\text{LO}) = 4$ then maximum $C_i(\text{EX})$ becomes equal to 3. Hence $\Delta^{\text{HI}} = 3$ and $S^{\max} + \Delta^{\text{HI}} = 8$. Therefore the job set fits into the frame size of 8, with a switch time of 5.   □

Rather than iterating through potential candidate values for S in the manner described above, we can construct a single **linear program** (LP) for determining a suitable value for S – see Fig. 1. In this linear program

- δ_i denotes the amount of execution that is "moved" from $C_i(\text{EX})$ to $C_i(\text{LO})$; the first two constraints of the LP restrict this amount to (i) be positive and (ii) not exceed the value of $C_i(\text{EX})$.
- The next two constraints are an LP representation of the makespan resulting from applying McNaughton's rule to the LO-criticality execution requirements of the HI-criticality jobs.
- The fifth constraint represents the requirement that the synchronization barrier should not be moved beyond $S^{\max}$ (since doing so could result in LO-criticality jobs failing to complete even in LO-criticality behaviors).
- The final two constraints are an LP representation of the makespan resulting from applying McNaughton's rule to the excess (i.e., HI-criticality minus LO-criticality) execution requirements of the HI-criticality jobs.

Since a linear program can be solved in time polynomial in its representation, this LP-based approach allows us to determine, in polynomial time, whether an instance can be scheduled using our improved approach (The iterative approach could require time proportional to $S^{\max} - S^{\min}$; in pathological cases, it could thus have a run-time that is pseudo-polynomial in the representation of the instance to be scheduled.).

MINIMIZE $(S + S')$ subject to

(1). $\delta_i \geq 0$ for each i : $\chi_i = \text{HI}$

(2). $\delta_i \leq C_i(\text{EX})$ for each i : $\chi_i = \text{HI}$

(3). $S \geq C_i(\text{LO}) + \delta_i$ for each i : $\chi_i = \text{HI}$

(4). $S \geq \Big(\sum_{i:\chi_i=\text{HI}} (C_i(\text{LO}) + \delta_i) \Big) / m$

(5). $S \leq S^{\text{max}}$

(6). $S' \geq C_i(\text{EX}) - \delta_i$ for each i : $\chi_i = \text{HI}$

(7). $S' \geq \Big(\sum_{i:\chi_i=\text{HI}} (C_i(\text{EX}) - \delta_i) \Big) / m$

Fig. 1. A linear program for determining the switching point S

4 Periodic Task Systems

We now consider instances in which the workload is specified as periodic tasks rather than as individual jobs. In this section, we again focus upon dual-criticality systems.

Let us assume that there are k minor cycles in the major cycle of the cyclic executive we seek to construct, with k being an integer power of 2. As before, we assume that we have m parallel cores. Application tasks are assumed to have *harmonic* periods that are k or $2k$ or $4k$ etc. times the size of the minor frame (e.g. $\in \{25\,\text{ms}, 50\,\text{ms}, 100\,\text{ms}, 200\,\text{ms}, 400\,\text{ms}, \ldots\}$). For the purposes of illustration in the following discussions we will assume that there are 8 minor cycles to the major cycle (i.e., $k = 8$).

We now describe how we construct cyclic executives for such dual-criticality periodic task systems. For each of the k sets of frames we seek to compute a switch point $S_1, S_2, \ldots, S_k$; we do not require these switch points to be the same in each minor cycle.

First the tasks with period equal to the minor cycle must be allocated to all the minor cycles. These can be dealt with by the job-based procedures described in Sect. 3.

To add tasks with longer periods a number of approaches are possible. The simplest, and the one that is most appropriate if computation times for these tasks are relatively small (and hence compatible with the jobs already allocated), is to allocate each job of these tasks to exactly one minor cycle. So, for example, a task with period equal to twice the minor cycle duration will be allocated exactly once each in cycles $\{1, 2\}$, $\{3, 4\}$, $\{5, 6\}$, and $\{7, 8\}$. And a task with period four times the minor cycle duration will be allocated exactly once each in cycles $\{1, 2, 3, 4\}$ and $\{5, 6, 7, 8\}$. Finally tasks with period equal to the major cycle can be allocated to any one of the minor cycles. To manage this allocation, common forms of heuristics may be applied. First-Fit or Worst-Fit for example, with the tasks been allocated largest $C(\text{LO})$ first. As tasks are added to each cycle the analyses of Sect. 3 above for the set of frames that make up that cycle are applied. Different switch points for each cycle will emerge, but if the full task set can be accommodated then allocation is complete and the system is schedulable by construction.

This process of allocating jobs to single cycles can fail if tasks with larger periods have larger computation times ($C(\text{LO})$ or $C(\text{HI})$) that are not easily accommodated within a single frame. To accommodate such tasks, jobs need to be split between minor frames. (This is a common approach with single processor cyclic executives and is considered to be one of the disadvantages of the cyclic executive approach.) Two forms of splitting are possible, *explicit* or *implicit*. With explicit splitting the code of the task is actually partitioned (statically). So for a task with period equal to twice the minor cycle the code will be 'cut' in half (approximately). Each portion can then be analysed to determine its $C(\text{LO})$ and $C(\text{HI})$ values. The first half will be allocated to cycles 1, 3, 5 and 7; and the second half will be allocated to cycles 2, 4, 6 and 8. These jobs are added to the existing jobs corresponding to tasks with periods equal to the duration of a single frame, and the earlier analysis of Sect. 3 again applied.

Although this explicit splitting is optimal from a scheduling point of view (if the code can be partitioned exactly into two parts with the same $C(\text{LO})$ and $C(\text{HI})$ values), this approach suffers from a number of significant practical problems:

- The lack of available tool support for splitting code into exact portions that can give rise to identical estimates of worst-case execution time.
- Code structures may not be amenable to such partitioning.
- Even if approximate splitting is possible, modifications to the code due to upgrades or bug fixes, will require re-splitting, and re-testing. This is an expensive process.

For these reasons we reject explicit splitting and employ an implicit scheme similar to that used earlier for job splitting. But for a task with two estimates of worst-case execution time there is the issue of when to trigger the migration. (Note the migration here is to the next cycle; it may or may not involve a move to a different core.)

Reducing a task that runs every 50 ms, say, to one that runs every 25 ms is very similar to the use of period transformation [11] to reduce a task's period (and hence raise its priority in a rate-monotonic system). The application of period transformation to mixed criticality systems has been discussed in a number of papers [1,8,15]. Here we make use of the main techniques which is to divide $C(\text{HI})$ by the number of parts the task is split into. So if the 50 ms task has WCET estimates of 8 and 12 and is split into two parts, its computation time in the first cycle will be all at the "normal" or LO-criticality level (so it has $C(\text{LO}) = 6$ and $C(\text{EX}) = 0$). In the second cycle it could again have $C(\text{LO}) = 6$ and $C(\text{EX}) = 0$, but this would be conservative in that the task is being allocated $6 + 6 = 12$ units even at the LO-criticality level – it would be more efficient to have $C(\text{LO}) = 2$ and $C(\text{EX}) = 4$. Moreover, if the LO-criticality load on the first cycle is too high it could reduce its requirement in that cycle to be $C(\text{LO}) = 5$, and then in the second cycle we have $C(\text{LO}) = 3$ and $C(\text{EX}) = 4$. Alternatively if the second phase of the cycle is overloaded in the second cycle (i.e. $C(\text{EX}) = 4$ is too high) then the first cycle could have $C(\text{LO}) = 8$ and $C(\text{EX}) = 2$, and the second cycle $C(\text{LO}) = 0$ and $C(\text{EX}) = 2$. This potential movement of work from one cycle to another is exploited in the following scheme.

We need additional notation to denote per-cycle parameterisation. We will add '$[x]$' to the previously defined terms to denote the xth cycle. A task, τ_i, with a period equal to k minor cycles is split into k jobs, $\tau_i[1] \dots \tau_i[k]$. Its computation times will be denoted by $C_i[x](\text{LO})$, $C_i[x](\text{HI})$ and, by construction, $C_i[x](\text{EX}) \overset{\text{def}}{=} C_i[x](\text{HI}) - C_i[x](\text{LO})$.

We now describe the allocation process for dual critically systems. The following steps will be undertaken:

1. Allocate all single cycle tasks (i.e. tasks with period equal to the minor cycle) using the job-based analysis developed earlier (discussed in Sect. 3 above).
2. Allocate all remaining HI-crit tasks using the period transformation scheme (as detailed below).
3. If the above step is not successful, move work to later cycles until all HI-crit work is scheduled (or declare task set is unschedulable).
4. Allocate all remaining LO-crit tasks.

We will now describe these steps in more detail.

Initially the HI-crit tasks are allocated to the cycles with the computation time of each part of the task τ_i being defined by:

$$C_i[x](\text{LO}) = \min\left(\frac{C_i(\text{HI})}{p}, C_i(\text{LO}) - \frac{(x-1)C_i(\text{HI})}{p}\right)_{\geq 0} \tag{8}$$

(here, the subscript ≥ 0 denotes that this value is capped to be no smaller than zero), and

$$C_i[x](\text{EX}) = C_i(\text{HI})/p - C_i[x](\text{LO}) \tag{9}$$

where p being the number of minor cycles that equal the period of the task and x goes from 1 to p.

To illustrate this, a task with $C_i(\text{LO}) = 8$ and $C_i(\text{HI}) = 12$ split over 4 cycles would have pairs of values for $C_i[x](\text{LO})$ and $C_i[x](\text{EX})$ of: (3, 0), (3, 0), (2, 1) and (0, 3).

As all minor cycles are the same following step one, we initially focus on the first cycle. The HI-criticality load from single cycle tasks is added to the extra load from the set of $C_i[1](\text{LO})$ and $C_i[1](\text{EX})$ values. The analysis of the job-based scheme is applied to give values of $S[1]^{\min}$, $\Delta[1]^{\text{HI}}$ and $\Delta[1]^{\text{LO}}$. If the size of the minor cycle is D, $S[1]^{\min} + \Delta[1]^{\text{HI}} \leq D$ and $S[1]^{\min} + \Delta[1]^{\text{LO}} \leq D$ then the first cycle is schedulable and the scheme moves on to the second cycle.

However if the first cycle is not schedulable then the next step is to fill the makespan (if there are 'gaps') by moving work from $C(\text{EX})$ to $C(\text{LO})$. Again this follows the job-based approach. If this is not sufficient then work needs to be moved from some task's (or tasks') $C_i[1](\text{LO})$ to $C_i[2](\text{LO})$ so as to reduce $S[1]^{\min}$.

Once $C_i[1](\text{LO})$ and $C_i[2](\text{LO})$ have changed then the relevant $C_i[1](\text{EX})$ and $C_i[2](\text{EX})$ values are recomputed.

To make the first cycle schedulable any task that is active in the following cycle may be chosen as the one to have its work moved from the first to the second cycle. The task or tasks to choose are those that will not have their criticality behaviour in the first cycle changed. This constraint is best illustrated by an example. If a task with $C(\text{LO}) = 5$ and $C(\text{HI}) = 10$ is split into two then all of the following schemes are valid for the two computation times in the two cycles: $(5, 0)$ and $(0, 5)$, or $(5, 1)$ and $(0, 4)$ etc. until $(5, 5)$ and $(0, 0)$. But if this task moves just a single unit of its LO-criticality execution requirement into the second cycle then the only valid scheme is $(4, 0)$ and $(1, 5)$.

Once the first cycle is made schedulable the process is repeated on the second and subsequent cycles. If in any cycle there is no available work to be moved forward (to another cycle), then the technique of moving work within a cycle from after the switching point to before may be attempted. If none of these schemes work then the task set is not schedulable.

Intuitively, work in being moved forward until $C(\text{LO})$ is satisfied. Then a task's work can be done as either $C(\text{LO})$ or $C(\text{EX})$ which gives more flexibility. So if with the example used earlier, with $C_i[x](\text{LO})$ and $C_i[x](\text{EX})$ values of: $(3, 0)$, $(3, 0)$, $(2, 1)$ and $(0, 3)$, only two ticks could be accommodated in any $S[x]^{\min}$ then work would be pushed through until the following is obtained: $(2, 0)$, $(2, 0)$, $(2, 0)$ and $(2, 4)$.

If the HI-criticality tasks can be allocated then the next step is to allocate the LO-criticality tasks. From the HI-criticality stage k switching times have been computed $S[1] \ldots S[k]$. The available space is therefore $D - S[1] + D - S[2] + \cdots + D - S[k]$. LO-criticality tasks are spread evenly across the cycles. Those that execute every cycle must go into every cycle, those that execute every two need to be spread across the first two, then third and fourth etc. This is continued until, again, the allocation is successful or the task set is deemed unschedulable.

4.1   An Example

We illustrate our technique for the following task set:

	χ_i	T	$C_i(\text{LO})$	$C(\text{HI})$
τ_1	HI	10	2	3
τ_2	HI	10	3	4
τ_3	HI	10	2	3
τ_4	HI	10	1	2
τ_5	LO	10	2	2
τ_6	LO	10	3	3
τ_7	LO	10	1	1
τ_8	HI	20	4	6
τ_9	HI	20	6	8
τ_{10}	LO	20	2	2

Here there are two criticality levels (HI and LO) and the minor cycle time is 10 ms. Tasks have periods of either 10 or 20, so only two minor cycles are needed in the system's major cycle. The hardware platform has two cores, so each of the two minor cycles contains two frames.

The two HI-criticality tasks with period of 20 must be split. So $\tau_8[1]$ has a computation time $C_8[1](\text{LO}) = 6/2 = 3$; and $\tau_9[1]$ has computation time $C_9[1](\text{LO}) = 8/2 = 4$. Adding 3 and 4 to the computation times of tasks τ_1 to τ_4 gives a makespan for $S[1]^{\min}$ of $(2 + 3 + 2 + 1 + 3 + 4)/2 = 7.5$.

The value of $\Delta[1]^{HI}$ is 2 which is acceptable, but the makespan for the LO-criticality jobs ($\Delta[1]^{\text{LO}}$) is 3. So $S[1]^{\max}$ is 7 and $S[1]^{\min} > S[1]^{\max}$ which breaks the invariant for schedulability. We need to move work out of the first cycle so that $S[1]^{\min}$ has a value of 7.

Choosing τ_9 we reduce its computation time in the first cycle to 3. This means that $S[1]^{\min}$ now has a makespan of $(2 + 3 + 2 + 1 + 3 + 3)/2 = 7$, which is acceptable.

In the second cycle τ_8 needs 1 in the LO-criticality mode and 2 more in the HI-criticality mode (i.e. $C_8[2](\text{LO}) = 1$ and $C_8[2](\text{EX}) = 2$). Task τ_9 now needs 3 in LO-criticality mode and 2 more in HI-criticality mode. So $S[2]^{\min}$ now has a makespan of $(2 + 3 + 2 + 1 + 1 + 3)/2 = 6$, and $\Delta[2]^{HI}$ in the second cycle is $(1 + 1 + 1 + 1 + 2 + 2)/2 = 4$. So $S[2]^{\min} + \Delta[2]^{HI}$ is 10, which is the upper bound.

Finally we add τ_{10}. There is no room in the first cycle, but it can be added to the second cycle. The value of $\Delta[2]^{\text{LO}}$ for the second cycle is now 4, from $(2 + 3 + 1 + 2)/2$, which is just acceptable as now $S[2]^{\min} + \Delta[2]^{\text{LO}}$ is again 10.

The analysis shows that the full task set is schedulable over two frames and two cycles with switching times of 7 in the first cycle and 6 in the second. In total 40 time units are required $(2 \times 2 \times 10)$. If one ignores the benefits of mixed criticality scheduling then the total requirement using $C(\text{HI})$ values is 52. This equates to the use of three frames (that is three cores) which is one core more than is required with criticality-aware scheduling.

5 Conclusions and Further Work

Single processor safety-critical systems are often constrained so that they can be implemented as a series of frames in a repeating cyclic executive. In this paper we have extended this approach to incorporate multi-core platforms and mixed criticality applications. We allow a minimum number of tasks to be split across frames and cycles, and propose a practical means of constructing the necessary cyclic schedule.

Under further work we will extend the use of Linear Programming from job-based to task-based scheduling. We will also look to demonstrate how the proposed model can be implemented in Ada. The Ada programming language provides support for various forms of scheduling on single and multiprocessor platforms. This includes direct support for a barrier synchronisation protocol, and controlled task migration. These features, together with execution-time monitoring and timing events, should enable the full model to be represented in Ada.

Once an appropriate multicore platform with full Annex D Ada support is available a demonstrator will be implemented.

References

1. Baruah, S., Burns, A.: Fixed-priority scheduling of dual-criticality systems. In: Proceedings of the 21st International Conference on Real-Time Networks and Systems, RTNS 2013, pp. 173–181. ACM, New York (2013)
2. Baruah, S., Burns, A.: Achieving temporal isolation in multiprocessor mixed-criticality systems. In: Proceedings of the 2nd International Workshop on Mixed Criticality Systems (WMC), Rome (Italy), December 2014
3. Baruah, S., Fohler, G.: Certification-cognizant time-triggered scheduling of mixed-criticality systems. In: Proceedings of the IEEE Real-Time Systems Symposium (RTSS), Vienna, Austria. IEEE Computer Society Press (2011)
4. Bate, I., Burns, A.: An integrated approach to scheduling in safety-critical embedded control systems. Real-Time Syst. **25**(1), 5–37 (2003)
5. Burns, A., Baruah, S.: Semi-partitioned cyclic executives for mixed criticality systems. In: Proceedings of the International Workshop on Mixed Criticality Systems (WMC), December 2015
6. Burns, A., Fleming, T., Baruah, S.: Cyclic executives, multi-core platforms and mixed criticality applications. In: Proceedings of 27th ECRTS, pp. 3–12 (2015)
7. Fleming, T., Baruah, S., Burns, A.: Improving the schedulability of mixed criticality cyclic executives via limited task splitting. In: Proceedings of the 24th International Conference on Real-Time Networks and Systems, pp. 277–286 (2016)
8. Fleming, T., Burns, A.: Extending mixed criticality scheduling. In: Proceedings of the International Workshop on Mixed Criticality Systems (WMC), December 2013
9. Giannopoulou, G., Stoimenov, N., Huang, P., Thiele, L.: Scheduling of mixed-criticality applications on resource-sharing multicore systems. In: International Conference on Embedded Software (EMSOFT), pp. 17:1–17:15, Montreal, October 2013
10. McNaughton, R.: Scheduling with deadlines and loss functions. Manag. Sci. **6**, 1–12 (1959)
11. Sha, L., Lehoczky, J., Rajkumar, R.: Solutions for some practical problems in prioritized preemptive scheduling. In: Proceedings of the Real-Time Systems Symposium. IEEE Computer Society Press (1986)
12. Socci, D., Poplavko, P., Bensalem, S., Bozga, M.: Time-triggered mixed critical scheduler. In: Proceedings of the International Workshop on Mixed Criticality Systems (WMC), pp. 67–72, December 20143
13. Tamas-Selicean, D., Pop, P.: Design optimization of mixed-criticality real-time applications on cost-constrained partitioned architectures. In: Proceedings of the IEEE Real-Time Systems Symposium (RTSS), Vienna, Austria. IEEE Computer Society Press (2011)
14. Tamas-Selicean, D., Pop, P.: Task mapping and partition allocation for mixed-criticality real-time systems. In: 2011 IEEE 17th Pacific Rim International Symposium on Dependable Computing (PRDC), pp. 282–283, December 2011
15. Vestal, S.: Preemptive scheduling of multi-criticality systems with varying degrees of execution time assurance. In: Proceedings of the Real-Time Systems Symposium, pp. 239–243, Tucson, AZ. IEEE Computer Society Press, December 2007

Directed Acyclic Graph Scheduling
for Mixed-Criticality Systems

Roberto Medina$^{(\boxtimes)}$, Etienne Borde, and Laurent Pautet

LTCI, Télécom ParisTech, Université Paris-Saclay, 75013 Paris, France
{roberto.medina,etienne.borde,laurent.pautet}@telecom-paristech.fr

Abstract. Deploying safety-critical systems into constrained embedded platforms is a challenge for developers who must arbitrate between two conflicting objectives: software has to be safe and resources need to be used efficiently. Mixed-criticality (MC) has been proposed to meet a trade-off between these two aspects. Nonetheless, most task models considered in the literature of MC scheduling, do not take into account precedence constraints among tasks. In this paper, we propose a multi-core scheduling approach for a model presenting MC tasks and their dependencies as a Directed Acyclic Graph (DAG). We also introduce an evaluation framework for this model, released as an open source software. Evaluation of our scheduling algorithm provides evidence of the difficulty to find correct scheduling for DAGs of MC tasks. Besides, experimentation results provided in this paper show that our scheduling algorithm outperforms existing algorithms for scheduling DAGs of MC tasks.

Keywords: Mixed-Criticality · Directed acyclic graphs · Mode transition · Real-time scheduling

1 Introduction

Having certified software is imperative to deploy applications in safety-critical systems. To ensure that critical tasks always meet their timing requirements (*i.e.* deadline), Certification Authorities (CA) require an overestimated Worst-Case Execution Times (WCET).

The Mixed-Criticality (MC) model was proposed in [15] to guarantee safety while efficiently using embedded resources. In this model, tasks with different *criticality* levels share the same hardware platform. This model ensures that, (i) *high-criticality* tasks of the system always perform their execution within their deadlines and (ii) resources are efficiently used by redistributing WCET overestimation of *high-criticality* tasks to *low-criticality* tasks.

Nonetheless, data dependencies between tasks on a MC model has seen very few contributions [6]. Our model represents MC tasks with a Directed Acyclic Graph (DAG), where vertices represent tasks and edges represent precedence constraints among them. Vertices that are not related by an edge can be executed in parallel. This is very interesting since embedded platforms use multi-core architecture nowadays.

© Springer International Publishing AG 2017
J. Blieberger and M. Bader (Eds.): Ada-Europe 2017, LNCS 10300, pp. 217–232, 2017.
DOI: 10.1007/978-3-319-60588-3_14

In this paper, we propose a new approach based on static List Scheduling (LS) to schedule DAGs of MC tasks for multi-core architectures. We also propose a random generation method of MC-DAGs[1], used to evaluate our scheduling algorithm. Our evaluation shows that our scheduler has a better schedulability rate compared to the reference algorithm of the literature [2].

The remainder of the paper is organized as follows: Sect. 2 presents the task model used in our contribution. The main difficulties that need to be overcome by our scheduling approach are presented in Sect. 3. In order to schedule the MC-DAG on multi-core architectures we propose a new scheduling algorithm in Sect. 4. The implementation of the MC-DAG test generator is described in Sect. 5. Section 6 presents the evaluation of our algorithm on the generated MC-DAG tests. Related works are discussed in Sect. 7 and we conclude in Sect. 8 with future research perspectives.

2   Task Model

In this section we present the task model our contribution relies on: DAGs of MC tasks. DAGs and the synchronous model of computation are widely used in industrial tools like SCADE from Esterel, Simulink from MathWorks among others. Therefore, including the MC approach to this model is of great interest.

2.1   Mixed-Criticality Tasks

MC scheduling [6] has become an appealing solution to integrate various tasks with different levels of criticality onto the same hardware platform.

MC scheduling was first presented by Vestal in [15]. Vestal's task model is based on the following observation: the higher the criticality level becomes, the more overestimated the WCET is. For instance, in a low criticality level tasks could have their WCET determined empirically (*i.e.* measuring execution times over multiple executions). While on a high criticality level, code coverage analysis and validation from a CA to determine a pessimistic WCET that cannot be exceed at any time, is required. Therefore the low criticality levels have a smaller WCET than high criticality levels. In order to mitigate the impact of overestimated WCET on resource dimensioning, MC models propose to identify operational modes, and to define different timing configurations of tasks for each operational mode. In particular when high-criticality tasks exceed their WCET of a low-criticality mode, the system performs a mode transition into a high-criticality mode where low-criticality tasks are stopped (discard approach) or have less processing power (elastic approach). However, this mode transition needs to be safe: **deadlines of high-criticality tasks must still be satisfied.**

We consider MC systems with two operational modes noted HI and LO. When the system is in LO mode (initial mode), all tasks can be executed on the platform until their WCET in LO mode (noted $C_i(LO)$ for a task τ_i). For

---

[1] Open source: https://github.com/robertoxmed/ls_mxc

each task τ_i, $C_i(LO) \leq C_i(HI)$ ($C_i(HI)$ is the WCET of τ_i in mode HI, it is a pessimistic WCET). If a task is able to complete its execution before its $C_i(LO)$, we suppose all estimated time budget is used, *i.e.* the processor would be idle until the $C_i(LO)$ is consumed. A Timing Failure Event (TFE) occurs when a task τ_i runs for a longer time than its $C_i(LO)$, and the occurrence of a TFE triggers a mode switch from LO to HI mode. In HI mode, tasks considered as highly critical (noted as HI tasks) are able to run until $C_i(HI)$ while lower criticality tasks (noted as LO tasks) are stopped: we adopt the discard approach.

2.2 DAG Mixed-Criticality Model

In addition to their criticality level, we consider tasks with precedence constraints modeled as DAGs. This representation allows us to identify clearly which parts of a computation can be run in parallel. Multi-core platforms are more and more used in embedded systems, parallel computation is an important challenge to improve resource usage. At the same time, MC studies often use independent task sets, however real applications are most likely going to have tasks communicating with each other. For example, Simulink and SCADE are tools that are used for designing and implementing embedded control systems [12]. We consider real-time systems modeled with **a single-DAG**, *i.e.* only one DAG of mixed-critical tasks is being executed by the platform. All tasks forming the DAG are constraint to meet a single deadline, can be preempted and can migrate from one CPU to another.

Our model, noted MC-DAG, is composed of tasks represented by vertices in the graph. Precedence constraints are materialized by edges. Each task τ_i is characterized by a criticality level $\chi_i \in \{LO, HI\}$, a WCET in LO mode $C_i(LO)$ and a WCET time in HI mode $C_i(HI)$ ($C_i(HI) = 0$ if $\chi_i = LO$). HI criticality tasks cannot depend on the output of LO criticality tasks for safety reasons: if the LO tasks fails to deliver its output, the HI criticality task can be compromised. For this reason we only allow three types of communications in our model: from HI to HI, from HI to LO and from LO to LO. Industrial standards like ARINC653 also apply this communication constraint for partitions for example.

In the remaining, we shall illustrate our contribution with the example of the MC-DAG presented in Fig. 1. White vertices represent LO criticality tasks and gray vertices are HI criticality tasks. Numbers on each vertex represent the execution times of tasks. The graph on the left has WCET for tasks in LO mode, while the right graph gives the WCET of HI tasks in HI mode. WCET are presented in Time Units (TU).

3 Problem Statement

Scheduling MC tasks on multi-core platforms is a difficult problem, specially due to transitions to higher criticality modes: deadlines of high-criticality tasks must be met, even when a TFE occurs. This scheduling problem becomes even more complex when there exist precedence constraints between tasks: if a task

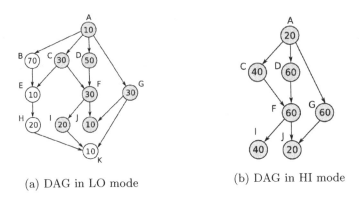

(a) DAG in LO mode   (b) DAG in HI mode

Fig. 1. Mixed-Criticality DAG example.

increases its WCET due to a switch to HI mode, all its successors are delayed in a domino effect.

In this paper, we aim at making sure a safe scheduling of a given MC-DAG exists. A MC system is considered to be safe if (i) tasks meet their deadlines in HI and LO modes, and (ii) the mode transition from LO to HI is safe: HI tasks meet their deadline even when a TFE occurs: the incrementation of the WCET (from $C_i(LO)$ to $C_i(HI)$) for HI tasks cannot compromise their deadline. Allocating MC tasks with data dependencies to a multi-core architecture is equivalent to an optimization problem that aims at minimizing the execution time of a MC-DAG while enforcing safe mode transitions for each possible date of a TFE. Ensuring the safety of a LO to HI mode transition is therefore a challenging objective.

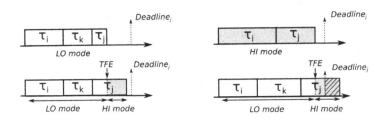

Fig. 2. Safe and unsafe mode transitions

Figure 2 provides scenarii for safe and unsafe mode transitions. The HI task τ_i completes its execution. Then, both the HI task τ_j and the LO task τ_k become ready to execute. Let us assume LO task τ_k starts its execution before the HI task τ_j. A TFE occurs during the execution of task τ_j. In other words, τ_j executes for a longer time than its LO WCET, $C_j(LO)$. Thus, a mode switch occurs. τ_k is stopped and τ_j's WCET is extended up to its HI WCET, $C_j(HI)$. In these two scenarii, the WCET $C_k(LO)$ differs: the WCET in the second scenario is greater than the one in the first scenario. In the first scenario, illustrated on the low left part of Fig. 2, the deadline of task τ_j is satisfied during the transition. In the second scenario, $C_k(LO)$ is greater and when the TFE occurs, task τ_j has not enough execution time available and eventually causes a deadline miss.

In addition to this problem, another issue is to evaluate scheduling algorithms for MC-DAGs in multi-core architectures. Since the MC-DAG model has mostly seen theoretical contributions, there does not exist yet a benchmarking framework to evaluate such DAG scheduling algorithms. Besides, benchmarking frameworks for MC-DAG have to consider lots of parameters that influence the degree of parallelism of tasks, the distribution of CPU utilization among tasks, the number of cores that are assigned to the DAG, as well as the topology of graph.

In the rest of this paper, we present the technical solutions we propose to answer these difficult problems.

4   Multi-core Scheduling for MC-DAGs

4.1   Scheduling Algorithms for DAGs on Multi-cores

Finding an optimal scheduling of DAGs on a limited number of processors (respecting the deadline and minimizing the scheduling time of the DAG) is a NP-complete problem [9]. List Scheduling (LS) is a polynomial approach to find near-optimal scheduling. It aims at producing a static scheduling for DAGs that minimizes the completion time of the DAG, also called *makespan*. Several different heuristics are based on LS and improve the resulting scheduling under some hypothesis. As explained before, the MC-DAG model increases the complexity of DAG scheduling, mainly because of the safety constraints on the LO to HI mode transition (satisfying the deadline of HI tasks after their WCET is incremented).

In order to reduce the complexity of this problem, we consider the following hypotheses: the scheduler executes tasks with a time-triggered semantics, and tasks execute exactly for their WCET: if tasks finish before their WCET, idle time is enforced at run time. These hypotheses increase the determinism of the schedule and reduce the number of possible scheduling scenarii, as well as the number of instants for which TFEs may occur.

4.2   Scheduling Algorithms for MC-DAG on Multi-cores

Scheduling MC-DAGs was first proposed by Baruah for uni-core architectures in [4]. LS was then used for scheduling this model into multi-core platforms [2]. The idea is to build two scheduling tables: one per mode. In HI mode, a static scheduling allocates time slots to HI tasks in a table by applying LS to the DAG in HI mode. In LO mode, another static scheduling table allocates time slots to tasks almost the same way. However, time slots are allocated for HI tasks as soon as they are ready. Then, time slots are allocated to LO tasks according to

LS when they are not preempted by HI tasks. In case a TFE occurs, the system switches to HI mode and applies the scheduling table in HI mode. Since HI tasks are always scheduled prior to LO tasks, there is a guarantee to have a safe mode transition.

We applied this approach to schedule MC-DAGs on uni-core architectures [11]. The objective was to evaluate availability of MC-DAG systems enriched with our recovery mechanisms to switch back to LO mode. In this context, we realized that preempting LO tasks as soon as a HI task is ready can produce inefficient schedules and could result in deadline misses whereas valid schedules exist.

Figure 3 highlights the problem with this approach. Figure 3a provides the schedule obtained with Baruah's method on the MC-DAG we described on Fig. 1. On this example, the deadline (180 TUs) is missed. Figure 3b illustrates the schedule obtained with our method on the same example.

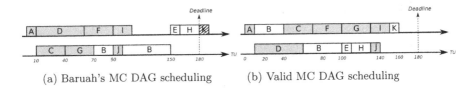

(a) Baruah's MC DAG scheduling   (b) Valid MC DAG scheduling

Fig. 3. Scheduling tables for the MC DAG

Intuitively, the main idea of our approach is to privilege HI tasks over LO tasks, **only** at specific instants for which it is required to prioritize HI tasks in order to ensure a safe mode transition. These specific instants are called Latest Safe Activation Instant (LSAIs). The main steps of our algorithm consist in calculating the HI scheduling table (S_{HI}) starting from the deadline of the graph. This way we obtain a LSAI for each HI task. The LO mode scheduling table (S_{LO}) is then obtained thanks to LS with preemption of HI tasks at their LSAI. We explain this method in the remaining of this section: in Sect. 4.3, we define a necessary condition in order to ensure mode transitions are safe. As explained in Sect. 4.4, we use this definition to compute the LSAIs of HI tasks in LO mode, as well as the scheduling table of HI tasks in HI mode. Finally, we explain in Sect. 4.5 how we compute the scheduling table of tasks in LO mode.

4.3   Safe Mode Transition: Necessary Condition

We introduce in this section a necessary condition (see Eq. (1)) ensuring that a mode transition can be performed safely. This condition is then used in Sect. 4.4 to compute (i) the LSAIs of HI tasks in LO mode, and (ii) the scheduling of HI tasks in HI mode.

$$\forall \tau_i \in \tau_{HI}, WCRT_i(LO) + C_i(HI) - C_i(LO) \leq D. \tag{1}$$

In this equation, τ_{HI} is the set of HI tasks of the graph and D is the deadline of the graph. $WCRT_i(LO)$ corresponds to the Worst Case Response Time, that is the time required for task τ_i to finish its execution in LO mode. The intuition behind Eq. (1) is that, for all $\tau_i \in \tau_{HI}$, τ_i has enough time to finish its execution in mode HI in case a TFE occurs while executing τ_i in LO mode. Figure 4 gives an illustration of Eq. (1):

- the upper part of the figure illustrates a scheduling scenario in which Eq. (1) is not respected, leading to a deadline miss;
- the lower part of the figure illustrates a scheduling scenario in which Eq. (1) is respected. This illustration helps to understand why, in the worst case (*i.e.* the time of the TFE equals $WCRT_i(LO)$) the deadline is still met after the transition to HI mode.

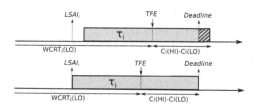

Fig. 4. Example of unsafe mode transition

Respecting Eq. (1) forces HI tasks in LO mode to start at a time that allows τ_i to switch to HI mode safely. The LSAI of τ_i, an exit vertex of the MC-DAG in HI mode, is illustrated on Fig. 4. As one can see on the figure, computing the LSAI of an exit vertex of the DAG is very easy: it is a straightforward application of Eq. (1). In the next subsection, we explain how we compute the LSAIs of all the HI tasks, which boils to compute the scheduling table of the MC-DAG in HI mode.

4.4 Building the HI Mode Table

We schedule HI tasks in HI mode **as late as possible** in order to compute the LSAIs of HI tasks in LO mode, leaving as much time as possible to schedule LO tasks in LO mode. In order to do so, we first compute the LSAIs of exit vertices as illustrated on Fig. 4. The LSAI of a task τ_i then becomes the virtual deadline for the predecessors of τ_i and we can compute the LSAIs of these predecessors by applying Eq. (1) with this virtual deadline. In other words, we *reverse schedule* the MC-DAG in HI mode: from the *deadline* of the graph, backwards time 0, we allocate time slots for HI tasks in HI mode. As a result, we obtain a scheduling table of HI tasks in HI mode, called S_{HI}, and the starting date of a task in this table corresponds to its LSAI. However, in order to start HI tasks in HI mode **as late as possible** we need to minimize the makespan of the *reverse schedule*.

For this purpose, we use a LS algorithm called Highest Level First with Estimated Time (HLFET) [1]. Indeed, HLFET is the most efficient LS algorithm to schedule DAGs on multi-cores [9]: HLFET is less computationally expensive than other LS algorithms (which are in general of polynomial complexity), and provides near-optimal makespans. In HLFET, the *level* of a vertex is given by the longest path from that vertex to an exit vertex, and the level of an exit vertex is equal to its execution time. For example, applying HLFET to the graph presented in Fig. 1b leads to the following levels for HI tasks: $\langle (A, 180), (C, 140),$ $(D, 160), (F, 100), (G, 80), (I, 40), (J, 20) \rangle$.

Algorithm 1. S_{HI} computation

1: **function** CALCSHI
2:    Calculate levels for each vertex in HI mode
3:    **for all** HI tasks τ_i **do**
4:        $RET[\tau_i] \leftarrow C_i(HI)$ /* Remaining execution time*/
5:    $t \leftarrow Deadline$
6:    **while** $t > 0$ **do**
7:        **for all** cores c **do**
8:            $\tau \leftarrow$ lowest level task s.t. all successors have been fully scheduled
9:            $S_{HI}[t][c] \leftarrow \tau$
10:           $RET[\tau] \leftarrow RET[\tau] - 1$
11:           **if** $RET[\tau] = 0$ **then** $LSAI[\tau] \leftarrow t$
12:       $t \leftarrow t - 1$
13:       **if** $\sum RET > t * NbCores$ **then**
14:           **return** NotSchedulable
15: **return** S_{HI} and $LSAI$

Algorithm 1 describes the algorithm we propose to compute the scheduling table of HI tasks in HI mode, called S_{HI}. The first step of the algorithm is to compute the levels of tasks with HLFET (using $C_i(HI)$ for their execution time). We build S_{HI} starting from the deadline and from the exit vertices of the DAG in HI mode. For each time slot, we schedule on each core the tasks (i) having the lowest level, and (ii) having all their successors completely scheduled. If all the tasks are completely scheduled before time 0 is reached, the system is schedulable in mode HI and table S_{HI} provides its scheduling in mode HI. Besides, the start date of τ_i in this table is also the LSAI of τ_i.

We illustrate the execution of this algorithm on the DAG provided in Fig. 1b. We assume we have two cores to execute this DAG and its deadline is 180 TUs. At the beginning we have two exit vertices with no successors: I and J. Tasks I and J are selected, they have the lowest levels. Once J has been fully allocated, at time 160 TU, the only task that can be executed is G (F has to wait until I is completely scheduled). AT 140 TU, F is scheduled until 80 TU, activating tasks C and D. Once D has been fully allocated, task A executes from TU 20 to 0. The final S_{HI} table is shown in Fig. 5, and the DAG is schedulable in HI mode. With S_{HI}, we also obtain the LSAIs of each task, depicted with vertical

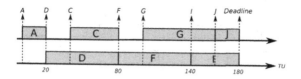

Fig. 5. S_{HI} table

arrows in Fig. 5: 160 for I, 140 for J, 100 for G, 80 for F, etc. As explained in the next section, these LSAIs are then used to calculate the scheduling table of tasks in LO mode, called S_{LO}.

4.5   Building the LO Mode Table

Algorithm 2 describes the algorithm we propose to compute the scheduling table of HI and LO tasks in LO mode. First, we calculate tasks levels using HLFET (using $C_i(LO)$ for tasks execution time). Then, we start allocating time slots to tasks from time 0, scheduling tasks towards the deadline. We schedule tasks with the highest level first, but we promote a HI task when its LSAI is reached. LSAI behaves as a virtual deadline that guarantees safe mode transitions. Promoted tasks preempt other tasks, and execute until completion. Preempted tasks can be resumed in another processor since task migration is allowed in our model. As explained previously, we thus guarantee that Eq. 1 is satisfied for all HI task.

Algorithm 2. S_{LO} computation

1: **function** CALCSLO
2:     Calculate levels for each vertex in LO mode
3:     **for all** tasks tau_i **do**
4:         $RET[\tau_i] \leftarrow C_i(LO)$ /* Remaining execution time */
5:     $t \leftarrow 1$
6:     **for all** timeslots $t \leq Deadline$ **do**
7:         **if** t is a LSAI **then** promote the corresponding HI task(s)
8:         **for all** cores c **do**
9:             $\tau \leftarrow$ highest level task s.t. all predecessors have been fully scheduled
10:            $S_{LO}[t][c] \leftarrow \tau$
11:            $RET[\tau] \leftarrow RET[\tau] - 1$
12:         **if** $\sum RET > (Deadline - t) * NbCores$ **then**
13:            **return** SchedulingException
14: **return** S_{LO}

Considering the MC-DAG provided in Fig. 1a, the levels of each task are given by: $\langle (A, 120), (B, 110), (C, 90), (D, 110), (E, 40), (F, 60), (G, 40), (H, 30), (I, 30), (J, 10), (K, 10) \rangle$.

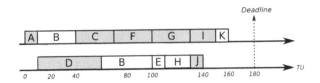

Fig. 6. S_{LO} table

Time 0 TU is a LSAI for task A so it is promoted and starts its execution. At 10 TUs, tasks B, C, D and G can run and no LSAI occurs. Thus, we select B and D, the tasks with the highest levels. At 20 TUs, we have a LSAI for D. However, D is already running so there is no preemption at this point. But, at 40 TUs, it is a LSAI for C which preempts B. At 60 TUs, D has finished its execution, B is resumed (on a different processor). Once C has finished its execution at 70 TUs, F runs until it completes at 100 TUs in parallel with B. Tasks G, E have met their precedence constraints and it is a LSAI for G, so G and E are selected. We continue this procedure until there are no more tasks to schedule. The final S_{LO} is presented in Fig. 6. Vertical arrows correspond to LSAIs of HI tasks.

In this section, we presented a scheduling approach for MC-DAGs. To evaluate this approach, we propose the benchmarking tool described in Sect. 5.

5   Mixed-Criticality DAG Synthesis

To evaluate our scheduling algorithm we need a benchmarking tool that automatically generates a significant number of MC-DAGs. No such tool is available in the literature: contributions to this subject have only presented theoretical work [2] or evaluation frameworks have not been released publicly [10]. We explain the different aspects we considered for developing our benchmarking tool.

The benchmarking tool takes into account different aspects of the various communities that are part of our work: DAG, Real-time on multi-core architectures, and MC scheduling.

- The objective of generating graphs randomly is to avoid topologies that might influence schedulability. We developed a DAG generation tool based on the Erdös-Rényi's method, which has been used in several research on DAGs scheduling for real-time systems [8,14].
- An important parameter for scheduling tasks sets on multi-core systems is the *utilization*. Distribution of utilization [5] is a method widely used in the real-time systems domain in order to benchmark scheduling algorithms. Task sets can be generated quite efficiently with a uniform distribution of utilization among tasks. However, these methods usually create independent tasks, *i.e.* without precedence constraints among them.
- When it comes to MC in DAG generation tools, it is important to parameterize the utilization of HI and LO tasks, as well as utilization of HI tasks in LO mode.

Our generator has three main stages: (i) generation of the DAG of HI tasks, (ii) reduction of HI tasks utilization in LO criticality mode, and (iii) completion of the DAG with LO tasks. The following parameters are used by the tool: e is the probability of having an edge between two vertices. p the maximum degree of "parallelism" in the DAG, *i.e.* the maximum number of vertices that are not transitively connected by an edge. CP, the critical path of the graph, *i.e.* the longest path in the DAG between an entry vertex to an exit vertex. U_{HI}, the utilization (of HI tasks) in HI mode. U_{HIinLO}, the utilization of HI tasks in LO mode ($U_{HIinLO} < U_{HI}$). U_{LO}, the utilization (of all tasks) in LO mode.

The first step of the MC-DAG generation creates the DAG in HI mode using a parameter U_{HI}. This step is iterative: each iteration adds vertices until the utilization U_{HI} is reached. More precisely, we create in each iteration a random number (between 1 and p) of vertices. When creating vertices, we distribute U_{HI} by giving each vertex a $C_i(HI)$. An edge can be added between two vertices, with a probability e, if (i) the vertices were created in different iterations (enforcing the degree of paralellism p), and (ii) if adding the edge does not increase the critical path (thus enforcing parameter CP).

As a second step, we generate the LO part of HI tasks. Parameter U_{HIinLO} gives an upper bound of the utilization of HI tasks in LO mode. HI tasks' $C_i(LO)$ is randomly generated between 1 and a bound starting at $C_i(HI)$.

We iteratively try a $C_i(LO)$ for each task and check if U_{HIinLO} is satisfied after the reduction. If it is not the case, a new iteration tries other values for $C_i(LO)$, but this time between 1 and the previous value tested. As a consequence, values for $C_i(LO)$ decrease until U_{HIinLO} is satisfied. In addition, if all HI tasks become unitary (*i.e.* $C_i(LO) = 1$) the reduction phase stops.

On the last step of the generation, LO tasks are added to the graph. We distribute a utilization of $U_{LO} - U_{HIinLO}$ to LO tasks (U_{HIinLO} is the final real value obtained after the reduction phase). We use a process similar to the one used in step one in order to complement the DAG of HI tasks. However, we prevent the process from adding edges from LO tasks to HI tasks. Finally, we check whether the CP was reached while creating the DAG. If not, we add a last task (either HI or LO) that completes the CP.

Our benchmarking tool is open sourced and can be found on GitHub[2]. Figure 7 shows a MC-DAG that was created with our generator. HI tasks are presented in gray and LO tasks are presented in white. Numbers represent estimated execution times in TUs. This MC-DAG was obtained using the following parameters: $U_{LO} = 4$; $U_{HI} = 3$; $U_{HIinLO} = 1.5$; $p = 6$; $CP = 30$; $e = 40\%$.

---

[2] https://github.com/robertoxmed/ls_mxc.

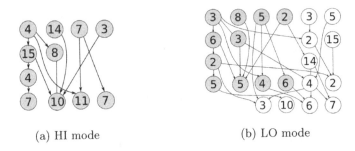

(a) HI mode   (b) LO mode

Fig. 7. Generated MC DAG

6   Evaluation of the Scheduling Algorithm

In this section we present our experimental results, and compare our approach to Baruah's [2] algorithm. The comparison criteria we used is the *acceptance rate*, defined as follows: given a set of MC-DAGs of tasks, supposed to be schedulable in HI and LO mode, the *acceptance rate* is the ratio of MC-DAGs for which a safe schedule (*i.e.* also ensuring safe mode transitions) was found.

6.1   DAG Generator Parameters

In our experiments, we have considered execution platforms of 2, 4, and 8 cores. The DAG parameters used for generation were chosen as follows: parallelism degree p was set twice the number of cores. Here is the rationale: for p greater than the number of cores, DAGs have mainly entry vertices. For p much smaller than the number of cores, we consider the hardware platform is oversized. The probability of having an edge between two vertices, e, was increased progressively from 20 to 60%. Utilization in HI and LO mode U_{LO}, U_{HI}, was increased progressively as well from half of the number of cores, to the number of cores (*e.g.* $U_{LO/HI}$ varied from 4 to 8 for a hardware platform of 8 cores). Utilization of HI tasks in LO mode U_{HIinLO} is given by $\frac{min(U_{HI}, U_{LO})}{2}$, that way we always reduce HI tasks' execution time in LO mode. The CP was fixed to 30 TUs for all the tests, and we considered the deadline equals to CP (see definition on Sect. 5).

6.2   Results

Obtained results, with 8 cores, are shown in Fig. 8. We do not provide results obtained with 4 or 2 cores because they are very similar to results presented here. Each subfigure represents results obtained with an edge probability e set to 20, 40 and 60%. Each line represents the acceptance rate for a given U_{LO}, varying from 4 to 8. Continuous lines correspond to results obtained with our method, whereas dashed lines are results obtained with Baruah's MC-DAG scheduler. The x-axis represents the U_{HI}, also varying from 4 to 8. Each point of the figure gives the acceptance rate obtained on a set of 200 DAGs for each combination of parameters U_{LO}; U_{HI}; U_{HIinLO}; p; e; CP.

6.3   Analysis of Results

Except when $U_{LO} = 4$, Baruah's scheduler has a much lower acceptance rate than our algorithm. This was predictable: forcing LO preemptions each time a HI tasks can be executed is suboptimal. The difference becomes very significant when U_{LO} increases: on Fig. 8a, with $e = 20$ and $U_{LO} = 7$, our method has an acceptance rate very close to 100% whereas Baruah's algorithm produces an acceptance rate below 40%. Clearly, relaxing the preemption condition to only LSAIs gives a better acceptance rate.

More generally, we can see on Fig. 8a that increasing U_{LO} impacts significantly the acceptance rate of a scheduling method. In practice, U_{LO} is expected to be high in a MC-DAG: increasing U_{LO} may either enable the inclusion of more functionalities, or reduce the probability of TFEs by overestimating WCET in mode LO. Experimental results show that the acceptance rate obtained with our method begins to decrease when U_{LO} is above 7. For instance, on Fig. 8a, with

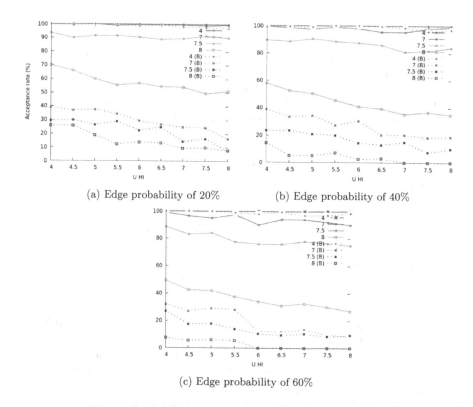

(a) Edge probability of 20%   (b) Edge probability of 40%

(c) Edge probability of 60%

Fig. 8. Acceptance rates for different edge probabilities.

$e = 20$ and $U_{LO} = 7$, the acceptance rate is around 100%. With $U_{LO} = 7.5$, the acceptance rate drops to approximately 90%. It decreases progressively between 70 to 50% when $U_{LO} = 8$ and U_{HI} increases. LSAIs of HI tasks are the main reason for this behavior. Each time a HI tasks preempts a LO one, the completion time of this LO task is increased, potentially ending in a deadline miss. However, the acceptance rate provided is still very good for high levels of utilization $U_{HI} = 8$ and $U_{LO} = 7.5$ on 8 cores. Therefore a vast number of LO tasks can be included into the system and we would still be able to ensure a safe scheduling.

With higher values of e, 40 and 60%, (*i.e.* the DAGs have more edges) we have similar results except that the acceptance rate for U_{LO} above 7.5 decreases. However, it remains above 75% in all subfigures of Fig. 8.

Our scheduling algorithm is very efficient when it comes to finding schedulers for DAGs. At each step of the allocation phase, the scheduler tests if there are enough slots to schedule the remaining of the DAG, which discards non-feasible cases rapidly. On average, the scheduling phase of our experiments took 70 s for 200 DAGs that were a combination of parameters $U_{LO}; U_{HI}; U_{HIinLO}; p; e; CP$. However, since the complexity of HLFET is polynomial, the running time of our scheduling algorithm can increase significantly depending on the number of nodes contained in the graph.

7   Related Works

In this section, we position our approach with respect to existing contributions aiming at scheduling DAGs for Real-Time systems.

Saifullah *et al.* [14], adapted preemptive and non-preemptive Earliest Deadline First (EDF) to schedule DAGs. In this work, authors transform the DAG of tasks into a set of independent tasks scheduled with EDF by synthesizing the scheduling parameters of these tasks (*i.e.* period, deadline). However, this approach *requires idle time* between the completion of the DAG and the deadline in order to compute the tasks parameters, which leads to an underutilization of the platform. DAGs in this work do not include tasks with different criticality levels.

Scheduling tests based on Worst-Case Response Time (WCRT) for multiple DAGs using DM and EDF are presented in [13]. Necessary conditions are found for systems running multiple DAGs by finding safe upper-bounds on their WCRT. However, these safe upper-bounds can be very pessimistic if applied to a single DAG, which is the scope of our contribution. DAGs can be judged as non-schedulable when in fact a valid schedule exists. In addition, each DAG has only one criticality level in this work.

A scheduling approach for multiple DAGs with mixed-criticality levels was presented in [10]. Authors use a federated approach to allocate cores to tasks: a single DAG can have various exclusive cores for its execution, while less demanding DAGs are scheduled in processors that are left. The task model used in this paper differs from ours since they use DAGs to describe the internal structure of a task: a task is modeled by jobs with precedence constraints among them. Criticality levels being assigned to tasks, means that this model forbids dependencies among tasks of different criticality levels (even dependencies of LO tasks on HI tasks). As opposed to our proposal, mixed-criticality tasks are independent tasks in this model.

The federated approach was also considered on the latest work of Baruah [3] to schedule multiple DAGs into one multi-core architecture. DAGs with a high utilization value will have exclusive cores assigned to them and LS is applied to find the scheduling tables for these exclusive cores. Tasks with a low utilization are distributed to the remaining cores and are considered to be sequential, so any real-time scheduling algorithm can be applied for them. The model differs from the one in [10] where DAGs are assigned with a single criticality level, while Baruah's model allows vertices to have different criticality levels in the same DAG. Nonetheless the approach to schedule multiple DAGs still considers HI tasks with the highest priority over LO tasks (like in [2]), which still causes delays on LO tasks for the scheduler in LO mode, this can be avoided with our scheduling approach.

Existing contributions do not aim at finding a minimal execution time for a single DAG of tasks with mixed criticality levels. As a consequence, these contributions would perform poorly when aiming at scheduling a single-DAG with criticality levels.

8   Conclusion

This paper presents an efficient and safe scheduling algorithm for real-time systems modelled with a DAG of MC tasks. Being based on a heuristic that minimizes the completion time of the DAG, our algorithm takes advantage of multicore platforms to find a near optimal allocation of tasks. Evaluation results provided in the paper show the capacity of our algorithm to find feasible schedules, even when the utilization of the multi-core platform is significant. Last but not least, our algorithm ensures safe mode transitions: higher criticality tasks will meet their deadline even in case timing failures occur. This paper also presents the very first benchmarking tool that generate randomly DAGs of MC tasks. As we believe this task model will become more and more popular in real-time domain, this open-source tool should be of great interest for the community.

Our future works will consider multiple DAGs being executed into a single multi-core platform with different periods and deadlines. In addition, we plan to integrate our work in design methodologies aiming at code generation [7] and safety analysis [11].

Acknowledgment. This research work has been funded by the academic and research chair Engineering of Complex Systems.

References

1. Adam, T.L., Chandy, K.M., Dickson, J.R.: A comparison of list schedules for parallel processing systems. Commun. ACM **17**(12), 685–690 (1974)
2. Baruah, S.: Implementing mixed-criticality synchronous reactive systems upon multiprocessor platforms. University of North Carolina at Chapel Hill, Technical report (2013)
3. Baruah, S.: The federated scheduling of systems of mixed-criticality sporadic dag tasks. In: 2016 IEEE Real-Time Systems Symposium (RTSS), pp. 227–236. IEEE (2016)
4. Baruah, S.K.: Semantics-preserving implementation of multirate mixed-criticality synchronous programs. In: RTNS (2012)
5. Bini, E., Buttazzo, G.C.: Measuring the performance of schedulability tests. Real-Time Syst. **30**(1–2), 129–154 (2005)
6. Burns, A., Davis, R.: Mixed Criticality Systems - A Review. Department of Computer Science, University of York, Technical report, January 2016 (2013)
7. Cadoret, F., Robert, T., Borde, E., Pautet, L., Singhoff, F.: Deterministic implementation of periodic-delayed communications and experimentation in aadl. In: ISORC, June 2013
8. Cordeiro, D., Mounié, G., Perarnau, S., Trystram, D., Vincent, J.M., Wagner, F.: Random graph generation for scheduling simulations. In: Proceedings - ICST (2010)
9. Kwok, Y.K., Ahmad, I.: Benchmarking and comparison of the task graph scheduling algorithms. J. Parallel Distrib. Comput. **59**(3), 381–422 (1999)
10. Li, J., Ferry, D., Ahuja, S., Agrawal, K., Gill, C., Lu, C.: Mixed-criticality federated scheduling for parallel real-time tasks. In: RTAS (2016)
11. Medina, R., Borde, E., Pautet, L.: Availability analysis for synchronous data-flow graphs in mixed-criticality systems. In: Proceedings - SIES (2016)
12. Pagetti, C., Saussié, D., Gratia, R., Noulard, E., Siron, P.: The rosace case study: From simulink specification to multi/many-core execution. In: 2014 IEEE 20th Real-Time and Embedded Technology and Applications Symposium (RTAS), pp. 309–318. IEEE (2014)
13. Parri, A., Biondi, A., Marinoni, M.: Response time analysis for G-EDF and G-DM scheduling of sporadic DAG-tasks with arbitrary deadline. In: RTNS (2015)
14. Saifullah, A., Ferry, D., Li, J., Agrawal, K., Lu, C., Gill, C.: Parallel real-time scheduling of DAGs. IEEE Trans. Parallel Distrib. Syst. **25**, 3242–3252 (2014)
15. Vestal, S.: Preemptive scheduling of multi-criticality systems with varying degrees of execution time assurance. In: RTSS (2007)

Software Time Reliability in the Presence of Cache Memories

Suzana Milutinovic[1,2]([envelope]), Jaume Abella[1], Irune Agirre[3],
Mikel Azkarate-Askasua[3], Enrico Mezzetti[1], Tullio Vardanega[4],
and Francisco J. Cazorla[1,5]

[1] Barcelona Supercomputing Center (BSC), Barcelona, Spain
{suzana.milutinovic,jaume.abella,enrico.mezzetti,
francisco.cazorla}@bsc.es
[2] Universitat Politècnica de Catalunya, Barcelona, Spain
[3] IK4-IKERLAN, Arrasate-Mondragòn, Spain
{iagirre,MAzkarateAskasua}@ikerlan.es
[4] University of Padova, Padova, Italy
tullio.vardanega@math.unipd.it
[5] IIIA-CSIC, Barcelona, Spain

Abstract. The use of caches challenges measurement-based timing analysis (MBTA) in critical embedded systems. In the presence of caches, the worst-case timing behavior of a system heavily depends on how code and data are laid out in cache. Guaranteeing that test runs capture, and hence MBTA results are representative of, the worst-case conflictive cache layouts, is generally unaffordable for end users. The probabilistic variant of MBTA, MB_PTA, exploits randomized caches and relieves the user from the burden of concocting layouts. In exchange, MBPTA requires the user to control the number of runs so that a solid probabilistic argument can be made about having captured the effect of worst-case cache conflicts during analysis. We present a computationally tractable Time-aware Address Conflict (TAC) mechanism that determines whether the impact of conflictive memory layouts is indeed captured in the MBPTA runs and prompts the user for more runs in case it is not.

Keywords: Probabilistic Timing Analysis · WCET · Representativeness · Cache memories

1 Introduction

Measurement-based timing analysis (MBTA) is widely adopted in the real-time domain [22]. The obtained worst-case execution time (WCET) estimates, however, are reliable insofar as the user is capable of designing test scenarios whose conditions are close to those that can arise during operation. Complex hardware and software, e.g. caches, introduce numerous sources of jitter (*soj*) that are difficult to analyze and control. For example, how program objects, such as

© Springer International Publishing AG 2017
J. Blieberger and M. Bader (Eds.): Ada-Europe 2017, LNCS 10300, pp. 233–249, 2017.
DOI: 10.1007/978-3-319-60588-3_15

code or stack, are assigned to memory defines their memory addresses, which in turn determines how they are mapped to cache sets and, ultimately, the program's pattern of hits and misses. Controlling the effect of memory layout to avoid incurring bad scenarios is not always feasible in practice. Existing techniques are typically exploitable only at the end of the development process as any analysis result obtained on single software units gets inevitably disrupted after integration. This inherently clashes with the principle of incrementality in software development and analysis, which is a fundamental cross-domain industrial concern [16].

Measurement-Based Probabilistic Timing Analysis (MBPTA) [2,6,21] exploits Extreme Value Theory (EVT) [14] and time-randomization to increase the confidence on WCET estimates. MBPTA uses EVT to model the probability of extreme events and, in particular, the combined probability of the events whose impact is captured in the execution time observations. EVT treats the system as a black box, focusing just on its output, hence providing no help to derive an argument of whether all *soj* are properly covered. And here is where time randomization comes to the rescue: higher coverage of *soj* can in fact be obtained by injecting time randomization in the operation of complex jittery resources to replace hard-to-control deterministic behavior, so that the corresponding *soj* exhibit probabilistic behavior. Interestingly, this feature also allows reasoning on whether enough measurement runs have been made, which will be the case when the residual probability of missing a significant behavior of the *soj* becomes provably negligible. For instance, if the extreme behavior of a *soj* has a probability of appearance of $P_{event} = 0.1$ per run, the probability of not observing it in $R = 1,000$ runs is $P_{nobs} = (1 - P_{event})^R = (1 - 0.1)^{1000} = 1.7 \times 10^{-46}$.

Time-randomized caches (*TRc*) [11] are MBPTA's preferred cache designs and have been demonstrated on FPGA implementations [9]. *TRc* use random placement, mapping memory addresses to random cache sets at each run, giving rise to random *cache (set) placements* across runs. As in deterministic set-associative caches, when the number of addresses mapped to a cache set exceeds its associativity (W), systematic cache conflicts may occur and eventually result in increased execution times. With *TRc* we do not need to control the cache mapping to avoid or trigger some specific scenarios, as the effect of cache placement is transparently exposed. Still, it must be guaranteed that the effect of placement is conveniently captured at analysis time. And this is not given since, *conflictive cache placements* may occur with a probability high enough to impact the timing budget of the system, but low enough to defy observation in the analysis runs [3,17,20]. For example, for an application that accesses 5 addresses in its execution, the probability that all of them are randomly mapped to the same set in a 32-set 4-way cache is $10^{-6} \approx (1/32)^4$, which can be of relevance for the domain safety standards. If $R = 1,000$ analysis runs are performed, a typical value for MBPTA, the probability of mapping the five addresses in at least one run to the same set is very low ($\approx 10^{-3}$). So far, this issue has been solved in limited scenarios, which assume that either the program addresses memory uniformly [3] or it accesses a small number (≤ 15) of cache lines [18].

In this paper we present the Time-aware Address Conflict (TAC) approach, a general and computationally-tractable method that, from the program's
sequence of accessed addresses, determines whether the number of runs performed by MBPTA, referred to as R, suffices to capture conflictive cache combinations with sufficient probability. Else it derives a higher number of runs,
referred to as R', for which this can be asserted. TAC derives a list of address
combinations that, when mapped to the same set, result in a high miss count.
For each combination, TAC determines its probability and by means of a lightweight cache simulator, the number of misses that would be incurred when the
addresses in each combination were mapped to the same set – while the rest of the
addresses are randomly mapped. This results in a $<probability, misscount>$ pair
for each combination. The user is then advised to explore random cache placements with the cache simulator until the probabilistic worst-case miss-count
(pWCMC) curve derived with EVT eventually upperbounds the pairs determined by TAC. This occurs when enough address combinations (R') singled out
by TAC have been simulated and the number of observed miss counts becomes
sufficient for EVT to converge to an exponential tail approximation [6]. The user
is then instructed to perform R' runs on the actual system to assure a reliable
application of MBPTA.

Results with EEBMC Autobench [19] and a railway case study running on a
time-randomized FPGA show that TAC successfully identifies conflictive address
combinations and determines the number of runs R' required to bring the assurance level of the WCET obtained with MBPTA to a desired threshold.

2 Background

MBTA aims at deriving a WCET estimate that holds during system operation.
This requires evidence that measurements taken at analysis occur under conditions similar to or worse than those that can arise during operation. Providing
such evidence is out of reach of standard MBTA approaches, as pointed out
in Sect. 1. MBPTA, by deploying EVT (see Fig. 1), derives the probability that
bad behavior of several of the sources of jitter (soj), whose impact has been
captured in the analysis-time runs, is simultaneously triggered in the same run,
leading to high execution times. Furthermore, randomization makes that soj
events affecting execution time (including those leading to high execution times)
have a probability of appearance. Hence, a probabilistic argument can be built
on whether those events are captured in the measurements performed during the
analysis phase.

Representativeness defines whether the impact of any random *relevant event*
is properly upper-bounded at analysis time. Relevant events are those occurring
with a probability above a threshold (e.g. $P_{rel} = 10^{-9}$). With the number of
runs R carried out at analysis, only events with a relatively high probability
(observable probability or P_{obs}) are (probabilistically) likely to be observed in the
measurement runs. This number of runs (R) determines the lowest probability
of occurrence of an event such that the probability of not observing it in the

analysis time measurements is below a cutoff probability, e.g. 10^{-9}. P_{obs} is a function of the probability of occurrence per run of the event, P_{event}, and the number of runs R (observations) collected by MBPTA at analysis time. For instance, for a cutoff probability of 10^{-9} and $R = 1,000$ runs, we can guarantee that if $P_{event} \geq 0.021$ the event will not be observed with a probability smaller than 10^{-9} (and vice versa). That is, $10^{-9} \geq (1 - 0.021)^{1000}$. It follows that with a higher number of runs, events with lower probability can be captured, though this increases the overhead on the user to deploy MBPTA. *Hence, the relevant events that may not be observed (for $R = 1,000$) with a sufficiently high probability (e.g. $> 10^{-9}$) are those in the range $P_{event} \in [10^{-9}, 0.021]$.*

Benefits and properties of *TRc*: Software complexity in current complex systems is handled via incremental software integration. In the timing domain, caches make the memory layout of existing modules change across integration [16]. This has disruptive effects on time composability since the WCET estimate derived for a software unit in isolation – during system early design stages – is not valid as software integrates. This loss of time composability has potential significant costs since, on every integration, regression tests are required to re-assess the WCET estimate of already-integrated software. Furthermore, timing analysis is pushed and compressed near the end of the development process where the detection of timing violations leads to unacceptable increase in product cost and time to market. *TRc* break the structural dependence among the memory address given to program code/data and its cache set location. The user is not required to control the effect of memory layout but just needs to make sure that its impact on timing has been accounted for performing enough execution time measurements at analysis time. This enables performing measurements *in isolation* factoring in the impact of any cache alignment independently of the memory placement produced by future integration. This has the potential of enabling incremental software integration – and its benefits– in the presence of caches. *TRc* hash addresses with a random number[1] to compute the (random) sets where addresses are placed [11]. The random number remains constant during program execution so that an address is placed in the same set during the whole execution, but it is randomly changed across executions so that the particular set where an address is placed is also random and independent of the placement for the other addresses across executions. Thus, the probability of any two addresses to be placed in the same set is 1/S where S is the number of sets.

We call conflictive address combinations, aC_i, those combinations of $W + 1$ or more addresses that, when mapped to the same set, cause a conflictive cache (set) placement that results in a non-negligible increase in execution time. Table 1 summarizes notations used in this paper.

HoG (Heart of Gold) method [3]: *HoG* shows that, whenever up to W addresses are mapped into the same set, after some random evictions, each

---

[1] Random numbers are generated with a pseudo-random number generator that provides sequences with long periods to prevent any correlation.

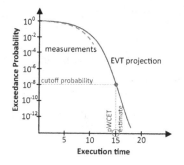

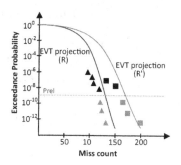

Fig. 1. pWCET (EVT) estimate.

Fig. 2. Application of *TAC*.

address can be stored in a different cache line in the set, thus not causing further misses. Conversely, if more than W cache line addresses compete for the cache set space, then they do not fit and evictions will occur often. This scenario represents a random event with high impact on execution time as noticed also in [17,20]. Hence, a correct application of MBPTA requires ensuring that (i) either those events are captured in the measurement runs; or (ii) their probability is low enough to be considered irrelevant. HoG assumes that *the impact of all addresses on execution time is similar*. This may happen when addresses are accessed homogeneously. However, in the general case not every combination of addresses – when mapped to the same set – results in an execution time increase of the same magnitude. This general case is addressed in this paper.

ReVS (Representativeness Validation by Simulation) method [18]: *ReVS* considers all combinations of the most accessed cache line addresses with a cardinality bigger than W, i.e. $\forall aC_i : |aC_i| > W$, and captures their impact in a cache simulator. However, the number of address combinations with a cardinality bigger than W is huge: $\sum_{k=W+1}^{U} \binom{U}{k}$ for a sequence $\mathcal{Q}_i$, where $U = |@(\mathcal{Q}_i)|$. Hence, evaluating in the cache simulator all potentially conflictive combinations of addresses is *not feasible in the general case* due to its exponential dependence on the number of addresses.

Overall, while MBTA lacks a quantitative measure of coverage of those events that can affect execution time, MBPTA enables deriving a probabilistic argument about whether events impacting execution time are captured in analysis-time tests. Yet, current approaches to derive the number of runs are either non-scalable [18] or assume homogeneous accesses over all program addresses [3]. TAC provides a low-overhead solution to handle the more general case of arbitrary access patterns. For controlled scenarios where ReVS can be applied, e.g. until $U = 15$ addresses, ReVS provides *exact* results with which we compare TAC results to show that TAC covers all conflictive aC_i. We also evaluate TAC in general scenarios, including a real industrial case study.

Table 1. Definitions used in this paper.

Term	Description
aC_i; $|aC_i|$	Address combination, i.e. set of unique addresses; cardinality of aC_i
K	Cardinality of (number of addresses in) a combination
$\mathcal{Q}_i$	Sequence of accesses
$@(\mathcal{Q}_i)$; $|@(\mathcal{Q}_i)|$	Set of unique addresses in $\mathcal{Q}_i$; Number of unique addresses in $\mathcal{Q}_i$
U	Number of unique addresses in a sequence
X_i	Subsequence of accesses between 2 accesses to the same address
q	Number of distinct addresses in a subsequence X_i
R (R')	Number of measurements to collect determined by MBPTA (TAC)
T	Number of conflictive combinations to return by TAC

3   TAC Mechanism

For a sequence of addresses, TAC focuses on identifying *address combinations*, aC_i that, when mapped to the same cache set, cause high execution times. The application of TAC comprises the following steps.

Step 1. List creation. Rather than considering all address combinations with a cardinality bigger than W as ReVS does, TAC provides a list of potential conflictive aC_i ranked according to their expected impact on execution time (the size of the list is specified later in this section). To that end, TAC builds an *Address Guilt Matrix* (Sect. 3.1) to quickly retrieve those combinations of addresses that, when mapped to the same set, can cause high miss counts.

Step 2. Impact calculation. Each combination in the list is evaluated with a cache simulator. Several Monte-Carlo simulations are performed to derive the number of misses occurring when the addresses in the combination collide in the same set while the rest of the addresses are mapped randomly. The number of combinations in this list is fixed and, therefore, independent of the number of addresses in the program. ReVS, instead, simulates *all* combinations of addresses, which has huge cost.

Step 3. Probability calculation. TAC upper-bounds the probability of occurrence of those aC_i – and combinations of them. The probability of every aC_i to occur is: $S \times (1/S)^{|aC_i|}$, where $|aC_i|$ is the number of addresses in aC_i. For the combined probability of several aC_i we pessimistically use the addition of their individual probabilities. In reality, due to dependences among aC_i, their combined probability is smaller than that [18].

Step 2 and *Step 3* result in a pair <probability, misscount> for each combination. Figure 2 presents a synthetic example where pairs are represented with different symbols: black triangles and squares represent the miss counts obtained for all aC_i – and their combinations – whose probability of occurrence is above

P_{rel}. Meanwhile, their gray counterparts are those below P_{rel}, which are discarded by TAC since their probability is deemed as negligible.

Step 4. pWCMC curve. TAC uses MBPTA on the miss counts obtained from cache simulations in which all addresses are randomly mapped, as it would occur in reality, to obtain a probabilistic worst-case miss-count (pWCMC) curve (see solid line in Fig. 2). The number of simulations, R, is determined by MBPTA.

Step 5. Assessment. In Fig. 2 triangles are those aC_i (and their combinations) whose miss count is covered by the pWCMC, while the miss counts of the aC_i marked with squares are not. Hence, by validating whether the pWCMC curve upper-bounds all conflictive mappings (i.e. <probability, misscount> pairs), we determine whether the number of runs R used by MBPTA suffices. If this is not the case, more runs are performed until the validation step is passed with $R' \geq R$ runs. Whenever it is passed, the number of runs R' is the minimum number of execution time measurements that MBPTA needs to use.

TAC builds on the correlation between miss counts and execution time that has been positively assessed for our target platform in [18]. If such correlation is weak, cache behavior would have low impact in execution time, which would have higher dependence on other *soj*. However, those other *soj* do not challenge MBPTA since probabilities of their events are higher than P_{obs} [3].

3.1   The Address Guilt Matrix

TAC follows an iterative process in which, across iterations, an incremental number of addresses K (starting from $K = W + 1$) is considered to be mapped to the same set. This creates a cache conflict scenario exceeding cache space in one set. The process stops when K is large enough so that the probability of occurrence of the event "K addresses mapped to the same set for the most relevant combinations of K addresses" is below a given cutoff probability[2] P_{cff}. In practice, we only need the most relevant combination for each value of K since EVT (part of MBPTA) already accounts for the probability of several of those events occurring simultaneously. Our results for controlled scenarios show that the worst combination is always among the TAC top-ranked ones, so we consider only the $T = 20$ most relevant combinations for each value of K. In our future work we will investigate how to choose an optimal parameter value for T.

TAC builds on the concept of *guilt*, which is intended to help identifying those aC_i that, if mapped to the same set, result in high miss counts. For a given access A_i with a non-null cache miss probability, guilt provides an approximation to the extent *each intermediate access* between A_i and A_{i-1} causes A_i to miss in cache. Note that this concept, although related, differs from the probability of miss since we are not interested in how many misses each access experiences, but how much certain addresses can impact each other address if placed in the

---

[2] Note that, while P_{rel} stands for the threshold probability of relevant events at analysis (e.g., 10^{-9}), P_{cff} relates to the probability of events during operation (e.g., 10^{-15}) [3].

same cache set. For instance, given a direct-mapped (i.e. single way) cache and the sequence $\mathcal{Q}_i = \{A_1 B_1 A_2\}$, if both addresses A and B are mapped to the same set, A_2 will miss in cache, and the cause of that is access B_1, so B_1 takes full guilt of A eviction. Later in this section we present an efficient mechanism to approximate guilt for arbitrarily complex sequences.

From probability of miss to guilt. Approaches [4] have been proposed to derive upper-bounds to the miss probability. However, in this work we are interested in the *actual* impact rather than on upper-bounds, and on guilt rather than on P_{miss}. Approaches exist to approximate [11] P_{miss} ($\tilde{P}_{miss}$) in the context of MBPTA. These approaches are as shown in Eq. 1, where $\sum \tilde{P}_{miss}(X_i)$ corresponds to the accumulated miss probability of the intermediate accesses.

$$\tilde{P}_{miss} = 1 - \left(\frac{W-1}{W}\right)^{\sum \tilde{P}_{miss}(X_i)} \tag{1}$$

While this approach provides good $\tilde{P}_{miss}$ approximations [18], it does not help identifying how much each intermediate access contributes to cause the miss.

TAC sorts address combinations based on their impact, which requires having means to estimate the relative impact that each address and group of addresses have on each other address (guilt) in terms of cache misses. To cover this gap we propose the $\tilde{P}_{guilty}$ estimator (see Eq. 2) that targets providing a precise relative value for guilt as needed by TAC, rather than approximating P_{miss}.

$$\tilde{P}_{guilty} = 1 - \left(\frac{W-1}{W}\right)^{exp} \qquad exp = \begin{cases} 0, & \text{if } q < W \\ q, & \text{if } W \leq q < K \\ K-1, & \text{otherwise} \end{cases} \tag{2}$$

When the number of intermediate addresses between A_i and A_{i-1}, q, is smaller than the number of cache ways W, they all would fit in a cache way, so misses may only be produced due to random replacement, whose impact is already captured with the default number of runs of MBPTA [3]. Hence, we assume that A_i results in a hit, so the guilt of intermediate accesses is 0. Hence, we ignore A_i and look for the next occurrence of A until $q \geq W$ or we reach the end of the sequence. The rationale behind this is that hits do not change cache state in TRc, thus they can be ignored. On the other hand, ignoring intermediate accesses due to having extra hits in between A_i and A_{i-1} would be misleading. For instance, let us consider $W = 2$ and $\mathcal{Q}_1 = \{A_1 B_1 A_2 C_1 A_3\}$. We cannot assume that A_3 will always hit in $\mathcal{Q}_1$ since sooner or later A will be evicted. Thus, A_2 is ignored and A_3 considers the guilt of B_1 and C_1. It can also be observed that we enforce exp to be smaller than K, the reason behind this is explained next.

Guilt estimation. When for an access A_i $\tilde{P}_{guilty} \neq 0$, its value is 'distributed' among the intermediate accesses between A_i and A_{i-1}. Each access is assigned a guilt value w.r.t. address A computed as shown in Eq. 3. For instance given a cache with $W = 2$ ways, the sequence $\mathcal{Q}_1 = (A_1 B_1 C_1 D_1 A_2)$ and $K = 3$, we obtain that $q = 3$ and $\tilde{P}_{guilty}(A_2) = 1 - (1/2)^2 = 0.75$ according to Eq. 2. In this scenario we assign a guilt of 0.375 to each of the $q = 3$ intermediate accesses. Note that the addition of guilt assigned to intermediate accesses is bigger than $\tilde{P}_{guilty}$. The idea is that for $K = 3$, TAC constructs 3-address combinations that in this case can be any of ABC, ABD, ACD, BCD. In all those containing A, we want to assign one half of the guilt to each of the two intermediate accesses. That is, for ABC one half of the guilt is assigned to B and another half to C. At any moment only $K - 1$ accesses will be simultaneously considered by TAC, so the guilt of a given access is not decreased because of having other intermediate accesses (more than K). As the value of K increases – as part of TAC iterative process – those other intermediate accesses will be considered simultaneously.

$$guilt = \begin{cases} \frac{\tilde{P}_{guilty}}{exp}, & \text{if } exp > 0 \\ 0, & \text{otherwise} \end{cases} \quad (3)$$

Based on the concept of guilt, which applies at access level, we build the *address guilt matrix* (adgm). The *adgm* comprises as many rows and columns as different (cache line) addresses are accessed in the program. Cell $adgm[A][B]$ captures the guilt of B on A, that is, a measure of to what extent misses of every access A_i are caused by any access to B_j. The *adgm* is built for every value of K. From the *adgm* we infer information about the impact that each address has on the evictions of each other address. To that end we use the technique in Sect. 3.2, which covers *Step 1* and *Step 2*. Steps 3 to 5 are applied as presented before.

The metric, obtained from the guilt, does not have a semantic meaning in the real world, yet it provides a way to rank address combinations so that if aCi is ranked higher than aCj, the actual impact in miss count (and execution time) of aCi is higher than that of aCj. This allows performing cache simulations for those highly ranked address combinations to measure their actual impact.

3.2 Smart Search of Address Combinations

Exhaustive Search. As reference we use an algorithm that exhaustively searches the *adgm* and later provide refinements to limit computational costs. For every value of K we build all potential combinations of K addresses out of U, so performing an Exhaustive Search. For each combination we query the *adgm* to obtain the expected impact if those addresses were mapped to the same set. The impact is obtained as follows: (1) for each address i in the combination aCi we compute a value M_i obtained as the highest minimum impact that W other addresses in the combination may have on it. Hence, we take the minimum M_i out of the highest W values in the *adgm* ($adgm[i][x]$ where x is any other address in the combination). Note that we care only about those W addresses that can create highest impact on the address of that row in the *adgm*, since $W + 1$ addresses suffice to exceed the cache set space. Then, we select the minimum value out of those to reflect that, if an address produces few evictions, the others will not produce more evictions than that one because other accesses will become hits. (2) Finally, we obtain the impact as the harmonic mean of all M_i values to, again, reflect that the number of evictions is limited by the address producing the lowest number of evictions. We exclude pairs for the same address (e.g., $adgm[A][A]$) since an address cannot create evictions on itself. If one or some of the addresses have little impact on the other addresses, then its M_i value is much lower and so the final impact, thus allowing to discard this combination. For instance, in the combination $aCi = \{A, B, C, D, E, F\}$, if F has almost zero impact on the other addresses, this combination will be discarded for $K = 6$. If the other 5 addresses have high impact among them, they will be conveniently considered for $K = 5$. Whenever all combinations are considered in the $adgm$ (without performing any cache simulation), we create a list of top ranked combinations (*Step 1*) for which cache simulations are performed to measure miss counts (*Step 2*).

Smart Search. Since the computational cost of considering this Exhaustive Search in the $adgm$ is prohibitive, we propose a smart search algorithm that comprises the following steps.

First, we discard the rows in the $adgm$ whose $\tilde{P}_{guilty}$ is below 1% of the highest $\tilde{P}_{guilty}$ in the table since their combinations with relevant addresses ($\tilde{P}_{guilty}$ above the 1% threshold) will already be accounted by those other addresses, and their impact on irrelevant addresses is deemed irrelevant as well. Then, we create address *buckets* in each row of the $adgm$ with all the addresses with the same guilt value w.r.t. the address of that row. Empirically, we observed that EEMBC and the railway case study produce a low number of buckets. Otherwise, some difference is tolerated among addresses in the same bucket to reduce their count.

Second, the relevant buckets for a certain address are only those whose relative impact w.r.t. the total guilt in the row is significant for the address of that row. Such significance threshold S_{th} (1% in our case) is used to explore combinations with meaningful impact. The remaining addresses (their guilt is below S_{th}) are simply regarded as irrelevant.

Third, we generate the combinations of K elements for each row by making all possible combinations with the address corresponding to that row and $K - 1$ elements from different buckets. For instance, assuming $K = 4$ and 2 buckets ($b1$ and $b2$), we make all combinations of 4 addresses using the one of the row and three addresses from the buckets: 3 from $b1$, 2 from $b1$ and 1 from $b2$, 1 from $b1$ and 2 from $b2$, and 3 from $b2$. We always choose those addresses with the highest $\tilde{P}_{guilty}$ in each bucket. We take into account the size of the bucket by computing how many combinations are expected to have the same impact to the representative ones. For instance, if $b1$ and $b2$ contain 4 and 5 addresses respectively, when picking 2 addresses from $b1$ and 1 from $b2$, we determine that there are 30 different combinations meeting those constraints. This is used to set the probability of the pair <probability, misscount> if these combinations have a sufficiently high impact to be simulated.

Fourth, when all addresses have been analyzed and the list with $T = 20$ combinations[3] for a particular value of K is obtained (*Step 1*), we perform cache simulations to determine their miss counts (*Step 2*). In the case of addresses in a bucket, we simulate only those with the highest $\tilde{P}_{guilty}$ and assume the same impact for other combinations that could be generated with other addresses in the bucket. While this may lead to a little pessimism in terms of the impact of those addresses, such pessimism is very limited given that addresses belong to the same bucket. This may result in pairs <probability, misscount> further challenging the reliability of the pWCMC curve, thus potentially rejecting some very tight (yet reliable) pWCMC estimates.

4   Evaluation

We model a pipelined in-order processor with 4KB 2-way-associative 32B-line separated first level instruction (IL1) and data (DL1) caches. Both caches deploy random placement and replacement policies [11], with DL1 implementing write-back (IL1 is read-only). DL1/IL1 access latency is 1 cycle for hits with 3 extra cycles for misses. The latter is added to the main memory latency (16 cycles).

We evaluate TAC on the EEMBC automotive benchmarks, widely used in the community to capture real-time automotive application features [19]. On average this suite has 6,500 Lines of Code, 2,500 Unique Instruction Addresses and 5,600 Unique Data Addresses per benchmark. In particular we use these benchmarks: `a2time` (a2), `aifftr` (at), `aifirf` (ar), `aiifft` (ai), `basefp` (ba), `bitmnp` (bi), `cacheb` (ca), `idctrn` (id) and `iirflt` (ii). We consider all addresses accessed by each benchmark. Additionally, we analyzed the same benchmarks in a *controlled scenario* in which we focus on a subset of the most accessed (cache line) addresses to allow for a comparison against *ReVS*, which hardly scales for higher values of U. While in this scenario we cover on average 58% of the accesses across all benchmarks – thus leaving some degree of uncertainty due to the remaining 42% accesses that are neglected in [18] – it allows comparing TAC against ReVS, with the latter guaranteeing exact results.

TAC vs ReVS. For this comparison we focus only on the $U = 15$ most accessed addresses for which ReVS is capable of exploring all address combinations.

Table 2 shows the number of runs that each of the methods regards as the minimum to use for a reliable MBPTA application. We show results for both IL1 and DL1. As shown, both approaches provide *exactly* the same number of runs (R') for these limited address traces. In particular, TAC identifies the same address combinations most of the times or, alternatively, address combinations with roughly the same impact as those regarded by ReVS as the most conflictive ones for each value of K. The exception to this comes from the case in which ReVS identifies for high values of K combinations which, in fact, are the addition

---

[3] One combination may be the representative of many others if addresses belong to buckets. Hence, simulating 20 combinations provides information of, at least, 20 actual address combinations, but generally many more than 20.

Table 2. Runs for TAC and ReVS for $P_{rel} = 10^{-9}$ and $U = 15$.

	R'_{IL1}		R'_{DL1}		R'	
	ReVS	TAC	ReVS	TAC	ReVS	TAC
a2	58,360	58,360	540	540	58,360	58,360
at	6,840	6,840	5,500	5,500	6,840	6,840
ar	21,390	21,390	11,530	11,530	21,390	21,390
ai	8,920	8,920	8,770	8,770	8,920	8,920
ba	82,080	82,080	20,010	20,010	82,080	82,080
bi	4,640	4,640	3,510	3,510	4,640	4,640
ca	18,610	18,610	7,950	7,950	18,610	18,610
id	65,770	65,770	47,700	47,700	65,770	65,770
ii	18,310	18,310	49,760	49,760	49,760	49,760

Table 3. Results for complete EEMBC benchmarks.

TAC				MBPTA	
R'_{IL1}	R'_{DL1}	R'	lik.(R')	R	lik.(R)
67,150	300	67,150	10^{-9}	300	0.911
300	4,760	4,760	10^{-9}	300	0.271
20,080	8,090	20,080	10^{-9}	14,260	10^{-7}
300	10,630	10,630	10^{-9}	300	0.557
78,220	300	78,220	10^{-9}	1,250	0.718
330	1,800	1,800	10^{-9}	300	0.032
19,840	1,500	19,840	10^{-9}	9,360	10^{-5}
67,460	43,040	67,460	10^{-9}	300	0.912
29,920	2,430	29,920	10^{-9}	300	0.812

of two or more independent combinations. For instance, ReVS identifies combinations for $K = 6$ that, in reality correspond to two combinations of $K = 3$ occurring at the same time. As explained before, EVT needs to observe high-impact events, but not their combination. Thus, this difference has no influence on R'.

Execution time cost. For $U = 15$ ReVS requires on average 27 h per benchmark with 1,000 cache simulations per address combination on a cluster running 100 jobs in parallel. TAC is 148 times faster requiring 2 s on average per program on a laptop computer to derive the address combinations and their cost, and around 11 min per benchmark to run cache simulations for the limited address combinations considered on the same cluster. For full benchmarks, i.e. unrestricted U, ReVS could not be applied while TAC required 1 min per program to generate the pairs <probability, misscount> and around 38 min per program to perform cache simulations in our cluster.

TAC evaluation on full benchmarks. In Table 3 we report the number of runs required by TAC to guarantee that relevant events can only be missed with a probability below a *parametrizable residual threshold*, e.g. 10^{-9}. We also show the runs requested by MBPTA together with the probability of missing those events with the default number of runs required. MBPTA takes as input the number of execution times belonging to the tail of the distribution that need to be observed in measurements, in our case 50 values [2]. Then, starting from 300 runs, MBPTA inspects whether enough tail values are observed. If this is not the case, it asks for more runs until this condition is satisfied and EVT converges.

As shown, $R' \geq R$: in many cases we observe that the likelihood of missing critical address combinations in the default runs (R) determined by MBPTA only is high. This does not mean that pWCET estimates are necessarily wrong, but indicates that there is non-negligible risk of not observing some high-impact timing events in the analysis runs if TAC is not used.

When comparing the number of runs of TAC with full address traces w.r.t. only 15 addresses, we observe in most of the cases a limited variation in R'.

However, in some cases R' decreases noticeably (e.g. R'_{IL1} for `aifftr` (at)) because there are many combinations with similar impact that cannot be observed with only 15 addresses. This makes that the probability of observing one of those combinations is much higher and thus, fewer runs are needed to observe one of them. In any case, differently to ReVS, which is limited to 15 addresses, TAC can deal with arbitrary access patterns without any explicit limit. Thus, TAC removes the uncertainty brought by ReVS due to non-analyzed addresses.

5 Railway Case Study

We use as railway case study a safety function part of the European Vital Computer (EVC): the central safety processing unit of the European Train Control System (ETCS) reference architecture. The EVC is responsible of executing all safety functions associated to the travelling speed and distance supervision. As a fail-safe system, whenever an over-speed of the train is detected, the ETCS must switch to a safe-state where the emergency break is active. This safety function shall be provided with the highest integrity level defined in the railway safety standards, SIL-4, and has strict real-time requirements. Accordingly, we apply MBPTA to estimate the WCET for the safety function from the moment of reading the input sensors until the activation of the safe-state. The end user (IK4-IKERLAN) controls input vectors' impact on execution path coverage and in their current timing analysis practice they focus on observed paths. We stick to those paths and apply TAC to all of them. We plan to cover scenarios where the user lacks this control as part of our future work.

Address traces were collected from a LEON3-based FPGA board using existing tracing capabilities of the platform. We have applied TAC to the case study for 10 different input sets (TEST0 to TEST9). The case study comprises around 8,500 Lines of Code, 2,994 Unique Instruction Addresses and 597 Unique Data Addresses for the largest input set.

Table 4 reports the results we obtained, in terms of the number of runs that MBPTA and TAC require in the miss domain. For each test we show whether (Y) or not (N) MBPTA's default number of runs (R) and that reported by TAC (R') suffice to upper-bound the pairs <probability, misscount>. As it can be seen, the default application of MBPTA failed to upper-bound some address combinations for data and instructions for many input sets. Furthermore, in those cases where $R < R'$, confidence on having enough runs for a reliable application of MBPTA cannot be had.

This is illustrated in Fig. 3 for TEST7 and the DL1 where TAC <probability, misscount> pairs (points in the plot) are not upper-bounded by the pWCMC curve (lower straight line in the plot) when using $R = 300$, the number or runs required by MBPTA. Instead, if we use $R' = 4,400$, as determined by TAC, the pWCMC curve properly upper-bounds those pairs.

For this industrial application, TAC required, on average, $1,828$ runs per input set, which is affordable in a usual test campaign. TAC took 1.3 min to derive the conflictive combinations and 0.35 min per test for cache simulations.

Table 4. Runs needed by TAC and MBPTA to achieve a confidence of 10^{-9}.

	IL1		DL1	
	R	R'	R	R'
TEST0	300(Y)	300(Y)	370(N)	1,300(Y)
TEST1	300(N)	600(Y)	3,800(Y)	3,800(Y)
TEST2	300(N)	600(Y)	300(N)	1,000(Y)
TEST3	300(N)	1,600(Y)	300(N)	850(Y)
TEST4	300(N)	1,200(Y)	750(N)	1,100(Y)
TEST5	300(N)	2,100(Y)	480(N)	900(Y)
TEST6	300(N)	500(Y)	890(Y)	890(Y)
TEST7	300(N)	500(Y)	300 (N)	4,400(Y)
TEST8	300(N)	700(Y)	300 (N)	2,300(Y)
TEST9	300(N)	4,800(Y)	1,740(Y)	1,740(Y)

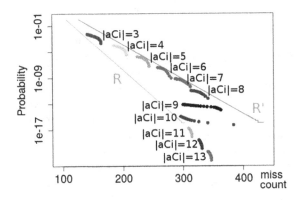

Fig. 3. pWCMC for *TEST7* (DL1) by applying MBPTA (R) and TAC+MBPTA (R').

6   Related Work

A recent work comparing static (deterministic) timing analysis techniques (SDTA) and MBPTA [1] shows that there is not a dominant technique but the relation between the application working set and the cache size is the factor affecting the most which technique performs better.

MBPTA-compliant hardware. The concept of MBPTA-compliant hardware has been defined in [13]. Hardware techniques provide MBPTA compliance for some specific resources like caches [11] or buses [10]. Software randomization techniques have been shown to enable the analysis of deterministic caches with MBPTA [12]. Time-randomized caches were originally proposed in [11]. Recently some variants have been proposed combining benefits of modulo placement while keeping the randomization required by MBPTA [9]. Some of these random placement designs have been shown to be implementable in FPGA prototypes [9].

Probabilistic Analysis. Some works study random caches in terms of the coverage of conflictive cache placements and complex timing effects, as noted in [3,17, 20]. Other studies cover aspects related to control-flow dependences and data-dependences in the context of MBPTA. We refer the reader to [13,23] for details on how to handle control and data dependences.

Applying EVT on software programs brings the dependence of execution times on input-data [15,23] into the equation. Static and measurement based approaches tackle input-data dependence by requiring program features like loop bounds or recursion level to be bounded to derive WCET estimates. Hence, input vectors mainly affect the paths traversed. Current practice in MBPTA, and our assumption here, is to operate on a set of representative input vectors provided by the user. This is also the practice followed by IK4-IKERLAN for the rail case study. In the context of MBPTA, this assumption can be lifted by synthetically extending the input set, with the same effect of full path coverage [23].

EVT has also been used to estimate WCET on top of non-MBPTA-compliant (deterministic) architectures [5,7,8]. The main challenge of those architectures is providing evidence of the representativeness of the execution time observations passed to EVT. To the best of our knowledge, the representativeness challenge has not been studied on non-MBPTA platforms [13].

7   Conclusions

MBTA cannot quantify the degree of coverage attained for the jitter caused by platform events. For caches, while the end user can perform many tests, it is hard to argue about whether conflictive cache mappings leading to high execution times have been covered in the tests. In the context of MBPTA and building on the properties of *TRc*, on every new run a random cache mapping is explored. This enables building a coverage argument. Yet, it is necessary to determine the number of runs to perform to capture conflictive cache mappings. We propose TAC, a low-overhead mechanism that determines whether the number of runs is enough to cover the cache mappings of interest to a given quantifiable threshold. If this is not the case, TAC requests an increased number of runs to the user until the threshold is reached. Results with EEMBC Automotive and a real railway case study show that TAC successfully identifies conflictive address combinations and increases the number of runs accordingly so that reliable WCET estimates can be obtained for programs with arbitrary access patterns.

Acknowledgments. The research leading to these results has received funding from the European Community's FP7 [FP7/2007-2013] under the PROXIMA Project (www. proxima-project.eu), grant agreement no 611085. This work has also been partially supported by the Spanish Ministry of Science and Innovation under grant TIN2015-65316-P and the HiPEAC Network of Excellence. Jaume Abella has been partially supported by the Ministry of Economy and Competitiveness under Ramon y Cajal postdoctoral fellowship number RYC-2013-14717.

References

1. Abella, J., Hardy, D., Puaut, I., Quiones, E., Cazorla, F.J.: On the comparison of deterministic and probabilistic WCET estimation techniques. In: 2014 26th Euromicro Conference on Real-Time Systems, pp. 266–275, July 2014

2. Abella, J., Padilla, M., del Castillo, J., Cazorla, F.: Measurement-based worst-case execution time estimation using the coefficient of variation. ACM Trans. Des. Autom. Electron. Syst. (to appear)

3. Abella, J., Quiones, E., Wartel, F., Vardanega, T., Cazorla, F.J.: Heart of gold: Making the improbable happen to increase confidence in MBPTA. In: 2014 26th Euromicro Conference on Real-Time Systems, pp. 255–265, July 2014

4. Altmeyer, S., Davis, R.I.: On the correctness, optimality and precision of static probabilistic timing analysis. In: 2014 Design, Automation Test in Europe Conference Exhibition (DATE), pp. 1–6, March 2014

5. Bernat, G., Burns, A., Newby, M.: Probabilistic timing analysis: an approach using copulas. J. Embed. Comput. 1(2), 179–194 (2005). http://content.iospress.com/articles/journal-of-embedded-computing/jec00014

6. Cucu-Grosjean, L., Santinelli, L., Houston, M., Lo, C., Vardanega, T., Kosmidis, L., Abella, J., Mezzetti, E., Quiones, E., Cazorla, F.J.: Measurement-based probabilistic timing analysis for multi-path programs. In: 2012 24th Euromicro Conference on Real-Time Systems, pp. 91–101, July 2012

7. Edgar, S., Burns, A.: Statistical analysis of WCET for scheduling. In: Proceedings 22nd IEEE Real-Time Systems Symposium (RTSS 2001) (Cat. No.01PR1420), pp. 215–224, December 2001

8. Hansen, J.P., Hissam, S.A., Moreno, G.A.: Statistical-based WCET estimation and validation. In: Holsti, N. (ed.) 9th International Workshop on Worst-Case Execution Time Analysis, WCET 2009, OASICS, Dublin, Ireland, 1–3 July 2009, vol. 10. Schloss Dagstuhl - Leibniz-Zentrum fuer Informatik, Germany (2009). http://drops.dagstuhl.de/opus/volltexte/2009/2291

9. Hernandez, C., Abella, J., Gianarro, A., Andersson, J., Cazorla, F.J.: Random modulo: a new processor cache design for real-time critical systems. In: 2016 53nd ACM/EDAC/IEEE Design Automation Conference (DAC), pp. 1–6, June 2016

10. Jalle, J., Kosmidis, L., Abella, J., Quiones, E., Cazorla, F.J.: Bus designs for time-probabilistic multicore processors. In: 2014 Design, Automation Test in Europe Conference Exhibition (DATE), pp. 1–6, March 2014

11. Kosmidis, L., Abella, J., Quiones, E., Cazorla, F.J.: A cache design for probabilistically analysable real-time systems. In: 2013 Design, Automation Test in Europe Conference Exhibition (DATE), pp. 513–518, March 2013

12. Kosmidis, L., Curtsinger, C., Quiones, E., Abella, J., Berger, E., Cazorla, F.J.: Probabilistic timing analysis on conventional cache designs. In: 2013 Design, Automation Test in Europe Conference Exhibition (DATE), pp. 603–606, March 2013

13. Kosmidis, L., Quiones, E., Abella, J., Vardanega, T., Broster, I., Cazorla, F.J.: Measurement-based probabilistic timing analysis and its impact on processor architecture. In: 2014 17th Euromicro Conference on Digital System Design, pp. 401–410, August 2014

14. Kotz, S., Nadarajah, S.: Extreme Value Distributions: Theory and Applications. EBL-Schweitzer, Imperial College Press (2000). https://books.google.es/books?id=tKlgDQAAQBAJ

15. Lima, G., Dias, D., Barros, E.: Extreme value theory for estimating task execution time bounds: a careful look. In: 2016 28th Euromicro Conference on Real-Time Systems (ECRTS), pp. 200–211, July 2016

16. Mezzetti, E., Vardanega, T.: A rapid cache-aware procedure positioning optimization to favor incremental development. In: 2013 IEEE 19th Real-Time and Embedded Technology and Applications Symposium (RTAS), pp. 107–116, April 2013

17. Mezzetti, E., Ziccardi, M., Vardanega, T., Abella, J., Quiones, E., Cazorla, F.: Randomized caches can be pretty useful to hard real-time systems. Leibniz Trans. Embed. Syst. 2(1), 01:1–01:10 (2015). http://ojs.dagstuhl.de/index.php/lites/article/view/LITES-v002-i001-a001

18. Milutinovic, S., Abella, J., Cazorla, F.J.: Modelling probabilistic cache representativeness in the presence of arbitrary access patterns. In: 2016 IEEE 19th International Symposium on Real-Time Distributed Computing (ISORC), pp. 142–149, May 2016

19. Poovey, J.A., Conte, T.M., Levy, M., Gal-On, S.: A benchmark characterization of the eembc benchmark suite. IEEE Micro 29(5), 18–29. http://dx.doi.org/10.1109/MM.2009.74

20. Reineke, J.: Randomized caches considered harmful in hard real-time systems. Leibniz Trans. Embed. Syst. 1(1), 03:1–03:13 (2014). http://ojs.dagstuhl.de/index.php/lites/article/view/LITES-v001-i001-a003

21. Wartel, F., Kosmidis, L., Gogonel, A., Baldovino, A., Stephenson, Z., Triquet, B., Quiones, E., Lo, C., Mezzetta, E., Broster, I., Abella, J., Cucu-Grosjean, L., Vardanega, T., Cazorla, F.J.: Timing analysis of an avionics case study on complex hardware/software platforms. In: 2015 Design, Automation Test in Europe Conference Exhibition (DATE), pp. 397–402, March 2015

22. Wilhelm, R., Engblom, J., Ermedahl, A., Holsti, N., Thesing, S., Whalley, D., Bernat, G., Ferdinand, C., Heckmann, R., Mitra, T., Mueller, F., Puaut, I., Puschner, P., Staschulat, J., Stenström, P.: The worst-case execution-time problem—overview of methods and survey of tools. ACM Trans. Embed. Comput. Syst. 7(3), 36:1–36:53. http://doi.acm.org/10.1145/1347375.1347389

23. Ziccardi, M., Mezzetti, E., Vardanega, T., Abella, J., Cazorla, F.J.: Epc: extended path coverage for measurement-based probabilistic timing analysis. In: 2015 IEEE Real-Time Systems Symposium, pp. 338–349, December 2015

Author Index

Printed in the United States
By Bookmasters